DATE DUE

DEMCO 38-296

THE
2000 ANNUAL:
Volume 2
Consulting

(The Thirty-Fifth Annual)

THE 2000 ANNUAL: Volume 2 Consulting

(The Thirty-Fifth Annual)

Edited by Elaine Biech

Jossey-Bass Pfeiffer

San Francisco

Printed in the United States of America

Published by

Jossey-Bass
Pfeiffer
350 Sansome Street, 5th Floor
San Francisco, California 94104-1342
(415) 433-1740; Fax (415) 433-0499
(800) 274-4434; Fax (800) 569-0443

www.pfeiffer.com

Acquiring Editor: Matthew Holt
Director of Development: Kathleen Dolan Davies
Editor: Rebecca Taff
Senior Production Editor: Dawn Kilgore
Senior Manufacturing Supervisor: Becky Carreño

Printing 10   9   8   7   6   5   4   3   2   1

 This book is printed on acid-free, recycled stock that meets or exceeds the minimum GPO and EPA requirements for recycled paper.

PREFACE

Welcome to the *2000 Annual: Volume 2, Consulting*. This year represents the twenty-ninth year the *Annuals* have been published. The sixth that they have been published as a set of two: Volume 1, Training, and Volume 2, Consulting. The materials in the training volume focus on skill building and knowledge enhancement, as well as on the professional development of trainers. The materials in the consulting volume focus on intervention techniques and organizational systems, as well as on the professional development of consultants. The performance-improvement technologist, whose role is one of combined trainer and consultant, will find valuable resources in both volumes.

As we begin our trek into the 21st Century and all that it promises for us, it is natural for us to look back to see where the profession has been, as well as forward to where it is going. The two volumes this year are representative of both. We all remember fifteen years ago or so when some leaders in our profession were predicting the end of the training profession. It was thought that most learning would occur via the computer and that imprecise measures of the ROI of training would be discouraging to organizations. To the contrary, computers seem to have increased the need for training. In addition, the need for training professionals has grown as companies everywhere recognize the value of training. Yes, training has changed. The performance-improvement technologist has been added to the list of professions, more companies are outsourcing their training, the profession has expanded to the executive suite, we are using web-based training, the "learning organization" has been added to our jargon, and hundreds of other things have developed. Training is alive and well.

The same can be said of the consulting field. The number of consultants is growing by 20 percent each year. Certainly the traditional consultants abound, including management development consultants and organizational development consultants. In addition, many of these consultants specialize in areas that did not exist ten years ago: web-page design consultants, diversity consultants, environmental consultants, executive coaches, and those who focus on spirituality in the workplace. It's been said that all of us will spend a portion of our career as a consultant—even if for just a short time.

Whether you are a trainer or a consultant, or a bit of both, the *2000 Annuals* will be your companions as you begin your HRD journey into the new century. Experiential learning activities range from the basic topic of learning transfer to the high-tech topic of computer communication. Instruments measure a wide variety of issues important to individuals, teams, and organizations: attitudes toward sexual harassment, performance of teams, aptitude for mentoring, and an organization's ability to adapt to the future. Articles address age-old topics such as decision making and strategic planning; articles also address cutting-edge topics such as spirituality in the workplace and web-based training. Articles will also stretch you by challenging you to use improvisational theater games as a training technique and aligning teams with the organization's values as a consulting process.

Both volumes provide a broad spectrum of material. We have tried to balance the basics you've come to us for in the past with the mind-stretching cutting-edge ideas you'll need in the future.

One aspect of the *Annuals* that will never change is the way in which they continue to enhance your professional competence. You will find experiential learning activities, instruments, and articles that you may use to develop workshops and seminars for many or use for mentoring and coaching one-on-one. We want you to use everything you find in the *Annuals,* and we want to make it easy for you to use them. All of the materials in the *Annuals* are yours to duplicate for educational and training purposes. You may also adapt and modify the materials to meet your audience's needs. Please ensure that the credit statement found on the copyright page is included on all copies you make. If the materials are to be reproduced in publications for sale or are intended for large-scale distribution (more than one hundred copies in twelve months), *prior written permission is required.* Reproduction of material that is copyrighted by another source (as indicated in a footnote) requires written permission from the designated copyright holder. Please call us if you have questions. We believe our liberal copyright policy makes it easier for you to do your job.

All this is possible due to professionals in the HRD field like you. Our contributing authors—your colleagues—who through their work as trainers, consultants, facilitators, educators, and performance-improvement technologists have experimented with and perfected new material in real-life settings with actual participants and clients. They have contributed activities, techniques, models, instruments, theories, and methods that they have developed and used to meet real-world needs. This is your reassurance that the activities produce results, the instruments measure what they claim, and the articles have given value to others prior to publishing.

We would like to invite you to submit materials to be considered for publication in the *Annuals.* At your request we will provide a copy of the guidelines for preparing your material. We are interested in receiving experiential learning activities (based on the five stages of the experiential learning cycle: experiencing, publishing, processing, generalizing, and applying); inventories, questionnaires, and surveys; and presentation and discussion resources (articles that include theory related to practical application). Contact the Jossey-Bass/Pfeiffer Editorial Department at the address listed on the copyright page and we will send you our guidelines for contributors. In addition, we welcome your comments, ideas, and questions. You may contact me through Jossey-Bass, or e-mail me directly at *ebbiech@aol.com*.

Thank you to the dedicated people at Jossey-Bass/Pfeiffer who produced the *2000 Annuals:* Arlette Ballew, Laurel Bergman, Jamie Corcoran, Kathleen Dolan Davies, Matthew Holt, Ocean Howell, Dawn Kilgore, Carol Nolde, Susan Rachmeler, and Rebecca Taff. Thanks also to Beth Drake of ebb associates inc, whose patience and persistence ensures that we make all the impossible deadlines. And, most importantly, thank you to our authors, who represent the rich variety in the fields of training and consulting. In-house practitioners, consultants, and academically-based professionals have shared the best of their work so that other professionals like you may benefit. Your generosity contributes to professional development for many of us.

Elaine Biech
Editor
August 1999

About Jossey-Bass/Pfeiffer

Jossey-Bass/Pfeiffer is actively engaged in publishing insightful human resource development (HRD) materials. The organization has earned an international reputation as the leading source of practical resources that are immediately useful to today's consultants, trainers, facilitators, and managers in a variety of industries. All materials are designed by practicing professionals who are continually experimenting with new techniques. Thus, readers and users benefit from the fresh and thoughtful approach that underlies Jossey-Bass/Pfeiffer's experientially based materials, books, workbooks, instruments, and other learning resources and programs. This broad range of products is designed to help human resource practitioners increase individual, group, and organizational effectiveness and provide a variety of training and intervention technologies, as well as background in the field.

CONTENTS

---

*See Experiential Learning Activities Categories, p. 7, for an explanation of the numbering system.

**Topic is "cutting edge."

GENERAL INTRODUCTION
TO THE 2000 ANNUAL

The 2000 Annual: Volume 2, Consulting is the thirty-fifth volume in the *Annual* series, a collection of practical and useful materials for professionals in the broad area described as human resource development (HRD). The materials are written by and for professionals, including trainers, organization-development and organization-effectiveness consultants, performance-improvement technologists, educators, instructional designers, and others.

Each *Annual* has three main sections: *experiential learning activities; inventories, questionnaires, and surveys;* and *presentation and discussion resources.* Each published submission is classified in one of the following categories: Individual Development, Communication, Problem Solving, Groups, Teams, Consulting and Facilitating, Leadership, and Organizations. Within each category, pieces are further classified into logical subcategories, which are identified in the introductions to the three sections.

The last category, Organizations, made its debut in the 1999 *Annual.* This addition reflects the changing nature of the field, as professionals take on more and more responsibilities in their organizations or as consulting professionals to organizations. The more widely accepted role of performance-improvement technologist brings with it more broadly defined responsibilities, often more "organizational" in nature. In addition, after four years of publishing a separate consulting volume, the need to incorporate the broader Organization category in the *Annual* series became self-evident. We encourage you to broaden your perspective to include this category as you consider submitting material for future *Annuals.*

A new subcategory, "Technology," was also added last year. Much has changed for the HRD professional in recent years, and technology has led much of that change. Given the important role technology plays, we will continue to publish material that relates technology to the HRD field and how the HRD professional can use technology as a tool.

Another addition, beginning in 1999, is the identification of "cutting edge" topics. This designation highlights topics that present information, concepts, tools, or perspectives that may be recent additions to the profession or that have not previously appeared in the *Annual.*

The series continues to provide an opportunity for HRD professionals who wish to share their experiences, their viewpoints, and their processes with their colleagues. To that end, Jossey-Bass/Pfeiffer publishes guidelines for potential authors. These guidelines are available from the Pfeiffer editorial department at Jossey-Bass Inc., Publishers, in San Francisco, California.

Materials are selected for the *Annuals* based on the quality of the ideas, applicability to real-world concerns, relevance to current HRD issues, clarity of presentation, and ability to enhance our readers' professional development. In addition, we choose experiential learning activities that will create a high degree of enthusiasm among the participants and add enjoyment to the learning process. As in the past several years, the contents of each *Annual* span a wide range of subject matter, reflecting the range of interests of our readers.

Our contributor list includes a wide selection of experts in the field: in-house practitioners, consultants, and academically-based professionals. A list of contributors to the *Annual* can be found at the end of the volume, including their names, affiliations, addresses, telephone numbers, facsimile numbers, and e-mail addresses. Readers will find this list useful if they wish to locate the authors of specific pieces for feedback, comments, or questions. Further information is presented in a brief biographical sketch of each contributor that appears at the conclusion of each article. We publish this information to encourage "networking," which continues to be a valuable mainstay in the field of human resource development.

We are pleased with the high quality of material that is submitted for publication each year and often regret that we have page limitations. In addition, just as we cannot publish every manuscript we receive, you may find that not all published works are equally useful to you. Therefore, we encourage and invite ideas, materials, and suggestions that will help us to make subsequent *Annuals* as useful as possible to all of our readers.

Introduction
to the Experiential Learning Activities Section

Experiential learning activities ensure that lasting learning occurs and should be selected with a specific learning objective in mind. Although the experiential learning activities presented here all vary in goals, group size, time required, and process[1], they all incorporate one important element: questions that facilitate the learning. This final discussion, led by the facilitator, assists the participants to process the activity, to internalize the learning, and to relate it to their day-to-day situations. It is this element that creates the unique experience and learning opportunity that only an experiential learning activity can bring to the group process.

Readers have used the *Annuals'* experiential learning activities for years to enhance their training and consulting events. Each learning experience is complete and includes all lecturettes, handout content, and other written material necessary to facilitate the activity. In addition, many include variations of the design that the facilitator might find useful. Although the activity as written may not fit perfectly with your objective, within your time frame, or to your group size, we encourage you to use these variations as well as your own variations. Should you wish to look beyond this volume for additional experiential learning activities, we encourage you to peruse the "Experiential Learning Activities Categories" chart that immediately follows this introduction.

The 2000 Annual: Volume 2, Consulting includes thirteen activities, in the following categories:

Individual Development: Sensory Awareness

657. Secret Sponsors: Mirroring the Self by Gary Gemmill and Barbara Hanson

---

[1] It would be redundant to print here a caveat for the use of experiential learning activities, but HRD professionals who are not experienced in the use of this training technology are strongly urged to read the "Introduction" to the *Reference Guide to Handbooks and Annuals* (1999 Edition). This article presents the theory behind the experiential-learning cycle and explains the necessity of adequately completing each phase of the cycle to allow effective learning to occur.

Individual Development: Self-Disclosure

658. Spirituality at Work: Enhancing Spiritual Values Through Renewal by Krista Kurth and Suzanne Adele Schmidt

Individual Development: Diversity

659. Unearned Privilege: Understanding Dominant-Culture Advantage by Julie O'Mara and Aja Oakman

Communication: Awareness

660. Supreme Court: Examining Organizational Rules by Frank A. Prince

Communication: Building Trust

661. What to Say: Telling the Truth in Organizations by Barbara Pate Glacel and Emile A. Robert, Jr.

Communication: Conflict

662. Retaliatory Cycle: Introducing the Elements of Conflict by Daniel Dana

Problem Solving: Generating Alternatives

663. Deck of Cards: Using Deming's Funnel Experiment by Kristin J. Arnold

Problem Solving: Consensus/Synergy

664. Shift Happens: Dealing with Different Information by Steve Sugar and Robert C. Preziosi

Problem Solving: Action Planning

665. Make a Mark: Experiencing the Importance of Planning by Edward Earl Hampton, Jr.

Groups: Competition/Collaboration

666. Powerful Exercise: Exploring the Dynamics of Power in Teams by Andy Beaulieu and Karon West

Teams: How Groups Work

667. Share the Load: Experiencing Intragroup and Intergroup Problem Solving by Terry Murray

Teams: Roles

668. Appreciative Introductions: Building Teams by Sherene Zolno

Consulting and Facilitating: Facilitating Skills

669. Continuum: Exploring the Range of Facilitator Interventions
by M.K. Key

Other activities that address goals in these and other categories can
be located by using the "Experiential Learning Activities Categories" chart
that follows, or by using our comprehensive *Reference Guide to Handbooks and
Annuals.* This book, which is updated regularly, is an index of all of the *Annuals* and all of the *Handbooks of Structured Experiences* that we have published
to date. With each revision, the *Reference Guide* becomes a complete, up-to-
date, and easy-to-use resource for selecting appropriate materials from all of
the *Annuals* and *Handbooks.*

EXPERIENTIAL LEARNING ACTIVITIES CATEGORIES

Vol. Page

NDIVIDUAL DEVELOPMENT

Sensory Awareness

Feelings & Defenses (56)	III	31
Lemons (71)	III	94
Growth & Name Fantasy (85)	'72	59
Group Exploration (119)	IV	92
Relaxation & Perceptual Awareness (136)	'74	84
T'ai Chi Chuan (199)	VI	10
Roles Impact Feelings (214)	VI	102
Projections (300)	VIII	30
Mastering the Deadline Demon (593)	'98–1	9
Learning Shifts (643)	'00–1	11
Secret Sponsors (657)	'00–2	11

Self-Disclosure

Johari Window (13)	I	65
Graphics (20)	I	88
Personal Journal (74)	III	109
Make Your Own Bag (90)	'73	13
Growth Cards (109)	IV	30
Expressing Anger (122)	IV	104
Stretching (123)	IV	107
Forced-Choice Identity (129)	'74	20
Boasting (181)	'76	49
The Other You (182)	'76	51
Praise (306)	VIII	61
Introjection (321)	'82	29
Personality Traits (349)	IX	158
Understanding the Need for Approval (438)	'88	21
The Golden Egg Award (448)	'88	89
Adventures at Work (521)	'95–1	9
That's Me (522)	'95–1	17
Knowledge Is Power (631)	'99–2	13
Spirituality at Work (658)	'00–2	15

Sex Roles

Polarization (62)	III	57
Sex-Role Stereotyping (95)	'73	26
Sex-Role Attributes (184)	'76	63
Who Gets Hired? (215)	VI	106
Sexual Assessment (226)	'78	36
Alpha II (248)	VII	19

Vol. Page

Sexual Values (249)	VII	24
Sex-Role Attitudes (258)	VII	85
Sexual Values in Organizations (268)	VII	146
Sexual Attraction (272)	'80	26
Sexism in Advertisements (305)	VIII	58
The Promotion (362)	IX	152
Raising Elizabeth (415)	'86	21
The Problem with Men/ Women Is . . . (437)	'88	9
The Girl and the Sailor (450)	'89	17
Tina Carlan (466)	'90	45

Diversity

Status-Interaction Study (41)	II	85
Peer Perceptions (58)	III	41
Discrimination (63)	III	62
Traditional American Values (94)	'73	23
Growth Group Values (113)	IV	45
The In-Group (124)	IV	112
Leadership Characteristics (127)	'74	13
Group Composition (172)	V	139
Headbands (203)	VI	25
Sherlock (213)	VI	92
Negotiating Differences (217)	VI	114
Young/Old Woman (227)	'78	40
Pygmalion (229)	'78	51
Race from Outer Space (239)	'79	38
Prejudice (247)	VII	15
Physical Characteristics (262)	VII	108
Whom To Choose (267)	VII	141
Data Survey (292)	'81	57
Lifeline (298)	VIII	21
Four Cultures (338)	'83	72
All Iowans Are Naive (344)	IX	14
AIRSOPAC (364)	IX	172
Doctor, Lawyer, Indian Chief (427)	'87	21
Life Raft (462)	'90	17
Zenoland (492)	'92	69
First Impressions (509)	'94	9
Parole Board (510)	'94	17

Vol. Page

Fourteen Dimensions (557)	'96–2	9
Adoption (569)	'97–1	9
Globalization (570)	'97–1	19
Generational Pyramids (571)	'97–1	33
People with Disabilities (594)	'98–1	15
Expanding the Scope of Diversity Programs (617)	'99–1	13
Tortuga Place and Your Place (644)	'00–1	15
Unearned Privilege (659)	'00–2	25

Life/Career Planning

Life Planning (46)	II	101
Banners (233)	'79	9
Wants Bombardment (261)	VII	105
Career Renewal (332)	'83	27
Life Assessment and Planning (378)	'85	15
Work-Needs Assessment (393)	X	31
The Ego-Radius Model (394)	X	41
Dropping Out (414)	'86	15
Roles (416)	'86	27
Creating Ideal Personal Futures (439)	'88	31
Pie in the Sky (461)	'90	9
What's in It for Me? (463)	'90	21
Affirmations (473)	'91	9
Supporting Cast (486)	'92	15
Career Visioning (498)	'93	13
The Hand You're Dealt (523)	'95–1	23
Living Our Values (548)	'96–1	25
Career Roads (549)	'96–1	35
Collaborating for Success (572)	'97–1	45
High Jump (573)	'97–1	57
Issues, Trends, and Goals (595)	'98–1	21
Bouncing Back (596)	'98–1	35
Work Activities (597)	'98–1	43
From Good Intentions to Results(645)	'00–1	27

657. Secret Sponsors: Mirroring the Self

Goals

- To acknowledge our projections and thereby incorporate them into self-expression.

- To experience our own nonthreatening, wise, and positive qualities.

Group Size

Eight to twenty participants.

Time Required

This activity will have the most impact when conducted within a multi-session workshop setting of at least four total hours in duration. The initial instructions take about five minutes. The core part of the activity, letter writing, will be done outside the main workshop sessions (e.g., in the evening). About ten minutes are required during each workshop session for participants to read the letters they receive. When the final letters are distributed, about forty to fifty minutes are required.

Materials

- Slips of paper on which to write the names of each participant.
- A container for the slips of paper (e.g., a hat or bowl).
- A pad of paper and writing instruments for each participant.
- Four or five envelopes per participant.

Physical Setting

Any training session in a large, comfortable room.

Process

1. Prior to the workshop, write the name of each participant on a slip of paper, fold each piece of paper in half, and place them all in a hat or some other container.

2. At the beginning of the first session, explain to the participants that they will each become a "secret sponsor" to someone else in the group. Tell participants that they are to observe their charges closely to find the issues they are struggling with in their lives, both within and outside the formal group setting. They are to focus on what they believe would be useful to the people whose names they draw in terms of sustaining and accelerating that person's personal growth.

3. Ask participants to draw a name from the hat. Tell the participants not to reveal the names they draw and not to identify themselves as secret sponsors to the persons whose names they draw.

4. Explain that they will be asked to write letters of guidance and encouragement to their charges—once again without revealing their identity. Tell participants to *make copies of the letters they send* for use later in the workshop. Tell participants that during the last training session they will write a final letter and have the opportunity to give any small symbolic gift they wish, such as a flower, a poem, or a drawing. (*Note:* For this activity to be effective, participants must have the opportunity to write two or three letters to their charges between sessions.)

5. Explain that the letters will be delivered during a predetermined session. Hand out the appropriate number of envelopes to each participant. Tell them that they will put their letters inside envelopes, disguise their handwriting, and write the recipient's name on the outside of each envelope.

6. Prior to any session when you will be collecting letters, remind participants to bring their letters and provide a large shopping bag or other container for them to place their letters anonymously.

7. Distribute the letters to the group members at the beginning of the designated session and give everyone about ten minutes to read what they have received. Ask participants to share their reactions with the rest of the group. The following questions can be used to promote discussion:

   - What are you feeling about the letter you received?
   - How does the information in the letter help you?
   - Do you think your "secret sponsor" sees you clearly? Why so?

- What do you want to say to your secret sponsor?

(Fifteen minutes.)

8. During the final session of the workshop, ask participants, in turn, to read their letters, discuss the gifts they have received (if applicable), and then try to guess which other group member has acted as a secret sponsor. (Usually participants are quite excited and believe that their secret sponsors see them rather clearly.) (Fifteen minutes.)

9. After everyone has read their letters and tried to guess who sent them, ask participants to study their copies of the letters they sent and pretend that the letters were written to themselves. In place of "you" (i.e., the recipient's name) they are to substitute "I" and their own names. Tell them to also acknowledge the message to themselves in the letters. Ask volunteers to read letters aloud from that perspective. (The point is to become aware of their projections, see the importance of the words they used to describe the other person, and learn how other people function as a mirror for viewing one's inner self. Steer the conversation in this direction.)

10. Bring closure to the activity with these discussion topics and questions:

Taking on and being in the role of a secret sponsor to others pushes us to more clearly see the secret sponsor within ourselves. This represents our own deep-level ability to nurture ourselves and others spiritually and positively.

As a result of the group sharing and hearing what others have done, people discover a number of different ways of guiding and nurturing themselves and others.

Use the following questions to help bring out these learnings:

- What happens when you take on the role of a secret sponsor to others?
- What did you learn about nurturing yourself and others?
- How can you play this role with others back on the job?

(Thirty minutes.)

Submitted by Gary Gemmill and Barbara Hanson.

Gary Gemmill, Ph.D. is professor emeritus of organizational behavior in the School of Management at Syracuse University. His publications focus on personal and group transformation. His articles have appeared in Human Relations, Small Group Research, *and* Consultation. *Professor Gemmill consults with the top management of several organizations on issues of leadership development and group transformation.*

Barbara Hanson is an independent consultant who specializes in the design and development of interpersonal communication skills training. She has a master's degree in instructional design, development, and evaluation from Syracuse University. She has more than ten years of experience creating training programs for corporations such as Eastman Kodak and Apple Computer.

658. Spirituality at Work: Enhancing Spiritual Values Through Renewal

Goals

- To offer individuals a framework for reflecting on their spirituality.

- To identify actions through which individuals may enhance spiritual renewal at work.

Group Size

Fifteen to twenty-five people.

Time Required

One and one-half to two hours.

Materials

- One Spirituality at Work Handout for each participant.
- One Spirituality at Work Self-Assessment for each participant.
- One Spirituality at Work Worksheet for each participant.
- Paper and pencils for each participant.
- Art supplies for each participant.

Physical Setting

Space at tables for each participant to draw freely.

Process

1. Begin by saying, "We are living in a time of the *Overworked American*, which is also the title of a book by Juliet Schor. We must be the best, the fastest, the most competitive, and the busiest. As we continue to meet

others' expectations at work, many of us have a desire to renew ourselves. This is one of the reasons for the recent increased interest in spirituality and renewal at work. Let's think back to some situations at work in which you felt renewed and some in which you did not."

2. Ask participants to get comfortable, close their eyes if they wish, and recall a time when they felt off balance or overwhelmed at work—a time when they were not performing well. Speaking slowly, ask the following questions, pausing between: "What were you doing? . . . What was your inner state like at the time? . . . Your mental, emotional, physical, and spiritual state? . . . How did you feel? . . . What were some of the attributes of your experience? . . . What impact did your state of mind have on your work and on those around you?" Pause for a few minutes to allow participants to re-create their experiences. (Ten minutes.)

3. After about five minutes ask participants to open their eyes. Hand out paper and pencils and place the art supplies within easy reach. Ask participants to capture the experiences they have remembered on paper by using the art materials or to write down how they felt about the experience they remembered. Allow about five minutes and then ask participants to set aside their work. (Five minutes.)

4. Ask participants to recall another time—a time when they felt that they were performing very well, to their maximum potential—when they felt full of enthusiasm for their work or were very creative. Again, slowly ask, "What were you doing at that moment? . . . What was your mental, emotional, physical, and spiritual state like? . . . Specifically, how did you feel? . . . What were some of the attributes of your experience? . . . What impact did your inner state have on your work and those around you?" Pause for a few minutes to allow participants to re-create that experience. (Ten minutes.)

5. After about five minutes ask participants to open their eyes. Again, ask them to capture their experiences on paper using the art materials or to write words that describe the experiences they remembered. (Five minutes.)

6. Have participants pair up to discuss the experience. (Five minutes.)

7. After five minutes reconvene the large group and ask the following questions:

   ■ What were the differences between the two experiences that you remembered?

- How did your mental, emotional, physical, and spiritual states differ between the two experiences?

- What impact do you believe each experience had on your work? On those around you?

- Would it be valuable to you, your colleagues, and/or your employer to be able to re-create the second state more often? How could you do that?

(Ten minutes.)

8. Say to the group: "This discussion of a time when you felt full of enthusiasm for your work may have been a time when you experienced spiritual renewal at work and a spiritual connection to your work. Let's take this subject of spirit and work to the next level and assess your own spiritual renewal at work."

9. Distribute the Spirituality at Work Handout. Use the handout to describe the four areas of spiritual renewal briefly. Answer any questions and draw out examples from the group. (Ten minutes.)

10. Distribute the Spirituality at Work Self-Assessment and ask the participants to take about ten minutes to complete it. (Fifteen minutes.)

11. When everyone has finished, ask participants to look at the results of their assessments and determine the area in which they have the largest gap, that is, the greatest difference between their present frequency of activities and their interest in increasing those activities.

12. After everyone has identified the area in which he or she has the largest gap, form subgroups of three to five participants who have identified the same gap area.

13. Provide the Spirituality at Work Worksheet to each participant and ask the subgroups to identify specific actions they could take to enhance their spiritual values and to provide renewal at work in the area they identified. Allow about ten minutes. (Fifteen minutes.) (The Worksheet lists all four areas, participants can be encouraged to complete the other three areas on their own.)

14. Reconvene the large group and ask each subgroup for a few of the actions they identified. Summarize with the following questions:

- What did you learn about yourself through this activity?

- How likely are you to implement some of the suggestions you discussed? Why or why not?

- What benefits do you see to enhancing your spirituality and finding ways for renewal at work?
- What will you do differently at work from now on?

(Twenty minutes.)

Submitted by Krista Kurth and Suzanne Adele Schmidt.

Krista Kurth, Ph.D., co-founder of Renewal Resources LLC, has been exploring, conducting programs on, and speaking about renewal in the workplace for over a decade. Her own personal experience and her abiding interest in helping people be more true to themselves at work inspired her original research on spiritual renewal in business. She brings her love of service and her extensive background in business organization development, psychology, and spiritual and renewal practices to her work with individuals and organizations. Dr. Kurth personally puts her work into practice by meditating, reading inspirational literature, and playing with her children.

Suzanne Adele Schmidt, Ph.D., co-founder of Renewal Resources LLC, has been leading renewal retreats and addressing issues related to the impact of nonstop change on the human and organizational spirit for the last fifteen years. Her life-long passion is to facilitate the continuous learning of individuals and groups in the workplace. She blends her great enthusiasm and care for people with her corporate and academic expertise in her work with clients. Dr. Schmidt incorporates renewal in her own life by journaling, praying, listening to music, and creating celebrations.

SPIRITUALLY AT WORK HANDOUT

We have opportunities to renew ourselves spiritually in four main areas: transcendental, personal, relationships, and community. Descriptions of these four areas are provided below.

Transcendental. Focusing explicitly on a divine being or consciously bringing a spiritual awareness into your daily work life and engaging in spiritual activities at work is known as transcendental renewal. Actions that might express such an explicit focus include being in silence together, offering your work to a higher being, praying for co-workers or about a business decision, meditating during the work day, talking with others at work about spiritual issues, and engaging in work that is in alignment with your spiritual values.

Personal. A personal renewal can include such things as being committed to your personal growth and to living with integrity. This leads to self-reflection, seeing challenging situations as opportunities to learn, and being vigilant of your actions as you do your work.

Relationships. Establishing caring relationships with others at work based on trust, love, and respect is another way to renew oneself. This necessitates communicating openly and honestly, actively supporting others' growth, and responding to co-workers' needs as human beings.

Community. Building communities in and caring for the environments in which you work by creating an atmosphere of acceptance, open communication, diversity, cooperation, and belonging is the fourth way to build a sense of renewal. This also includes focusing on the structure and policies of the organization to ensure that they support a sense of community. Depending on your organization, it may also support the broader community and the environment outside the organization itself.

SPIRITUALITY AT WORK SELF-ASSESSMENT

Instructions: Respond to each question twice, first according to current frequency (How often do you engage in the action now?) and second by degree of interest in engaging in the action more often (How interested are you in engaging in the action more often?).

Transcendental Area

Do you bring a spiritual awareness into your work day by any of the following:

1. Engaging in spiritual practices at work, by yourself or with others?

Present Frequency	*not at all*	*sometimes*	*often*	*very often*
Interest in Increasing	*not interested*	*somewhat interested*	*interested*	*very interested*

2. Focusing on the connectedness of life or seeing the divine in others?

Present Frequency	*not at all*	*sometimes*	*often*	*very often*
Interest in Increasing	*not interested*	*somewhat interested*	*interested*	*very interested*

3. Talking about your deeply held spiritual values and/or spiritual issues at work with co-workers?

Present Frequency	*not at all*	*sometimes*	*often*	*very often*
Interest in Increasing	*not interested*	*somewhat interested*	*interested*	*very interested*

4. Engaging in work that is aligned with your spiritual or deeply held values?

Present Frequency	*not at all*	*sometimes*	*often*	*very often*
Interest in Increasing	*not interested*	*somewhat interested*	*interested*	*very interested*

Personal Area

Do you focus on learning to live authentically and with integrity by:

5. Engaging in personal refection, personal growth activities, or spiritual practices?

Present Frequency	not at all	sometimes	often	very often
Interest in Increasing	not interested	somewhat interested	interested	very interested

6. Maintaining awareness of and control over your actions and emotions?

Present Frequency	not at all	sometimes	often	very often
Interest in Increasing	not interested	somewhat interested	interested	very interested

7. Acting in accordance with your spiritual values, behaving ethically?

Present Frequency	not at all	sometimes	often	very often
Interest in Increasing	not interested	somewhat interested	interested	very interested

8. Seeing situations at work as opportunities to learn, maintaining a positive, accepting attitude toward life?

Present Frequency	not at all	sometimes	often	very often
Interest in Increasing	not interested	somewhat interested	interested	very interested

Relationship Area

Do you build caring relationships at work by:

9. Accepting, having empathy, and treating co-workers and customers with love and respect?

Present Frequency	not at all	sometimes	often	very often
Interest in Increasing	not interested	somewhat interested	interested	very interested

10. Being present to listening receptively and responding to the needs of others and the situation at hand?

Present Frequency	not at all	sometimes	often	very often
Interest in Increasing	not interested	somewhat interested	interested	very interested

11. Actively supporting others' growth and development by encouraging them to explore and live their personal visions?

Present Frequency	not at all	sometimes	often	very often
Interest in Increasing	not interested	somewhat interested	interested	very interested

12. Speaking and encouraging truthful, open communication and confronting others in caring, non-denigrating ways?

Present Frequency	not at all	sometimes	often	very often
Interest in Increasing	not interested	somewhat interested	interested	very interested

Community Area

Do you create a caring community at work by:

13. Building shared visions and encouraging participation and collaboration at work?

Present Frequency	not at all	sometimes	often	very often
Interest in Increasing	not interested	somewhat interested	interested	very interested

14. Creating an organizational culture that embraces diversity, allows for others' self-expression, and encourages open communication?

Present Frequency	not at all	sometimes	often	very often
Interest in Increasing	not interested	somewhat interested	interested	very interested

15. Establishing a sense of community and belonging through celebrations, rituals, and fun events?

Present Frequency	not at all	sometimes	often	very often
Interest in Increasing	not interested	somewhat interested	interested	very interested

16. Structuring groups and the organization and developing policies and procedures based on spiritual values and principles?

Present Frequency	not at all	sometimes	often	very often
Interest in Increasing	not interested	somewhat interested	interested	very interested

SPIRITUALITY AT WORK WORKSHEET

Instructions: Read the Spirituality at Work Handout again and use the definitions there to identify actions in each of the areas that would enhance your spiritual values and provide renewal for you at work. Be as specific as you can by stating exactly what you would do, when, where, with whom, in each area.

Transcendental Area

Personal Area

Relationship Area

Community Area

659. UNEARNED PRIVILEGE: UNDERSTANDING DOMINANT-CULTURE ADVANTAGE

Goals

- To acquaint participants with the concept of "privilege" as it pertains to diversity (unearned advantage or opportunity afforded members of the dominant culture).

- To provide an opportunity for participants to identify, examine, and study examples of privilege in the workplace.

- To develop participants' awareness that privilege is inherent in organizations.

- To explore how awareness of privilege can encourage the effective use of human resources in participants' organization(s).

Group Size

Twelve to thirty participants of diverse backgrounds (racial, ethnic, gender, sexual orientation, age, ability/disability, and/or work group). All participants should be members of the same organization.

(*Important Note for the Facilitator:* This activity may produce a high level of affect. It is advised that you use the activity only if you have extensive experience in dealing with diversity issues. Also, the activity is best positioned in a diversity program that is at least one day long and in which topics such as prejudice, discrimination, and stereotyping are addressed in depth early. Under these circumstances the activity is best used in mid-afternoon to late afternoon, after the participants have acquired some background in and understanding of diversity issues. In preparation for answering questions and leading discussion, the facilitator should study the references listed after "Variations.")

Time Required

Approximately one hour and thirty minutes.

Materials

- Copies of the Unearned Privilege Theory Sheet for all participants.
- A flip-chart poster listing the following questions:
    - To what degree do you believe the statements on the handout are experienced by people in your organization? In your department or unit?
    - What examples of "white privilege" have you experienced, observed, or heard about?
- Masking tape for posting.
- A flip chart and markers for each subgroup and for the facilitator.

Physical Setting

A room large enough for subgroups of four or five members each to work without distracting one another. Movable chairs should be provided; a table for each subgroup is optional.

Process

1. Introduce the activity by defining "privilege" as it relates to diversity and by reviewing the goals. State that the concept of privilege may be new to some and may cause some persons to feel uncomfortable and/or resistant. Emphasize that the concept of privilege is complex and that the focus of this activity is to open the door to basic understanding of privilege. (Five minutes.)

2. Form subgroups of four or five persons each, ensuring that the members of each subgroup represent a variety of diversity dimensions (race, ethnicity, gender, sexual orientation, age, ability/disability, or work group). Ask the members of each subgroup to convene at a different table or to form their chairs into a circle. Give each subgroup a flip chart and several felt-tipped markers.

3. Distribute copies of the theory sheet and ask participants to read it. (Five minutes.)

4. Display the poster of prepared questions. Explain that members of each subgroup will have fifteen minutes to discuss briefly their reactions to the twenty theory-sheet statements and then to concentrate on their responses to the posted questions. Ask each subgroup to appoint a recorder to list responses to the posted questions on the flip chart. Monitor the subgroups as they work to ensure that they do not get stuck on the reaction phase and have plenty of time to respond to the posted questions. (Spending no more than five minutes on reactions works well.)

5. Ask the members of each subgroup to choose:

   ■ One statement they believe is especially true;

   ■ One example that they discussed in support of one of the statements; and

   ■ One statement they believe is *not* true (unless they cannot identify one).

   Explain that the recorder should record each subgroup's choices; then the subgroup should appoint a spokesperson to share those choices with the total group, as well as any highlights of their discussion. Again monitor the subgroups as they work, reminding them periodically of the remaining time. (Fifteen minutes.)

6. After fifteen minutes call time and reconvene the entire group. Ask the spokespersons to take turns reporting; limit each subgroup to three minutes. When denials of privilege are brought up, immediately facilitate a discussion on the subject. (*Note:* It is not uncommon for white persons to deny the existence of privilege. They may not feel particularly privileged in their lives or in the organization; they may believe that education and training in diversity issues and equal opportunity employment have reduced or eliminated disparate treatment. Emphasize that although they may not feel privileged individually and personally, as members of the dominant culture they possess both power and opportunity and, thus, have advantages that have not been earned.) (Twenty-five minutes.)

7. Explain that now each subgroup is to meet again to select one of the following dominant cultures in North American organizations and to choose two or three examples of unearned privilege for that group:

   ■ Men

   ■ Heterosexuals

   ■ People without disabilities

Ask the recorders to list the examples on their flip charts. State that each subgroup has ten minutes to complete this task and then ask the subgroups to begin. Monitor their work, keeping them apprised of the remaining time. (Fifteen minutes.)

8. After ten minutes call time and reconvene the entire group. Ask the spokespersons to take turns presenting examples; limit each spokesperson to two minutes. After each spokesperson reports, ask for brief questions or comments from participants. (Twenty minutes.)

9. To conclude, lead a discussion based on the following questions:

- What are your key learnings on privilege as it pertains to diversity?

- Why might some persons in a dominant culture deny they have unearned privilege?

- How does unearned privilege impact your organization?

- How might you use what you have learned during this activity in your work life?

(Ten minutes.)

Variations

- Instead of using the theory sheet as a handout, give a lecturette on its first few paragraphs (not including the twenty statements) and then distribute copies and form subgroups. (*Note:* This variation may produce an especially high level of affect; if so, extra time may be needed to process this affect.)

- After Step 6 lead a concluding discussion, thereby limiting the focus to white privilege only.

- To ensure that all three categories in Step 7 are covered, either assign a category to each subgroup or ask each subgroup to list examples for every category.

- In Step 9 ask participants to discuss actions that the organization can take to minimize the negative impact of privilege.

References

Cose, E. (1993). *Rage of a privileged class: Why are middle-class blacks angry?* New York: HarperCollins.

Kendall, F. (1997). *Barriers to clarify or what keeps white people from being able to see our privilege.* Unpublished manuscript. Albany, CA: Kendall and Associates (510) 559-9445.

Kendall, F. (1997). *Understanding white privilege.* Unpublished manuscript. Albany, CA: Kendall and Associates (510) 559-9445.

Maier, M. (1997). *Invisible privilege: What white men don't see.* Teaneck, NJ: The Diversity Factor.

McIntosh, P. (1992). White privilege and male privilege: A personal account of coming to see correspondences through work in women's studies." (pp. 70–81). In M.L. Anderson & P.H. Collins (Eds.), *Race, class and gender.* Belmont, CA: Wadsworth.

Submitted by Julie O'Mara and Aja Oakman.

Julie O'Mara *is the president of O'Mara and Associates, an organization development, leadership, and diversity consulting firm. She is co-author of* Managing Workforce 2000: Gaining the Diversity Advantage, *author of* Diversity Activities and Training Designs, *and other articles and booklets. A former national president of ASTD, she teaches at John F. Kennedy University, serves on the Board of World Trust, a nonprofit organization on transformative learning, and produced* The Way Home, *a diversity video.*

Aja Oakman *is a student at Las Positas Community College in Livermore, California. She will attend San Francisco State University in fall 1999 majoring in sociology.*

Unearned Privilege Theory Sheet

"Privilege" as it pertains to diversity is the unearned advantage or opportunity one receives just because one is a member of a dominant culture. Being in the dominant culture means you hold power and have unearned access to opportunities and, often, but not always, are in the majority. *Random House Webster's Unabridged Dictionary* (2nd ed., 1998) defines privilege as "a right, immunity, or benefit enjoyed only by a person beyond the advantages of most."

In North America, the privilege afforded white people is the most prevalent type of unearned advantage. Privilege is also commonly experienced by men, heterosexuals, and persons without disabilities.

It is important to distinguish between earned and unearned advantage. For example, earning a higher salary or having access to resources because one holds a doctoral degree is *earned* privilege. The distinction between earned and unearned can become muddied, however. Some individuals in a dominant culture (a group in power) may be accepted into a doctoral program more readily because of their race, gender, or sexual orientation. Thus, while they truly earned the degree and therefore merit the rewards it brings, unearned privilege may have played a role in their gaining acceptance into the graduate program from which they earned that degree.

People who have unearned privilege often are unaware they have it. But those who do not have privilege usually are very aware when others have it. Persons who have this kind of privilege take certain things for granted and consider them normal. For example, heterosexuals frequently and without concern put a spouse's photo on their desk, while most gays/lesbians/bisexuals probably think twice before displaying a photo of their same-sex partners. To do so may cause anxiety and discomfort. To do so may even cause someone in the organization to deny gays and lesbians promotional opportunities.

Among the goals of diversity work are (1) to develop people's understanding of the concepts of earned and unearned privilege, (2) to enable all individuals access to earned privilege, and (3) to mitigate the unearned privilege that some members of organizational populations have.

The following statements, each of which should be prefaced with the phrase "If I am white," represent the typical attitudes and feelings experienced by white persons in North America:

If I am white . . .

1. I am not concerned that people may think I was hired to mirror workforce demographics or fill a quota, rather than for my abilities.

2. and I must relocate for my job, I need not limit my choice of neighborhood, I need not fear that I may be unwanted by my neighbors, and I need not feel I stand out because of my race.

3. I do not worry that people may assume I am incompetent or ignorant because of my race.

4. I need not think that my choices of clothing might be considered too "ethnic."

5. I do not feel obligated to contribute (time, effort, money, or other resources) to the betterment of the white community, nor do I feel obligated to mentor others of my race so that they may succeed in their endeavors.

6. I do not suspect that I might be mistaken for another white person who works in the same organization.

7. and I am being considered for a promotion, I am not concerned that I will be denied the promotion if there are other white people with the same experience and qualifications who have already filled the "slots" allotted for white persons.

8. and I lend my luxury car to my teenage child, I need not fear that the police may see my child driving and assume the car was stolen.

9. and I do not receive a promotion, I do not assume that my race was a factor.

10. and I have a few cocktails at a party sponsored by the organization, people do not necessarily assume I am an alcoholic.

11. I do not consider it unusual for my race to be well-represented at all organizational levels, and I am secure in the fact that I belong where I am in the organization.

12. it is not assumed that I know specific demographics and techniques to serve or market to others of my race.

13. and I am engaging in casual discussion with co-workers, I do not feel uncomfortable when negative comments and jokes are made about my race.

14. I do not worry that my promotability rests on having the "right" accent.

15. and I go into work after hours dressed in casual clothing that might be considered inappropriate for the work environment, I do not worry about being mistaken for someone who is there to do maintenance work or cleaning.

16. and I speak to a high-ranking person at my company, I am likely to be speaking to someone of my race.

17. and I excel in a special project or receive an award for my accomplishments, people do not mention my race.

18. and I travel for business, I do not feel that people will look at me in surprise or think it unusual if I fly first class.

19. and I am invited to make a significant presentation to a large audience and that presentation is not well-received, I do not feel that my performance reflects negatively on others of my race.

20. people do not assume that I only do certain types of work, such as computer programming, gardening, convenience store clerking, or taxi driving.

For most people, learning about unearned privilege is a long-term process. It is a difficult topic for most persons who have unearned privilege because the denial of its existence is strong. For example, many white persons do not believe that having white people in charge of hiring contributes to the hiring of white people, rather than the hiring decision being based entirely on skill. This is not to say that being white is the only reason someone is hired; however, race may contribute.

The subject of privilege is a complex one, and you are encouraged to research it further and broaden your understanding of the issues involved. Doing so will increase your effectiveness, both within your organization and in your private life as well.

660. Supreme Court:
Examining Organizational Rules

Goals

- To examine both written and unwritten rules of an organization.
- To discuss the impact of rules.
- To take action on outmoded rules.

Group Size

Any number from the same organization.

Time Required

Forty to fifty minutes.

Physical Setting

Any comfortable setting with surfaces on which to write.

Materials

- One copy of the Supreme Court Rules Sheet for each participant.
- Pencils or pens for each participant.
- Flip chart and felt-tipped markers.

Process

1. Introduce the activity by explaining how rules within organizations are sometimes written and sometimes not. Ask for a few examples of each type in the participants' organization and write them on the flip chart for reference. Tell participants that they will create lists of both written and unwritten rules for their organization.

2. Give each participant a copy of the Supreme Court Rules Sheet and a pencil. Tell participants to first list the rules that are written within the organization. Encourage them to write as many as possible and not to begin the list of unwritten rules until told to do so. (Five to ten minutes.)

3. When everyone has finished, ask participants to create a second list, this time of unwritten rules within their organization. Once again, encourage them to write as many as possible. (Five to ten minutes.)

4. If the group is large, form pairs to share and consolidate the lists.

5. Go around the group, asking for items—first for written rules, then for unwritten. Write what they say on the flip chart.

6. Lead a brief discussion of their organizational rules with the participants, using the following questions:

   ■ Which rules are similar in scope and purpose?

   ■ Which rules are different?

   ■ Were any rules listed of which you were unaware?

   ■ Are there any rules with which you disagree? Which ones? Why?

   ■ Which list was easier to create? Why?

   ■ What is the impact of having both written and unwritten rules on individuals in this organization?

   (Twenty minutes.)

7. Conclude with a brief discussion about the impact of both written and unwritten rules on individuals and the organization.

   ■ How do these different rules impact the organization as a whole?

   ■ What actions could you take when you return to work as a result of this discussion?

   Encourage them to discuss the impact of unwritten rules in particular on newly hired people, long-time employees, customers, the organizational culture, friendships, and reporting relationships. (Ten minutes.)

8. Encourage participants to take action on any outdated rules when they return to work and to be explicit about unwritten rules.

Variations

- If you have a large group (more than twenty-four), this activity could be completed in subgroups of six to eight people. Each group could then present its list to the other groups on flip-chart sheets.
- Action plans can be developed if desired.

Submitted by Frank A. Prince.

*Frank A. **Prince** is founder of Involvement Systems Inc., Dallas, Texas. He is the author of seven books, including* C and the Box: A Paradigm Parable, *a best seller from Jossey-Bass/Pfeiffer. Mr. Prince is recognized as a global leader in the field of creativity and delivers motivational keynote addresses that spark innovation in organizations.*

SUPREME COURT RULES SHEET

Instructions: You have been appointed to the Supreme Court of your organization. This is a very special role, with the task of reviewing the "rules" of your organization. A number of rules have been established, some of which have been around for a very long time. Some rules are written down—and even etched in stone. Other rules are unwritten and must be learned through time and experience. First, list all written rules of your organization below. Wait until the facilitator calls time, then you will be asked to fill in as many unwritten rules as possible.

Written Rules	**Unwritten Rules**

661. What to Say:
Telling the Truth in Organizations

Goals

- To demonstrate that "truth" is subjective and depends on circumstances and priorities.

- To allow participants to express their own truths and to hear how others define truth.

- To assess the impact on an organization, employees, and client systems when truth is ambiguous.

Group Size

As many participants as will fit into the room may be involved, divided into discussion groups of five or six.

Time Required

From sixty to ninety minutes, depending on the number of situations discussed and the number of teams.

Materials

- A copy of the What to Say Lecturette for the facilitator.

- One copy of the What to Say Situations Sheet for each subgroup.

- One copy of the What to Say Tips for Telling the Truth in the Organization for each participant.

- A flip chart and felt-tipped markers.

Physical Setting

A room large enough to accommodate all subgroups, ideally at round table where they can work undisturbed.

Process

1. Divide participants into subgroups of five or six each, preferably at small, round tables. Deliver the What to Say Lecturette.

2. Announce the goals of the activity, briefly explaining that telling the truth in an organizational setting is a subjective process open to interpretation. Say that differing interpretations of the truth impact an organization's behavior, reputation, and success.

3. Distribute one What to Say Situations Sheet to each of the subgroups. Either assign one of the situations to each subgroup or let them choose a situation to discuss. When they have finished discussing one situation, they may choose to move to the next. Ask them not to begin reading the situations until they have read the instructions and understand them. Answer any questions participants may have and tell them to begin, giving them ten minutes for their first round of discussion. (Fifteen minutes.)

4. Now ask the subgroups to come to a consensus on what is the "truth" for each situation and on what action should be taken. Remind them that they are not to vote, draw straws, or use any other win-lose criteria, but to discuss each situation until they all can support one of the answers as "truth." (Fifteen minutes.)

5. Next ask the subgroups to discuss what the impact of their "truth" would be on the organization, the employees, and the clients. Call time after ten minutes and discuss their answers in the large group, posting responses on the flip chart. (Ten minutes.)

6. Ask group members to discuss what the impact on the organization, the employees, and the clients would be if a less "truthful" action were taken. Call time after ten minutes and discuss their answers in the large group, posting responses on the flip chart. (Ten minutes.)

7. Lead a discussion of the most significant learning points and post them on the flip chart.

8. Ask whether anyone has a similar situation in his or her own organization, in which organizational truth is not clear and in which conflicting priorities allow truth to be interpreted in a variety of ways. Ask the following questions about each example:

   ▪ What is the impact on the organization?

   ▪ On the employees?

- On the clients?

- Are there any other impacts?

List the important points on the flip chart, looking for similarities.

9. After wrapping up the discussion, hand out copies of the What to Say Tips for Telling the Truth in the Organization. Emphasize that telling the truth in organizations is a prerequisite for building trust in organizations, and that trust is the basis for high performance.

Variation

- Have participants create their own situations for discussion based on their organizational experiences. These situations may have more immediate applicability in reinforcing learning on the job.

Submitted by Barbara Pate Glacel and Emile A. Robert, Jr.

Barbara Pate Glacel, Ph.D., *is CEO of VIMA International. Dr. Glacel consults in team learning, executive coaching, and organization development for organizations such as Lockheed Martin Corporation, the MITRE Corporation, NASA, Motorola, and others in the United States, Europe, Africa, and the Pacific Rim. She is a frequent contributor to professional journals, an accomplished public speaker, an adjunct faculty member at the Center for Creative Leadership, and co-author of* Light Bulbs for Leaders: A Guide Book for Team Learning *(John Wiley, 1996).*

Emile A. Robert, Jr., Ph.D., *is COO of VIMA International. He has over thirty years' experience in human resource development and administration. He is an acknowledged authority in organization development, personnel assessment and evaluation, forecasting human resource needs, and professional development. Dr. Robert works with clients across the United States, as well as in Scotland, New Zealand, Southeast Asia, and South Africa. He is on the adjunct faculty at the Center for Creative Leadership. He is co-author of* Light Bulbs for Leaders: A Guide Book for Team Learning *(John Wiley, 1996).*

WHAT TO SAY LECTURETTE

Telling the truth—what's so hard about that? We are taught from the time we are young that we must tell the truth. We hear that our noses will grow if we tell lies. We hear the story of George Washington, founding father of the United States, who supposedly cut down a cherry tree and confessed to his father.

So, what's the big issue about telling the truth? If the importance of telling the truth is ingrained in us from infancy, why do we need to swear oaths in courts of law? Why do we need legislation to protect "whistle blowers"? In fact, why do we often attack people for simply telling the truth? Why is telling the truth such a big issue for organizations today?

The difficulty organizations are having in telling the truth is apparent from any newspaper. One recent headline read "Whistle-Blower Suit Stays Alive," and the article cited the lengthy appellate court process for a case in which an executive alleged his firm defrauded the Air Force. Another news story proclaimed that "Justice Department attorneys are nearing a decision on whether to prosecute" a multi-billion dollar company after former employees alleged that the company defrauded the U.S. government on a contract. In the same day's paper was an article saying that the news accounts about a certain large company's improper conduct were themselves "inaccurate and misleading," according to the office of the U.S. Inspector General. It can be difficult to find the truth in this morass of controversy.

The question for organizations is two-fold: How does company leadership respond to truth? Does the organization's culture allow learning from its mistakes?

By the time people join organizations, they have already been either rewarded or punished a multitude of times for telling the truth. Organizational leaders then either reinforce or contradict the lessons taught by earlier experience. These lessons are more powerful teachers than are the childhood lessons we learned about telling the truth.

In every possible instance, the leaders of organizations must tell the truth, painful as it may be. Other than sensitive company information or client-sensitive projects, information must be shared fully and spread widely. Rumors can be greatly diminished by telling the truth early and often.

Employees at all levels must be rewarded for telling the truth, even if it is bad news. Learning takes place by correcting errors. If errors are hidden, then the same mistakes occur again and again. In these days of continual change, we don't have time to make the same mistake twice. Telling the truth and publicizing it and the lessons learned allow for continuous process improvement.

WHAT TO SAY SITUATIONS SHEET

Directions:

1. In your small group, choose one or two of the situations that follow. *Individually*, decide what the "truth" is in each of the situations you chose and what the conflicting priorities are. Analyze as many of the situations as possible in the time allowed, but be sure to work on the same situations as other members of the group.

2. *As a group*, share your individual answers and try to reach a consensus on what is the "truth" and on what action should be taken. Consensus means picking one answer that all of you can support. Do not vote, draw straws, or use any other win-lose selection criteria. Spend the time available discussing and reaching agreement on as many of the situations as you can without rushing the consensus process.

3. Discuss what the impact would be on the organization, the employees, and the clients if your chosen "truthful" action were taken.

4. Discuss what the impact would be on the organization, the employees, and the clients if a less "truthful" action were taken.

5. Choose a spokesperson to report the results of your discussion to the total group.

Situation A

You are in charge of business development for your division. Corporate has told you that your division must lay off one hundred employees if revenues do not increase this quarter by 25 percent over last quarter. The sales force has devised a scheme to increase revenues by taking orders in advance for their clients. This would be against company policy, which calls for just-in-time shipments, but save those at risk of losing their jobs. It is your responsibility to present a business plan to your boss that will increase revenue enough to save the threatened jobs. What will you say?

Situation B

You are the sales representative for your company covering the entire sub-Saharan African continent. Often you feel that you are "out of sight, out of mind" when corporate promotions and bonuses come along. You need to make a splash with one huge sale that will capture the company's attention. Your competitor routinely pays bribes to African government officials to obtain their business. Your company prohibits the payment of bribes. This prohibition has hurt your career, especially when you work in a culture in which bribes are an accepted and expected way to do business. Your major client has offered to buy the largest single amount of product that you have ever sold, for just a 2 percent kickback. It is easy to bury that amount in your expenses. What will you do?

Situation C

You are the project manager on a huge manufacturing production contract for the government. At the end of the project, you will be entitled to a bonus depending on completion time, how much you are under budget, and certain quality specifications. The client, however, requires you to do so much paperwork to apply for the bonus that the time it takes to complete it will put you beyond the deadline. You are entitled to the bonus based on your production work, and your bookkeeper suggests that you figure in this amount as an "expense" of the job. Because the government offered the bonus as an incentive and you met the requirement for receiving it, this seems to be simply another way of calculating the amount due. What action will you take?

Situation D

You are a consultant to a government agency on how to implement quality programs. Based on your reputation, another agency asks you to bid on similar work. They would like to avoid the lengthy proposal process and bureaucratic billing procedures. Government regulations allow small jobs to be awarded without going through the bidding process, especially if the cost is below the limit for credit-card charges by individual contracting agents. The contracting agent asks you to break your consulting intervention into several smaller efforts and to bill them separately. To complicate matters, he asks that you bill the first part of the project in advance to use end-of-year funds. What will you do?

Situation E

An account manager, you are in a staff meeting and have just learned that your best client wants you to bid on work that will mean you have to double your production. Your gut is saying, "Go for it." The profit will blow the socks off the rest of the organization. On the other hand, you know your boss is a stickler for detail. She's sure to ask you "How?" if you say you can do it. You've never played fast and loose with estimates before, but you have seen your colleagues get away with blowing smoke and, if they deliver, they reap rewards that might have been yours if you had been a little more daring. You take a risk and announce that you want to bid on the project. Just as you feared, your boss asks, "What are you basing that on?" How will you respond?

Situation F

You are the team leader in your office, responsible for delegating work among the clerical staff. One member of the staff is having personal problems that are affecting his work. He is a single parent with high family medical bills, and he takes off an extraordinary amount of time. Co-workers have been covering for the employee, and you have kept the situation quiet from your supervisor. Morale is beginning to suffer as the personal situation drags on, and team performance is decreasing. When performance-review time rolls around, the supervisor wants your input as she determines performance bonuses, raises, and promotions. What will you tell her?

What to Say Tips for Telling the Truth in the Organization

- Leaders must tell the truth consistently, whether it is good news or bad. Informing employees and colleagues of all news allows them to contribute suggestions, solutions to problems, and possible business plans. Sharing bad news helps to build trust in leaders.

- Truthful information must be disseminated widely and in a timely manner. Telling the truth immediately stifles rumors and allows time to take action.

- Those who tell the truth about embarrassing issues must be rewarded. Do not "shoot the messenger" for bringing bad news or revealing situations that are to the detriment of the organization. Recognize and praise those who tell the truth for having the courage to reveal bad news before it becomes worse.

- Truth-tellers must not publish innuendo or spread rumors if they have not been confirmed. They should be especially careful about sharing information that is of a personal nature, which can feed the rumor mill and cause suspicion and fear, which are counterproductive.

- Mistakes that are revealed should be rigorously investigated to discover ways to improve. Organizational success is as dependent on finding out how not to repeat mistakes as on how to replicate successes.

- Results of any investigation of mistakes should be published widely so that all can learn from them. Those responsible for the mistakes should not be singled out, but the situation itself should become a learning opportunity.

- When the truth hurts, share the pain with others by sharing your own feelings. In the worst of times, people cope better with change and failure when they are shared and viewed as opportunities for improvement.

- Do not tolerate behavior that is untruthful. Tolerance will quickly erase all the gains achieved from rewarding people for telling the truth. Building trust is a slow and painstaking process, but it can be broken in a hurry, and the results are devastating to organizational performance.

662. Retaliatory Cycle: Introducing the Elements of Conflict

Goals

- To identify the five sequential elements that are present in every interpersonal conflict.
- To understand how conflict escalates (spirals up) and how it causes relationships to wither (spiral down.)
- To illustrate that conflict is always a reciprocal process.

Group Size

Eight to twenty.

Time Required

Forty minutes.

Materials

- One overhead transparency of the Retaliatory Cycle Model.
- One copy of the Retaliatory Cycle Handout for each participant.
- Overhead projector and screen.

Physical Setting

Any comfortable setting with a writing surface for participants.

Process

1. Introduce the activity by stating the objectives, pointing out that the retaliatory cycle describes the relationships among the cogitative (thinking), emotional (feeling), and behavioral (acting) components that are present in all interpersonal conflicts.

2. Display the overhead transparency of the Retaliatory Cycle Model, briefly explaining each step in the cycle. Use an actual example from your personal experience to illustrate each step. (Five minutes.)

3. Ask learners to form discussion pairs and give each person a copy of the Retaliatory Cycle Handout. Refer learners to their handouts as you read aloud each of the five questions.

4. Ask participants to form discussion pairs. Explain that each discussion partner will have about five minutes to describe a conflict in his or her personal experience (in terms of the model) to his or her partner. Explain that you will give a signal in five minutes to indicate that it is time to switch roles. Urge participants to use any extra time to answer the additional questions at the end of their handouts. (Fifteen minutes.)

5. After ten minutes have passed, draw out two or three examples from the group. Ask the participant whose example is being used to try to describe the cycle from the other person's point of view—that is, what was the trigger, perceived threat, and acting out, as experienced by the other person? Make the point that it is likely that the triggering event for the other person was the self-protective acting out behavior used by the first person. This discussion helps learners to appreciate the reciprocal nature of the retaliatory cycle and to recognize that the other's behavior makes sense in the context of how the situation was perceived. (Twenty minutes.)

Submitted by Daniel Dana.

Daniel Dana, Ph.D., *has been a mediator and conflict educator for over two decades and is credited as the originator of managerial mediation. Formerly a professor of organizational behavior at the University of Hartford, he is author of* Managing Differences, *published worldwide in five languages. His unique contribution to the field is the development of simplified mediation tools that enable nonprofessionals to use their quiet power in everyday work life to produce agreements where none seem possible.*

RETALIATORY CYCLE MODEL

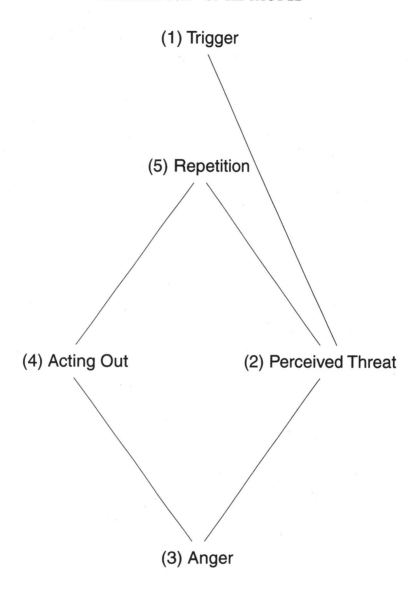

(1) Trigger

(5) Repetition

(4) Acting Out

(2) Perceived Threat

(3) Anger

Retaliatory Cycle Handout

Instructions: Think of a conflict that you have experienced with another person. Take turns with your discussion partner, and respond to the following questions. The facilitator will tell you when to change roles. Jot notes in the spaces provided to use during the group discussion to follow.

1. *Triggering Event.* What was said or done by the other person that triggered the conflict episode?

2. *Perceived Threat to Your Self-Interest.* This could arise from actual hostile intent or simply from carelessness by the other person. What did you assume was behind the other person's triggering action (cognition/thinking)?

3. *Anger.* Defensive anger is the natural emotional response to perceived threat, and it is necessary for mobilizing energy for self-protection. Describe your feeling of anger (emotion/feeling):

4. *Acting Out.* What did you do with your anger? How did you respond? Was your anger expressed through "noncommunication" (spiraling down) or "power play" (spiraling up) behavior or acting?

5. *Repetition.* How did the other person react to your acting out? What do you assume he or she perceived to be your intentions? What did the other person do to retaliate? Describe the next round of the retaliatory cycle from the point of view of the other person.

Additional Questions

- Were you able to break out of the retaliatory cycle?

- If yes, what did you or the other person do to end the conflict?

- Whether yes or no, was your relationship harmed by the conflict? In what way?

663. Deck of Cards: Using Deming's Funnel Experiment*

Goal

- To demonstrate the harmful effects of overadjusting a process.

Group Size

Four teams of up to five people each.

Time Required

Thirty minutes.

Materials

- Four colored dots to serve as the "targets," one colored dot for each subgroup.
- One deck of fifty-two playing cards per subgroup.
- Four small tape measures, one per subgroup.
- A dozen colored dots of a different color for Team B.
- Index cards on which the rules for each subgroup are written in advance.
- Paper and pencils for each subgroup.
- One copy of the Deck of Cards Trainer Notes for the facilitator.

Physical Setting

A room large enough for four groups of people to stand and work in small circles.

---

*This activity was inspired by W. Edwards Deming's Funnel Experiment, as discussed in his book, *Out of the Crisis*, Chapter 11: Common Causes and Special Causes. MIT Press, Cambridge, Massachusetts.

Process

1. Before using this activity for the first time, read through the rules and do a dry run with volunteers so that you are familiar with the results that each subgroup will achieve.

2. Prior to the session, place one colored dot or "target" on the floor to mark where each of the four subgroups will be located for this activity. Also write the rules and team designations (A, B, C, or D) on the index cards.

2. Ask the participants to form four small groups, with no more than five members each, and to assemble around one of the dots on the floor.

3. Tell the subgroups that they represent four different manufacturing teams, and that their objective is to deposit as many "products" (playing cards) as close to the target (the dot) as possible, while following their particular rules.

4. Tell the teams that they are to "deliver products" by dropping one playing card at a time from shoulder height. Demonstrate dropping a card perpendicular (not horizontal) to the colored dot or "target" on the floor. (This provides the most variation.)

5. Reiterate the goal for each subgroup: To deliver as many products, as close to the target as possible, while following the rule for the team. Hand out one deck of playing cards, a tape measure, one "rule card," and paper and pencils to each team. Give Team B the extra dots of a different color. Go over the rule that each team received with that team:

   ■ *Team A:* Do not adjust. Drop every card over the target.

   ■ *Team B:* After each drop, measure the distance (X) from the target to the spot where the card landed. Position your next drop at X distance from *the last position you used.* Use the additional colored dots to mark your last positions.

   ■ *Team C:* After each drop, measure the distance (X) from the target to the spot where the card landed. Set the next drop position X distance *from the target,* but in the opposite direction.

   ■ *Team D:* Set the next drop position directly over the spot where the last card you dropped landed.

6. Allow the teams to conduct a dozen drops. Pay particular attention to teams B and C, as their rules are the most difficult to follow.

7. After all have finished, review the activity with the entire group:

- What rule did your group follow?

- What results did you achieve? Why do you think that happened?

- Can you think of times on the job when this type of results happened?

- What happens to an organization as a result of overadjusting a process?

- What can you do in the future to prevent this type of problem in your organization?

Variation

- If time permits, do another round, allowing teams to make process improvements rather than following one rule. Have each team identify one improvement to make, test it, and then compare results. For example, one process improvement might be to hold the card parallel to the floor before dropping it. The result using Rule A will be that almost every card will settle down on top of the target!

Reference

Deming, W.E. (1986). *Out of the crisis.* Cambridge, MA: MIT Press.

Submitted by Kristin J. Arnold, MBA, CPCM

Kristin J. Arnold, MBA, CPCM, maintains a private consulting practice specializing in team facilitation services and training, with an emphasis on strategic planning, strategic partnerships, collaborative problem solving and team building. Ms. Arnold has extensive experience as both an internal and external consultant with a wide variety of manufacturing and service industries, as well as the government sector.

DECK OF CARDS TRAINER NOTES

Team A: The cards will tend to be *clustered around the target.* The distribution is stable with minimum variation around the target. Even if you have a bad process, you will get an even distribution. This is a stable process, and by far the best choice for delivering the most "product."

Team B: This variation explodes and is unstable but symmetrical around the target, as the group *tampers with the process.* The person knows where the standard is (the dot), but adjusts based on where the last card landed. When setting an oven to bake a cake, if we know from past experience that the oven was too hot, we adjust the control to be a smidgen less than we baked our cake before, rather than make wider variations.

Team C: The distribution explodes in opposite directions, as the team *overcompensates for errors.* This is the way most processes are overadjusted, going the opposite direction from the last time. Like a novice driver steering a car, the operator overadjusts (or management overreacts!), affecting the whole process.

Team D: The cards will *tend to drift.* The distribution is unstable and moves away from the target in one direction. This is the kind of process drift that can occur when we use the last piece produced as the standard for the next piece, instead of a universal product standard. Drifting also occurs when we let experienced employees show new employees "the ropes," without any training standard.

664. Shift Happens:
Dealing with Different Information

Goals

- To demonstrate how personal agendas influence group decision making.

- To generate discussion around multiple alternative solutions to a stated problem.

- To demonstrate the dynamics of reaching consensus in a group when it appears there is more than one correct answer.

Group Size

Fifteen to thirty participants, five per subgroup. There must be at least three subgroups.

Time Required

Approximately forty-five minutes.

Materials

- The appropriate Shift Happens Case Study Sheet (standard, positive, negative) for each participant. (*Note:* The three case studies are slightly different. Each version is indicated by the number of dots following the title. Case Study: Sandy Spriggs. denotes the *standard* version; Case Study: Sandy Spriggs.. denotes the *negative* version; and Case Study: Sandy Spriggs. . . denotes the *positive* version.) Prepare one copy of the standard version for each participant and one copy of the negative for one person each in one-third of the groups and one copy of the positive version for one person each in one-third of the groups.

- A copy of the Shift Happens Options Sheet for each participant.

- A flip chart and felt-tipped markers.

- Masking tape.
- Paper and pens or pencils for participants.

Physical Setting

A room large enough to seat all subgroups of five at round tables.

Process

1. Explain to the participants that they are members of the senior executive panel at MicroChip Company and that they must make a consensus decision on a personnel matter involving the customer service department.

2. Tell the participants that they will work first as individuals and then as members of a group, the "Senior Executive Panel."

3. Ask participants to form groups of five and seat themselves at separate tables. Distribute copies of the case study to each participant, following this process:

   - In the first group, all participants receive copies of the standard version;

   - In the second group, one participant receives a copy of the negative version and the rest of the group receives the standard version;

   - For the third group, one participant receives the positive version and the rest of the group receives the standard version.

   Repeat this distribution pattern for as many groups as you have.

4. Explain to participants that they have seven minutes to review their case studies *individually* and to choose one of the options as a solution. (Ten minutes.)

5. Call time at the end of seven minutes, making sure that each participant has made a selection.

6. Next, collect the case study sheets from the individual participants.

7. Distribute one Shift Happens Options Sheet to each participant.

8. Give participants ten minutes to discuss the options in their groups. Remind them that their goal is to reach consensus as a group on which option is preferred. (Ten minutes.)

9. Call time at the end of ten minutes and ask whether all teams have agreed on one option. Collect the option sheets from all the teams that have completed the task.

10. Instruct the teams that have not reached consensus to tally the number of votes for each option.

11. Ask each team to report its results verbally to the total group while you record them on the flip chart.

12. Debrief the exercise with the entire group. Record their responses and observations on the flip chart. The following questions will aid in the debriefing:

   - What specific behaviors in your group helped or hindered your ability to reach consensus?

   - Were the imposed time limitations an obstacle to the quality of the decision you made? Why or why not?

   - Were there major differences in how the data in the case was perceived? How were these addressed by the team?

   - Did anyone favor an option not listed among the choices? If so, how did the team react to this?

   - Did anyone's "personal agenda" cause a shift in the team's decision-making process?

   - Is there anything that you wish you had said or done differently during the discussion and consensus-seeking phase?

   - What specific learnings from this activity can you apply in the workplace?

   (Twenty to twenty-five minutes.)

Variations

- Divide smaller groups into two teams, with one team using the standard version of the case study and the other team using one negative case study sheet and the others receiving the standard version.

- Vary the time allowed to discuss the case study.

- Have one team conduct a "fish bowl" discussion while other teams observe. Do not allow other teams to discuss their own opinions until after they have seen the first team's discussion.

Submitted by Steve Sugar and Robert C. Preziosi.

Steve Sugar is the president of the Game Group. He is the author of Games That Teach *(Jossey-Bass/Pfeiffer) and* Games That Teach Teams *(Jossey-Bass/Pfeiffer). He has presented at many national training conferences and has been interviewed on learning games by the* Personnel Journal, Training & Development, *and* TRAINING *magazines. He is an editor-contributor to four ASTD* INFO-LINE *publications and contributor to the ASTD* Handbook of Training Design and Delivery *and the ASTD* Handbook of Instructional Technology. *He has been on the faculties of The Johns Hopkins University; University of Maryland, University College; and the New York Institute of Technology.*

Robert C. Preziosi, D.P.A., is a professor of management education in the School of Business and Entrepreneurship at Nova Southeastern University in Fort Lauderdale, Florida. He is also the president of Preziosi Partners, a consulting firm. He has worked as a human resource director, a line manager, and a leadership-training administrator and has consulted with all levels of management in many organizations, including CITRIX, Lennar, Siemens, and many hospitals and banks. Dr. Preziosi has been training trainers since the 1970s; his areas of interest include leadership, adult learning, and all aspects of management and executive development. In 1984 he was given the Outstanding Contribution to HRD Award by ASTD; in 1996 he received the Torch Award, the highest leadership award that ASTD gives, for the second time. He is the only person ever so honored. He is a regular contributor to the Annuals.

Shift Happens Case Study: Sandy Spriggs.

Sandy Spriggs has been the Senior Technical Rep at MicroChip Systems for seven years. Over the years Sandy has proven to be a mixed blessing. Sandy prefers to work alone and does not tolerate "stupid" questions from co-workers or clients alike. But when there is a technical emergency, Sandy is the one who usually resolves it, no matter how long it takes.

Yesterday, Sandy was walking by the customer service desk when an urgent call came in from SugarLand, MicroChip's largest client. The fast-food distributor had just suffered a crash of their entire inventory-control system. Without the system SugarLand could not respond to incoming orders. They were especially upset when they were told by the rep who answered the telephone that it usually required a MicroChip team two days to get a system functioning again.

When the MicroChip service rep asked Sandy a question about the system, Sandy took over the call. Because Sandy had designed the system and written the manual, he was able to talk directly to the SugarLand technical staff about the problem. Sandy asked a series of questions, walked the SugarLand technical staff through a trouble-shooting process, and was able to restore the system to full operation within forty-five minutes. After confirming that the system was up, Sandy then scolded the person from SugarLand for not providing appropriate maintenance procedures, which would have prevented this type of problem in the first place. Sandy then turned the call back to the MicroChip service rep and returned to his desk.

Later, the president of MicroChip received a call from the technical supervisor at SugarLand complaining that Sandy had upset some of her technical staff. After finishing the conversation, the president called for a meeting of the Senior Executive Panel to decide what to do about the SugarLand complaint. The panel includes the personnel director and vice presidents of Service, Manufacturing, Production, and Marketing.

SHIFT HAPPENS CASE STUDY: SANDY SPRIGGS. .

Sandy Spriggs has been the Senior Technical Rep at MicroChip Systems for seven years. Over the years Sandy has proven to be a mixed blessing. Sandy prefers to work alone and does not tolerate "stupid" questions from co-workers or clients alike. But when there is an technical emergency, Sandy is the one who usually resolves it, no matter how long it takes.

Yesterday, Sandy was walking by the customer service desk when an urgent call came in from SugarLand, MicroChip's largest client. The fast-food distributor had just suffered a crash of their entire inventory-control system. Without the system SugarLand could not respond to incoming orders. They were especially upset when they were told by the rep who answered the telephone that it usually required a MicroChip team two days to get a system functioning again.

Sandy insisted on taking over the call. Because he had designed the system, he felt that the problem was not the system but how it was being operated. Sandy interviewed the SugarLand reps on problems the system had before the crash, focusing on how the client operated and maintained the system. Sandy then walked the SugarLand reps through the process of trouble shooting and re-installation, sometimes barking instructions. After forty-five minutes of back-and-forth discussion, the system was restored to full operation. Sandy then severely scolded the reps, telling them that SugarLand caused the crash by not using proper operation and maintenance procedures. After completing the call, Sandy told the MicroChip technical rep that the system was up and returned to his desk.

Later, the president of MicroChip received a call from the technical supervisor at SugarLand bitterly complaining about how Sandy had upset her entire technical staff. After finishing the conversation, the president called for a meeting of the Senior Executive Panel to decide what to do about the SugarLand matter. The panel included the personnel director and vice presidents of Service, Manufacturing, Production, and Marketing.

SHIFT HAPPENS CASE STUDY: SANDY SPRIGGS...

Sandy Spriggs has been the Senior Technical Rep at MicroChip Systems for seven years. Over the years Sandy has proven to be a mixed blessing. Sandy prefers to work alone and does not tolerate "stupid" questions from co-workers or clients alike. But when there is an technical emergency, Sandy is the one who usually resolves it, no matter how long it takes.

Yesterday, Sandy was walking by the customer service desk when an urgent call came in from SugarLand, MicroChip's largest client. The fast-food distributor had just suffered a crash of their entire inventory-control system. Without the system SugarLand could not respond to incoming orders. They were especially upset when they were told by the rep who answered the telephone that it usually required a MicroChip team two days to get a system functioning again.

Knowing that Sandy had designed the system, the service rep begged Sandy to take the call. Putting aside his own project, Sandy initiated a troubleshooting session with the client. After a few minutes, Sandy determined that errors in operation and lack of maintenance had caused the problem. He then walked the SugarLand reps through a set-up and operational procedure. Within forty-five minutes the SugarLand system was restored to full operation. After confirming that the system was operational, Sandy insisted the client initiate new operational procedures and begin a rigorous preventive maintenance schedule. Sandy then returned the phone to the grateful MicroChip service rep and returned to his desk.

Later, the president of MicroChip received a call from the technical supervisor at SugarLand complimenting Sandy on restoring their system and saving them thousands of dollars. After finishing the conversation, the president called for a meeting of the Senior Executive Panel to decide what to do about the SugarLand matter. The panel included the personnel director and vice presidents of Service, Manufacturing, Production, and Marketing.

SHIFT HAPPENS OPTIONS SHEET

Instructions: Decide as a group which of the following options the Senior Executive Panel should implement.

- Give Sandy a raise for immediately correcting a problem caused by Sugar-Land technical staff and not mention the scolding incident.

- Give Sandy a bonus for solving the problem and ask him what caused the problem and how he was able to resolve it.

- Give Sandy the recognition he deserves for saving the SugarLand account, but remind him of MicroChip's policy of using customer protocol.

- Counsel Sandy about the way he dealt with the SugarLand staff and send him to customer service training.

- Fire Sandy, giving him the usual severance package, to show him and other employees the importance of properly dealing with customers.

665. MAKE A MARK:
EXPERIENCING THE IMPORTANCE OF PLANNING

Goals

- To demonstrate the necessity for setting goals prior to expending resources.
- To demonstrate that planning is necessary for goal achievement.
- To demonstrate the importance of a leader in group activities.
- To demonstrate how a sense of ownership affects group behavior.
- To demonstrate how chaos (the absence of patterns) can evoke reflex behavior.

Group Size

Any in subgroups of five to ten.

Time Required

Thirty to fifty minutes, depending on number of iterations.

Materials

- A large writing surface such as blackboard or flip chart for each group.
- Markers or chalk for each group.
- Stopwatch or timer.

Physical Setting

A room large enough to allow groups to be separated by at least ten feet; the greater the dispersion, the better.

Process

1. If there are more than ten participants, divide the group into teams of five to ten each and provide markers and a writing surface for each.

2. Ask team(s) to group around their writing surface(s).

3. Give groups the following vision:

   "Today is a day in which your creative energies will be totally unleashed. You have but one purpose: To create. Feel your creative energy! Let it flow! I want each member of the team to make one mark on your easel (or blackboard). Once you have done so, tell me, as a group, what you have created. Now we are short of time, so you only have one minute to do this as a group. I know you are up to this challenge! Let's have fun! Are you ready? Yes? Go!"

4. Observe teams making their marks. Ideally, a team will decide on an object to draw before beginning, but very few of them will do so. Most will immediately make a mark independent of other team members. This is preferable for purposes of the discussion, so the more time pressure you create, the better.

5. Verify that everyone in every team has contributed a mark. If not, instruct nonparticipants to do so. (Five minutes.)

6. Give each group one or two minutes to determine what the group has made.

7. Ask groups to share what they have made. Invite others to challenge each group's product and ask groups to redefine their products. For example, if a group says it has made a house, tell them it is an aerial view of a garden or it is a birthday cake. It does not matter what you come up with. The object is to create frustration and a sense of futility. (Five minutes.)

8. Repeat Steps 4 through 7 until people start to quit in frustration. They will either express this overtly or passive-aggressively through mutterings or body language.

9. Process the exercise at this point. Groups normally take one of two approaches: Either a group will execute a plan or it will not. Most groups who start with a plan will be most resistant to redirection. Even groups who do not start with a plan will become resistant. Bring closure with the following discussion questions:

   - *Leadership.* Who made the first mark? Why and why did he or she make that particular mark? How did this affect the rest of the group?

- *Purpose and planning and resource expenditure.* Was the purpose of the activity clear? How did group members react? Why did they respond by reflex to the opportunity? What was missing that could have provided clarity (*answer:* a plan)? How could a plan have made the group more productive? Was this costly in terms of resource expenditure? How could planning have made our expenditure of resources more efficient and/or effective?

- *Ownership.* Why did the group members become increasingly hostile with each iteration of change? What does this tell us about ownership? At what point in a project can a leader most effectively affect the outcome (*answer:* the beginning)?

- *Chaos.* If we define chaos as the "absence of patterns," can you see that the blank page at the beginning is chaos? Accepting this as chaos, what do our actions today tell us about how people will most likely respond to chaos if they are not given the benefits of goals and plans? Is such chaos an opportunity or a challenge? How can we make sure chaos is seen as an opportunity?

In summary, ask the group if they can see how this exercise represents daily activity, that is, that without adequate plans or goals, people will simply "make a mark." This should cause "a-ha's" and good discussion. (Twenty to thirty minutes.)

Variations

- You can be very hostile in redirection to bring out how aggressive leadership behaviors can disenfranchise people.

- To bring out discussion on leadership, select a leader and brief only him or her and have this person redirect the groups. This can underscore the importance of communication.

- Appoint a leader, but still give instructions publicly. Communicate only with him or her. This enhances discussion on how having information affects the group's reaction to the leader.

Submitted by Edward Earl Hampton, Jr.

Edward Earl Hampton, Jr., is president of Performance Perspectives and is currently interim director for the LEAD Scholars Program, a leadership development program for 350 competitively selected students at the University of Central Florida. He has been an active organizational effectiveness consultant since 1985. He specializes in strategic planning, team building, change management, leadership development, assessment-based training, process analysis, quality management, and executive coaching.

666. Powerful Exercise: Exploring the Dynamics of Power in Teams

---

Goals

- To determine the distribution of power within a group.

- To explore and address any perceived negative imbalances of power within a group.

- To examine personal responses to use of power in groups or teams.

- To identify and understand models of power used in groups or teams.

- To identify internal and external sources of power and the implications for group facilitators.

- To initiate an action plan for using power in positive and productive ways.

Group Size

Because this exercise may reveal information sensitive to the team, it is recommended for a single intact group or team of any size. With several facilitators in a training setting, up to three intact groups or teams may be used.

Time Required

One hour to one and one-half hours.

Materials

- One copy of the Powerful Exercise Contingencies Sheet for the facilitator.

- Colored poker chips of mostly one color with about a fifth of any other colors, for a total of five to seven chips per participant.

Physical Setting

Each intact team should be seated around a separate table. To permit sliding of poker chips to one another, the table surface should be smooth and flat.

Process

1. Prior to conducting this activity, read the Powerful Exercise Contingencies Sheet.

2. Tell participants the purpose and objectives of the exercise and divide them into their intact work groups if more than one group is present.

3. Place a pile of poker chips in the center of each team's table. Provide five to seven chips per team member, taking care to provide an amount that is not evenly divisible among team members (e.g., provide 28 chips to a team of 5 rather than 30 chips). Provide mostly chips of one color, with some other colors in the minority.

4. *Round 1:* Tell team members that in this round each of them is to *take* as many chips as he or she perceives reflects the amount of power he or she holds in the group, and to do so silently. Explain that they may take chips from the center of the table or from one another, but they may not give away any chips. Remind them that this is a nonverbal exercise. Tell them this stage of the exercise lasts two and one-half minutes. Ask them to observe their own reactions and thoughts and the behavior of the other members of the group. Tell participants to begin, observe the exercise, and stop the action when time has elapsed. (Five minutes.)

5. *Round 2:* Instruct team members that in this round they are to *give away* their own or others' chips as they perceive reflects the amount of power they feel *others* have in the group. Remind them that this is also a nonverbal exercise. Tell them this stage of the exercise lasts two and one-half minutes. Ask them to observe their own reactions and thoughts and the behavior of the other members of the group. Conduct the round by telling participants to begin, observing the exercise, and stopping the action when time has elapsed. (Five minutes.)

6. Debrief the exercise with participants using the following questions:

   ■ What thoughts and feelings did you have when you were given the instructions?

   ■ What thoughts and feelings did you have during the first part of the exercise? How about during the second part?

- How would you account for your reactions?

- What were the primary patterns that emerged during the first round? How many chips did you have at the end of Round 1? How many did you think you should have had?

- Who were you taking chips from? Who was taking them from you?

- What about Round 2? Who was giving chips away? Who were they giving them to? How did the outcomes from Round 1 compare to those from Round 2?

- Why wasn't the outcome the same?

- What would you say the exercise outcomes mean in terms of power on your team? What were you trying to tell one another?

- Are there imbalances of power on your team? If so, what positive consequences result? Are there any negative consequences?

- What would you consider the sources of power among individuals on your team? And how is that power applied both within and outside the team?

- Is there anything you would like to consider changing about the distribution of power in your group? What would you like to do differently? How will you go about making these adjustments? What do you think will happen? What do you want to happen?

(Forty to seventy minutes.)

Variations

- *Variation 1:* Sometimes even the most thought-provoking exercise can produce a somewhat dispirited debriefing when only group dialogue is used. Here are some other ways to debrief the exercise. Whenever possible, consider letting group members choose the type of debriefing of most interest to them. Similarly, letting the group decide how long to spend on the debriefing can help set expectations and increase feelings of self-control.

  - *Fishbowl.* Have team members form a circle and ask a small subset of the team to sit in the center of the circle. Ask these inner circle members to discuss the debriefing questions while the outer circle listens but does not participate. After awhile, switch the membership of the inner and outer circles. This approach works well with larger groups.

- *Samoan Circle.* This approach is similar to the fishbowl approach, except that members of the outer circle may join the conversation by "tagging in," walking up to the inner circle, selecting one seat, and having the current occupant of that seat move to the outer circle. Again, this approach would normally be used only with a larger group.

- *Pair Discussions.* Have participants pair up to discuss the exercise, then ask them to report out some of their findings.

- *Written Answers.* Provide the debriefing questions to participants in the form of a questionnaire. Allow participants up to twenty minutes to process and record their thoughts. Then ask them to discuss their written responses with the total group.

- *Posting.* Ask participants to take turns recording the group's answers to the debriefing questions on a flip chart.

- *Top-Ten List.* The popularity of David Letterman's "Top-Ten List" is no fluke. People like the familiar structure and goal-oriented approach it employs to present information. Ask participants to work together to create a top-ten list of findings (reactions, patterns, and meanings) from the exercise. They will then have material from which to identify and plan for needed changes in their collective uses of power.

- *Variation 2:* If you are working with an audience that will want to apply this simulation to their own audiences, the following process questions are helpful:

  - Did you like the exercise? Why or why not? Was the exercise effective? Do you think the exercise would give team members information they would use to improve the team's performance? Why or why not? What adjustments might you make?

  - Was the debriefing effective? Why or why not? Do you think the debriefing could help team members verbalize their feelings and agree to some changes? What other ways might you have conducted the debriefing?

  - Under what circumstances might you use this exercise? Are there any situations in which you would not want to use it? Why not?

  - What do you think of using a nonverbal approach to get team members talking about a pattern on the team? When else might you use a nonverbal exercise to get people talking about a controversial topic?

References

Hillman, J. (1995). *Kinds of power.* New York: Currency/Doubleday.

McGregor, D. (1960, 1985). *The human side of enterprise.* New York: McGraw-Hill.

Submitted by Andy Beaulieu and Karon West.

Andy Beaulieu has over ten years' experience as a performance improvement consultant, helping clients achieve rapid results from which they derive performance and developmental benefits. He has consulted to such organizations as American Airlines, British Petroleum, Veteran's Administration hospitals, National Association of Securities Dealers, Showtime Networks, World Bank, and Fidelity Investments. Mr. Beaulieu has published chapters in each of the two previous Pfeiffer Annuals, *as well as McGraw-Hill's 1999* Team and Organization Development Sourcebook.

Karon West has more than twenty years' experience as an organization and human resource development consultant and trainer. Her expertise includes strategic change management, organizational design, search conference technology, and management and team development. As a frequent speaker at major conferences in Canada and the United States, Ms. West communicates her expertise in topic areas such as organizational effectiveness, adult learning, personal and professional development, and ethics and social change. Ms. West also lectures at the university and community college levels. Among her past and present clients are American Express, IBM, Bell Canada, Glaxo-Wellcome, Honeywell, American Funds, Firstar Bank, Consumers Gas, and Saskatchewan Public Service.

POWERFUL EXERCISE CONTINGENCIES SHEET

With luck, your audience will react positively and enthusiastically to the exercise and use it as an opportunity to express concerns about power within their teams or groups. However, in some cases you may experience other outcomes. Some of these are described below, along with suggestions for addressing them.

1. No one is willing to take the chips from the middle or from others. This could signify that the team members are afraid to address the issue of power, probably due to the power of one member. If they cannot respond nonverbally, do not expect anyone to admit this verbally during the debriefing. Instead, try using an anonymous survey instrument that addresses power. The team could also feel powerless due to some external force. In this case, however, they probably will raise the issue verbally.

2. Participants all try to give the chips to one member, who vehemently gives them to others. In a case like this, make sure you focus on the patterns that emerged during the round, rather than on the final allocation of chips. Even if a participant is adept at deflecting chips during this type of round and ends up with the fewest, the message is still clear.

3. Participants claim the whole exercise would have been different if "X" had been there. Find out how many team members actually agree with that assessment and probe to understand what is happening on the team. Encourage participants to find a way to present this feedback to X, along with a plan for helping to change the behaviors of all involved. Do not encourage participants to rerun the exercise later when the missing person is available.

667. Share the Load: Experiencing Intragroup and Intergroup Problem Solving

---

Goals

- To develop the participants' skills in communicating effectively, working cooperatively, and solving problems.

- To develop the participants' awareness of their individual communication and problem-solving styles within a group.

- To provide an opportunity to compare and contrast subgroup products that contribute to a whole group task.

Group Size

Eighteen to thirty-six participants.

Time Required

One and one-half to two hours.

Materials

- One Share the Load Sample Structural Module Diagram for the facilitator.

- A cardboard storage box with a lid large enough to hold the prototype module constructed by the facilitator so that only the investigator for each subgroup can see it.

- One copy of the Share the Load Team Instructions for each subgroup.

- One Share the Load Observer Form and a pen or pencil for each observer.

- One container per subgroup with the following supplies:

  - A role of masking tape.

- Fifty flexible plastic straws.
- Twenty-five rigid plastic straws.
- One dozen rubber bands.
- Twelve self-adhesive colored dots.
- One ruler.
- One pair of scissors.
- One copy of the Share the Load Debriefing Sheet for each subgroup.

Physical Setting

A large, open room that will allow you to set up a series of construction communication lines as illustrated on the Share the Load Team Instructions. The box containing the module you construct should be on one table, accessible only by the investigators of the teams. Supplies for all teams should be on a separate table, accessible by the supplies managers only. In addition, each team needs a table for construction. If possible, the construction tables should be screened to keep teams from viewing one another's modules until the appropriate time.

Preparation

Prior to the activity, construct a prototype module by using the Share the Load Sample Structural Model Diagram and place it into a container with a lid. Place the container on a table near the center of the area where subgroups will be working.

Process

1. Divide the total group into subgroups of six individuals each. If the group is not divisible by six, assign the extra people as observers across all subgroups.

2. Introduce the activity by asking the subgroups to imagine themselves as part of a large company with several departments. Say that each "department" will be given the same task—to construct a module from a prototype that, when combined with modules from other departments, will support significant weight.

3. Give one copy of the Share the Load Team Instructions to each team and tell them to take no more than ten minutes to assign group members to carry out the following roles:

- *Investigator:* The team member who is authorized to actually inspect the prototype module inside the box and describe the construction of the module to the messenger.

- *Messenger:* The team member who is authorized to receive information from the investigator and transmit information to the construction team.

- *Construction Team:* The three team members who are authorized to actually construct the module.

- *Supplies Manager:* The member of the construction team who is authorized to obtain supplies from the team's supply container on the supply table.

- *Process Observer:* The group member who will observe the group's attempt to solve the problem, but not participate in the transmission of information or construction of the module.

(Fifteen minutes.)

4. Once teams have identified who will carry out assigned roles, give one copy of the Share the Load Observer Form and a pen or pencil to each observer. Then review the following ground rules from the instruction sheet with all teams:

- *Only* the investigator may inspect the module and may not take it out of the box.

- Communication *must* follow the lines established by the facilitator, that is, the investigator may only talk to the messenger, and the construction team may only talk to the messenger.

- All communication must be *verbal;* neither the investigator nor the messenger may draw diagrams of the prototype module.

- Project teams may not communicate with one another nor show their modules to one another.

- Only the materials provided may be used in constructing the modules. (*Note:* Additional materials not necessary to construct module are included in the supplies box.)

(Ten minutes.)

5. Once team roles have been identified, the ground rules shared, and any clarifying questions answered, give the teams forty minutes to attempt the task: to communicate the structure of the module through the system as defined in the instructions and actually construct as many modules as possible. The team members may meet to organize and plan their efforts, but once they begin viewing, communicating, and constructing, they must stay in assigned roles and communicate as outlined in the instructions. (Forty minutes.)

6. Act as timekeeper and inform the teams when twenty minutes have passed and when five minutes are left. Remind teams to keep their structures out of view of other teams.

7. As the end of the construction period, ask the teams to stop work on their modules, gather the group, and ask the teams, one at a time, to display their completed module(s). Defer detailed discussion of results until all modules have been displayed and tested. Once all modules have been displayed, they should be clustered for testing. (Fifteen minutes.)

8. Test the modules by placing a large sheet of cardboard or lightweight plywood on top of all the modules at once and then gradually adding weight (bricks, books, etc.) to test the carrying weight of the composite structure. (Ten minutes.)

9. After congratulating the teams on their efforts, ask the teams to reconvene and complete two more tasks:

   ■ First, the teams should hear feedback from their process observers. Remind participants of some guidelines for giving and receiving feedback and ask team members to listen actively and ask clarifying questions, but defer discussion of the feedback until after the process observer has completed his or her sharing. (Ten minutes.)

   ■ Next, ask the teams to use the Share the Load Debriefing Sheet to discuss their experiences. (Fifteen to twenty minutes.)

10. Call all the teams together for whole-group sharing. In addition to eliciting samples from each team, you may wish to add additional dimensions to the activity by focusing discussion on one or more of the following topics:

   ■ Quality versus quantity in construction.
   ■ Gender roles within the group.
   ■ Cooperation versus competition between subgroups.

   This final debriefing stage can vary in time depending on time available, productivity, and needs of the group. (Ten to twenty minutes.)

Variation

- To compare and contrast varying team problem-solving styles as an outcome of this activity, some of the teams can be structured as described, while others are allowed to blend roles and eliminate the messenger and supplies manager roles.

Submitted by Terry Murray.

Terry Murray, president of Creative Solutions, is a trainer and consultant who specializes in work with school districts, colleges, hospitals, and human service organizations. He designs and facilitates training events and provides consulting services in support of individual, group, and organizational growth and change. His work has focused on a broad range of group and organizational issues, including team building, organizational problem solving, planning, and visioning. As an adjunct professor in the Humanistic Education Program at the State University of New York at New Paltz, Mr. Murray teaches graduate courses in group dynamics, helping skills, workshop design, and organizational change.

SHARE THE LOAD SAMPLE STRUCTURAL MODULE DIAGRAM

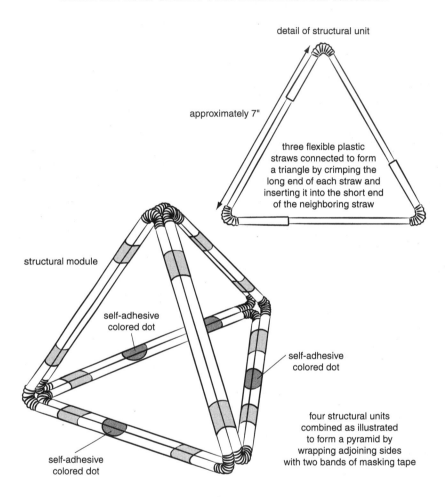

detail of structural unit

approximately 7"

three flexible plastic straws connected to form a triangle by crimping the long end of each straw and inserting it into the short end of the neighboring straw

structural module

self-adhesive colored dot

self-adhesive colored dot

self-adhesive colored dot

four structural units combined as illustrated to form a pyramid by wrapping adjoining sides with two bands of masking tape

SHARE THE LOAD TEAM INSTRUCTIONS

Objective: The challenge is to work as a team to construct structural modules from a prototype that, when combined with modules from other teams, will support as much weight as possible.

Instructions: After forming your team, meet together and do the following:

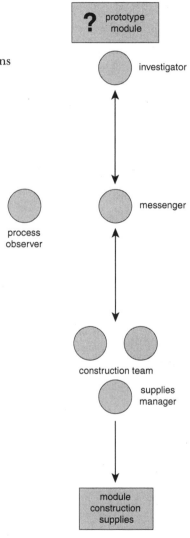

1. Review the following role descriptions and decide which person will play each role within your team.

   - *Investigator:* The team member who is authorized to actually inspect the prototype module inside the box and describe the construction of the module to the messenger.

   - *Messenger:* The team member who is authorized to receive information from the investigator and transmit information to the construction team.

   - *Construction Team:* The three team members who are authorized to actually construct the module.

   - *Supplies Manager:* The member of the construction team who is authorized to obtain supplies from the team's supply container on the supply table.

   - *Process Observer:* The group member who will observe the group's attempt to solve the problem, but not participate in the transmission of information or construction of the module.

2. Let the facilitator know when you have completed your role assignments. Send your process observer to receive further instructions.

3. When you have been assigned a work area, begin constructing as many modules as possible. Use the diagram on this page to remember how your team members are to communicate with one another.

4. At the end of your work period, you will be asked to display your module for others. Until that time, keep it hidden from view as well as you can. Modules will be tested for their weight-bearing ability.

Ground Rules

■ *Only* the investigator may inspect the prototype module and may not take it out of the box.

■ Communication *must* follow the lines established by the facilitator and shown in the diagram. The investigator may only talk to the messenger, and the construction team may only talk with the messenger.

■ All communication must be *verbal*. Neither the investigator nor the messenger may draw diagrams of the prototype model.

■ Project teams may not communicate with one another nor show their modules to one another.

■ Only the materials supplied by the facilitator for your team may be used in constructing the modules.

SHARE THE LOAD OBSERVER FORM

Instructions: Your task as an observer is to focus on the group process without participating or commenting. As your team attempts to solve the problem, watch and listen carefully and nonjudgmentally, focusing on interactions among group members and the roles they individually take on.

As you observe, answer the following questions in the spaces provided. *Do not share your observations until asked to do so by the facilitator.*

- How did the group members choose roles from the list? Did the group assess members' skills and experience when assigning roles? Were individual preferences taken into consideration?

- After roles were determined, how did the team go about solving the problem? How much preliminary discussion preceded their beginning to work?

- How would you describe the work climate as the team went about its task? Calm? Stressed? Focused? Unfocused? Spirited? Disinterested?

- Did the climate change as time progressed? If so, in what way?

- How would you describe the group's leadership?

- Were there differences of opinion? If so, how were they handled?

- What seemed to be the group's greatest challenges while building the modules? How were they solved?

Share the Load Debriefing Sheet

Directions: Discuss the following questions in your small group:

1. Imagine that your mind is a video camera that has captured the images and sound of your group's efforts. As you rewind your mental tape, what do you recall?

2. What feelings did this activity generate for you? Do other team members share your feelings? In what way did your feelings impact your performance?

3. What group dynamics were you most aware of as you participated in this activity?

4. What were the biggest challenges you faced as a team?

5. What criteria would you establish to assess a team's effectiveness in solving any problem? Based on these criteria, how would you assess your team's efforts in doing this task?

6. Does this activity remind you of any activities back on the job? If so, in what way? How would you like to change the way your actual work group structures tasks based on what you have learned?

668. Appreciative Introductions: Building Teams

Goals

- To introduce participants to one another and begin building an effective team environment.

- To create an "appreciative" understanding among team members.

- To develop participants' ability to formulate positive questions.

Group Size

All the participants who will be part of a new team or who are part of an intact work group. Optimum group size is eight to twelve.

Time Required

Approximately one hour and forty-five minutes.

Materials

- A prepared flip chart of Appreciative Introductions.
- A piece of blank flip-chart paper for each participant.
- Colored markers, and, if desired, scissors, colored paper, a variety of stickers (such as stars, hearts, shapes, animals, etc.), and tape or glue for use by the group.
- Paper and pencils for participants.
- Two flip charts with pads of paper.
- Felt-tipped markers.
- A roll of masking tape.

Physical Setting

A room in which tables have been arranged in a U shape, with enough table space so that participants can spread their flip-chart paper out on the tables. Adequate wall space is needed to post all flip charts. The two easels are placed near the front of the room.

Process

1. Introduce the goals of the activity, adding the following:

> "One way to understand the potential we have as a group is to view our process through the framework of social-constructionist theory. Social constructionists believe that people create organizations through their interactions with one another. Usually this process occurs outside of our awareness. However, we can choose to create our organizations in a deliberate way, either as individuals or as a team.
>
> "David Cooperrider, a social constructionist who created an approach to organization development called 'appreciative inquiry,' once said, 'The way we get to know one another is fateful.' He demonstrated in his work that our relationships will be affirming or negating, depending on whether our approach to engaging with one another is positive or negative. Cooperrider tells us that by becoming adept at framing our questions affirmatively, we can consciously create an affirmative culture within our teams.
>
> "Today, we will get to know one another in an appreciative way and thus begin to sharpen our skills in appreciative inquiry."

(Ten minutes.)

2. Give each person a piece of flip-chart paper and place some colored markers, stickers, colored paper, scissors, and tape in the center of each table.

3. Post the prepared flip chart, which has on it the following:

APPRECIATIVE INTRODUCTIONS

- What do you most value or appreciate about yourself?

- What makes you feel most alive, vital, and creative?

- Think of a previous satisfying team experience.
  What made it so satisfying?

- What will you value most in how we work together?

4. Explain the task, by saying, "Using symbols, words, and pictures and being as creative as you wish in helping others to know you, answer the questions on this flip chart on your own sheet of newsprint." (Five minutes.)

5. After twenty minutes, call time and reconvene the group. Ask each person in turn to post his or her flip-chart page and to take three to five minutes to present it to the group. (Twenty-five to sixty minutes, depending on group size.)

6. After participants have all presented their sheets, ask each person to select a partner for a discussion. Give each participant a pencil and a sheet of paper.

7. Write "MOST HOPEFUL ABOUT" at the top of one of the flip charts and say, "Now that we have heard one another's responses to the appreciative questions, please share with your partner what you are the most hopeful about in relation to accomplishing the task of this team."

   Continuing, write "OUR BEST WILL BE" at the top of the second flip chart and say, "Now, based on what you have learned about others in this group, write three statements on your paper that you would feel comfortable making about how we, as a team, will be at our best when working together." (Ten minutes.)

8. Allow ten minutes for pairs to discuss the two questions and write their answers. Then reconvene the group.

9. Lead a discussion based on the first question, writing participants' responses on the flip chart labeled "MOST HOPEFUL ABOUT." (Twenty minutes.)

10. Now ask the pairs to read the three statements they have written as you write them on the second flip chart, labeled "OUR BEST WILL BE."

11. Announce that you will save this flip chart and post it at subsequent meetings of the group. Conclude by stating that the "our best will be" statements are indicators of and guides for what the team members aspire to do and be in relationship to one another as they work together to accomplish the task ahead. (Fifteen minutes.)

   Note: These statements replace what are traditionally called "ground rules" or "operating guidelines" for a team, which are often generated by participants as they reflect on what did *not* work for them in the past, rather than on what did work, on what was the worst in other situations, rather than the best.

Variations

- An alternative would be to have all the participants post their individual flip-chart pages around the room and to allow three to five minutes for everyone to circle the room to look at what others have done. This would then be followed by the three-to-five-minute individual presentations.

- Send a memo in advance giving participants the questions and asking them to prepare and bring to the meeting their Appreciative Introduction flip charts.

- After they have read their statements aloud, have each pair turn in their written statements. Then have one person from the team transcribe all statements onto flip-chart paper to bring back to the next meeting for further discussion.

- Ask one person from the team to transcribe the group's statements onto 8½" x 11" paper and bring copies for everyone at the next meeting.

- Develop a checklist from the transcribed statements. Beginning with the next meeting, use the checklist at the end of meetings to evaluate the team members' ongoing commitment to being at their best.

Submitted by Sherene Zolno.

Sherene Zolno, M.S., executive director of The Leading Clinic, is a researcher, educator, and consultant whose expertise includes working with leadership teams to ready them for the future and assisting organizations in identifying strategic intentions, improving operations, and transforming the culture. Her research-based New Century Leadership™ program and Timeline for Tomorrow process are the foundations for systems change in several major organizations. Ms. Zolno has served on ASTD's OD Professional Practice Area Board; her articles have appeared in ASTD's Research Monograph *and OD Network's* VisionAction Journal.

669. Continuum: Exploring the Range of Facilitator Interventions

---

Goals

- To learn and practice a variety of group interventions, on a continuum from "doing nothing" to being "highly directive."

- To assist the group in solving some of its own thorny group-process issues.

Group Size

Ten to twenty members of an intact group, organized in small groups of about five members each.

Time Required

One and one-half hours.

Materials

- One overhead transparency of the Continuum of Facilitator Interventions.

- One copy of the Facilitator Intervention Definitions for each participant.

- Labels for each table on tent cards: 1, 2, 3, 4, etc.

- Several packs of index cards.

- Pens or pencils for participants.

- A flip chart and felt-tipped markers.

- An overhead projector.

Physical Setting

A room arranged with round tables for small group gatherings with moveable chairs.

Process

1. Prior to the session, label each table with a number, 1, 2, 3, etc., by using tent cards.

2. As a warm-up to a longer session for learning to facilitate groups or meetings, ask participants to form small groups. Hand out several index cards and pencils or pens to each group.

3. Ask the small groups to generate one or two group-process issues that have troubled them in the past or that they anticipate as problematic for the upcoming session. Ask a recorder from each group to write each of the issues on a separate index card, phrased as a question, and labeled with the table number. Give the example: "What do you do when there are side conversations?" (Fifteen minutes.)

4. Gather the cards and redistribute them to different tables.

5. Ask each group to discuss possible answers to the questions they have received among themselves. (Ten minutes.)

6. Present the Continuum of Facilitator Interventions transparency (Bentley, 1994) using the overhead projector. Define the terms and answer any questions from the participants. (Ten minutes.)

7. Instruct participants to examine each possible intervention on the continuum and to identify how each could be used in response to the problems on their cards. Encourage them to use a round-robin process so that all group members can participate. (Fifteen minutes.)

8. Next have groups discuss the probable outcome of each intervention and select their preferred intervention for each particular problem. (Fifteen minutes.)

9. Ask for a volunteer spokesperson from each table to present the group's assigned questions and their preferred interventions. Discuss that possibility and any others with the group that authored the question and the group at large. (Twenty minutes.)

10. Close with a discussion of the merits of various facilitator interventions and when each might be more effective. Post discussion notes on a flip chart.

Variation

- Have each group role play one of its issues in front of the group and ask the audience to decide which intervention to use. Conduct a group discussion of the best solutions.

Reference

Bentley, T. (1994). *Facilitation: Providing opportunities for learning.* New York: McGraw-Hill.

Submitted by M.K. Key.

M.K. Key, Ph.D., *is a clinical-community psychologist and the founder of Key Associates, LLC, in Nashville, Tennessee. She is a nationally recognized speaker on leadership, releasing the creative spirit, mediation of conflict, and team development. She has authored over thirty publications on such topics as change management, continuous quality improvement, strategic business issues, and leadership during turbulent times. Her most recent releases are* Corporate Celebration: Play, Purpose and Profit at Work, *with Terrence E. Deal (1998), and* Managing Change in Healthcare: Innovative Solutions for People-Based Organizations *(1998). Dr. Key also serves as adjunct professor of organization and human development at Vanderbilt University.*

CONTINUUM OF FACILITATOR INTERVENTIONS

Supportive

Highly
Facilitative

- Pausing
- Silence
- Nonverbal
- Validation
- Descriptive Feedback
- Evaluative Feedback
- Questions to Suggest Direction
- Debriefing
- Reframing
- Teaching
- Sharing Ideas
- Making Suggestions
- Guidance
- Mediation
- Direction
- Calling in Third Party

Based on the work of Trevor Bentley, *Facilitation: Providing Opportunities for Learning.* New York: Mc-Graw-Hill, 1994.

FACILITATOR INTERVENTION DEFINITIONS

Intervention is any action intended to help a person or group move in a healthy direction.

- *Pausing:* Choosing not to act, holding back and observing.
- *Silence:* Being still and using the quiet time to draw out others.
- *Nonverbal:* Using movement, voice, eye contact, and facial expression.
- *Validation:* Asking a question or paraphrasing to make sure that you understand.
- *Descriptive Feedback:* Playing back specific, behavioral observations without judgment, as a video camera would.
- *Evaluative Feedback:* In addition to the descriptive, adding a component to the feedback that summarizes it with a label or conclusion.
- *Questions to Suggest Direction:* Asking leading questions to invite the group to proceed, for example, "Why don't we move on to the next item?"
- *Debriefing:* Asking the group to examine with you what just happened.
- *Reframing:* Suggesting a new viewpoint or angle on a situation.
- *Teaching:* Giving instruction.
- *Sharing Ideas:* Revealing your thoughts on the matter.
- *Making Suggestions:* Proposing an idea about the best course of action.
- *Guidance:* In addition to verbal direction, actually leading in a suggestive way.
- *Mediation:* With situations involving conflict, drawing all parties into the room, hearing each faction's position and interest/rationale, and seeking a way with them to satisfy the interests of all in a creative way.
- *Direction:* Showing and telling in a stronger way.
- *Calling in Third Party:* After determined that you are not the best suited for this intervention, asking for the assistance of a consultant, counselor, or other qualified individual.

Introduction
to the Inventories, Questionnaires, and Surveys Section

Inventories, questionnaires, and surveys are important tools to the HRD professional. It may be difficult for participants and clients to look at themselves objectively. These feedback tools help respondents take stock of themselves and their organizations and understand how a particular theory applies to them or to their situations.

These instruments—inventories, questionnaires, and surveys—are useful in a number of training and consulting situations: privately for self-diagnosis; one-on-one to plan individual development; in a small group to open discussion; in a work team to help the team to focus on its highest priorities; or in an organization to gather data to achieve progress.

You will find that the use of inventories, questionnaires, and surveys enriches, personalizes, and deepens training, development, and intervention designs. Many can be combined with other experiential learning activities or articles in this or other *Annuals* to design an exciting, involving, practical, and well-rounded intervention.

Each instrument includes the background necessary for understanding, presenting, and using it. Interpretive information, scales, and scoring sheets are also provided. In addition, we include the reliability and validity data contributed by the authors. If you wish additional information on any of these instruments, contact the authors directly. You will find their addresses and telephone numbers in the "Contributors" listing near the end of this volume.

Other assessment tools that address a wider variety of topics can be found by using our comprehensive *Reference Guide to Handbooks and Annuals*. This guide provides an index to all the instruments that we have published to date in the *Annuals*. You will find this complete, up-to-date, and easy-to-use resource valuable for locating other instruments, as well as for locating experiential learning activities and articles.

The 2000 Annual: Volume 2, Consulting includes three assessment tools in the following categories:

Groups and Teams

Team Hope Survey: Enhancing Performance in Teams
by Susan B. Wilkes, Terry L. Hight, John D. DelCarmen,
and Melissa I. Figueiredo

Consulting and Facilitating

The Organizational Readiness Inventory (ORI):
Diagnosing Your Organization's Ability to Adapt to the Future
by James L. Moseley and Douglas J. Swiatkowski

Organizational Profile: Determining a Match by Scott B. Parry

TEAM HOPE SURVEY:
ENHANCING PERFORMANCE IN TEAMS

Susan B. Wilkes, Terry L. Hight,
John D. DelCarmen, and Melissa I. Figueiredo

Abstract: The concept of hope has gained attention recently as researchers are finding many positive attributes associated with individuals who have high levels of hope. The Team Hope Survey (THS) applies the concept of hope to group performance. It measures four dimensions of team functioning relevant to a team's sense of optimism about its future: *where* (purpose and goals), *way* (methods and plans), *we* (cohesion and caring), and *will* (motivation and confidence).

Team members respond to twenty questions regarding perceptions of their work team. Composite scores are obtained for the team on each of the four dimensions. Instructions are included for a team-development session based on the THS results.

Hope as a concept has been studied extensively by C.R. Snyder at the University of Kansas. Snyder (1994) defines hope as the will power and mental pathways one uses to reach goals. According to Snyder, hope has fundamentally three parts: goals, pathways to achieve those goals, and motivation to achieve the goals (Snyder et al., 1991). His research has shown that high-hope individuals characteristically display an optimistic outlook, perceive that they are in control of their lives, and demonstrate a capacity to solve problems. Additionally, high-hope individuals tend to have higher self-esteem and to feel less depressed than their lower-hope counterparts.

Based on the role that hope plays in enhancing individuals' lives, it seems worthwhile to also apply the concept of hope to teams, as more and more organizations seek to implement team-based approaches to work. The Team Hope Survey can be used to identify strengths and areas of weakness in work-team functioning. Having assessed these areas, consultants and trainers can then develop appropriate interventions for enhancing team performance. Practitioners who use the THS should possess a thorough understanding of group dynamics and have experience in leading team-building sessions.

DESCRIPTION OF THE INSTRUMENT

The Team Hope Survey is a self-scoring instrument containing twenty items, five items each on four scales. Respondents use a six-point Likert scale to rate critical elements of their team's performance and then receive feedback about their team's average scores on each of the four components that are necessary for a sense of hopefulness about the future of a team. These components are labeled "where," "way," "we," and "will." The instrument takes five to ten minutes to complete.

Results are scored using the Team Hope Survey Scoring Sheet. A Team Hope Survey Compilation Sheet is also included so that the facilitator can compile scores turned in by individuals. After group scores have been tabulated, they are plotted on a grid on the Team Hope Survey Interpretation Sheet. The instrument is best used as part of a team-development session in which, after the results are calculated, team members develop an action plan for enhancing their performance as a team.

PRESENTING THE THEORY

Distribute a copy of the Team Hope Survey Diamond Handout to each participant or display the diamond as a transparency, if desired. Go over the handout thoroughly with everyone, defining each dimension of the diamond, giving examples, and answering questions.

ADMINISTRATION AND SCORING

Explain that they will take a short survey to determine where their team is located in relation to the diamond. Remind them that the purpose is to give the team feedback so that team members can learn about one another's perceptions of team performance and plan for any necessary improvements. Tell the participants that their individual scores will not be revealed to anyone, but that group averages will be calculated and presented to the team.

Hand out copies of the Team Hope Survey (THS), the Team Hope Survey Scoring Sheet, and the Team Hope Survey Compilation Sheet. Instruct participants to be honest in their assessment of their team's functioning and to begin filling out the survey. As participants complete the survey, tell them to transfer their answers over to the Scoring Sheet. Assist any participants who need help. Tell them to transfer their totals on the four dimensions of the Scoring Sheet to the Compilation Sheet. As instructed on the Compilation Sheet, each person will tear his or her page into four strips that correspond with the corners of the diamond.

Ask for four volunteers to help tabulate the results on a copy of the Compilation Sheet printed on a flip chart. If the team is large, use pairs of volunteers for this task. Assign each person (or pair) one of the four components (where, way, we, and will). Have respondents pass the appropriate piece of paper to the volunteers as they move about the room. For a large group, give each of the volunteers a separate piece of flip-chart paper and a marker. Ask them to write the name of the component across the top of the page and then record the scores from the papers they receive. Remind the participants that their individual scores are private and not to inquire as to which scores came from which team members. Finally, have the volunteers calculate an average score for each component (total of all scores divided by the number of team members) and write that on the flip-chart page. Ask them to circle the average score so that everyone can see it easily.

INTERPRETATION

Hand out copies of the Team Hope Survey Interpretation Sheet and ask participants to plot all four scores from the flip-chart sheets along the appropriate axes. Show people how to do this by plotting the scores on a large piece of flip-chart paper. Next, have the participants connect the dots so that a diamond is formed. Connect the dots on the flip-chart page as an example. The result will be the team's "Hope Diamond."

Say that, like a diamond, a team's sense of hope is a very valuable attribute. Distribute the Team Hope Survey Individual Work Sheet and ask participants to spend ten to fifteen minutes filling it out in a thoughtful manner. Facilitate general discussion around the questions or, if the group is large, ask them to break into subgroups for discussion and then return to the main group after ten or fifteen minutes for a wrap-up discussion.

USING THE RESULTS IN TEAM ACTION PLANNING

Following the steps below, engage the team in developing a plan of action for enhancing team functioning and hope for future performance.

1. While the team members are completing their work sheets, make a separate flip-chart page for each of the four components. Write the name of the component across the top, make two columns by drawing a vertical line down the sheet, and then write as headers of the two columns "strengths" and "areas to improve."

2. Ask participants to share whatever information from their work sheets they feel comfortable saying in front of the group. Go through the four components one at a time, writing the strengths and areas for improvement as indicated by the group. For now, focus on putting everyone's ideas and thoughts up, rather than on critiquing the ideas.

3. After all pages have been completed, either on your own or with the group, decide on a reasonable number of areas for improvement that the group can work on. This can be determined by the amount of time allotted for the session as well as the time and energy the group has for implementing an action plan. It is better to develop a shorter, realistic action plan than one that is overly ambitious.

4. Give all group members a set of twelve stick-on stars or other self-stick dots or notes—*three for each point on the diamond.* (Fewer or more than three can be used, depending on the desired depth of the action plan.) Tell the group that each person is going to "vote" for the three items within each area he or she would most like the group to work on. Obviously, these should be items that they think are important and for which improvement is needed. Allow anyone who wishes to speak in favor of working on a particular item to do so before taking the "vote." Then ask team members to place their stars to the left of the items they want to vote for on the four flip-chart pages, one at a time.

5. On a new piece of flip-chart paper, write the three areas (or however many you desire) that received the most votes for each area. Brainstorm action steps the group could take within each area. (For example, if clarifying roles were selected as one area, the team would brainstorm specific things that could be done to help clarify roles.)

6. Next, lead the group in prioritizing the action steps and in committing to which steps will be taken. Again, help the group in selecting a realistic number of action steps to begin with. Remind them that other steps can be taken later. Agree on responsible parties who will make sure that each step is taken and on time frames for action.

7. Discuss and agree on any follow-up actions, such as having the flip-chart pages typed and distributed to members, agreeing on a date to check progress on action items, or other ideas the team may have for next steps.

8. Facilitate discussion on what team members learned during the session and the usefulness of the session.

PSYCHOMETRIC PROPERTIES OF THE INSTRUMENT

Demographics of the Sample

In order to test reliability and validity of the instrument, 164 people (a combination of university students and full-time employees from a variety of organizations) completed the Team Hope Survey. Of the employees, the majority (65.4 percent) were age forty-one or older and had significant work experience. Eighty-three percent of the employees had been team members for at least six months.

Racial breakdowns were as follows: 77.6 percent Caucasian, 20.7 percent African-American, and 1.7 percent other. Sixty-two percent of the group were females, while 38 percent were males.

Reliability

Internal consistency for the overall scale and each of the four sub-scales was calculated using Cronbach's alpha for the full sample of 164 participants. The internal consistency score for the overall scale of twenty items was very high, with an alpha of .953. Alpha coefficients for the sub-scales of where, way, we, and will were .85, .87, .84, and .86, respectively.

Test-retest correlations were calculated based on a sample of eighty-four individuals who took the survey once and then again two weeks later. The correlation on the overall survey score was .741. Test-retest correlations for the sub-scales where, way, we, and will were .693, .723, .744, and .589, respectively.

Validity

Validity of the instrument as a measure of hopefulness about one's team was assessed by examining the relationship between scores on the scales and ratings on two separate items about hope. These items were "I personally feel hopeful about the future of this team" and "I am optimistic about the potential of this group." Correlations between these items and the scales are noted in the table below.

	Item 1: Hopefulness	Item 2: Optimism
Total THS Score	.669	.669
Where Sub-Scale Score	.600	.630
Way Sub-Scale Score	.548	.551
We Sub-Scale Score	.641	.588
Will Sub-Scale Score	.634	.658

All of these correlations are significant at the $p < .001$ level.

In addition, two outside experts (one college professor specializing in group dynamics and one consultant who frequently conducts team-building sessions) were asked to rate the survey on the importance of the dimensions for team functioning, the relevance of the items to team performance, and the extent to which the survey covered the major areas in team development. On a five-point Likert scale, ranging from a low of 1 to a high of 5, the experts rated the survey a 4 or 5 on all three questions.

References

Coleridge, E.H. (Ed.). (1912). *The complete works of Samuel Taylor Coleridge* (Vol. 1). Oxford, England, United Kingdom: Clarendon.

Drucker, P. (1954). *The practice of management.* New York: Harper & Row.

Lynch, W. (1974). *Images of hope.* Notre Dame, IN: University of Notre Dame Press.

Snyder, C.R. (1994). *The psychology of hope: You can get there from here.* New York: The Free Press.

Snyder, C.R., Harris, C., Anderson, J.R., Holleran, S.A., Irving, L.M., Sigmon, S.T., Yoshinobu, L.R., Gibb, J., Langelle, C., & Harney, P. (1991). The will and the ways: Development and validation of an individual differences measure of hope. *Journal of Personality and Social Psychology, 60,* 570–585.

Susan B. Wilkes, Ph.D., *manages the Workplace Initiatives Program, a training and consulting unit in the Department of Psychology at Virginia Commonwealth University. She is an organizational psychologist who is a frequent workshop leader, consultant, and executive coach. Her areas of expertise include team performance, organizational change, performance improvement, conflict resolution, and leadership. Dr. Wilkes is a licensed professional counselor whose background also includes extensive experience in counseling and coaching individual employees for increased job satisfaction and efficacy.*

Terry L. Hight, M.S., M.A., *is a project coordinator in the Workplace Initiatives Program, a training and consulting unit in the Department of Psychology at Virginia Commonwealth University. He is a fourth-year doctoral student in VCU's APA-accredited counseling psychology program. His professional interests include facilitating performance enhancement and satisfaction in both career and marriage. Reflecting these interests, Mr. Hight has graduate degrees in counseling psychology and marriage and family therapy.*

John D. DelCarmen, M.S., *is a project coordinator for the Workplace Initiatives Program, a training and consulting unit in the Department of Psychology at Virginia Commonwealth University. He is a third-year doctoral student in VCU's social psychology program, which specializes in research in group dynamics. His professional* *goal is to teach at the collegiate level in conjunction with active consulting involvement in the business community.*

Melissa I. Figueiredo, M.S., *is project coordinator of the Workplace Initiatives Program, a training and consulting unit in the Department of Psychology at Virginia Commonwealth University. She is a fourth-year doctoral student in VCU's APA-accredited counseling psychology program. Her professional interests include health psychology and group dynamics. She has designed and led workshops on stress management and has facilitated small groups in supervisory skills and conflict resolution.*

TEAM HOPE SURVEY DIAMOND HANDOUT

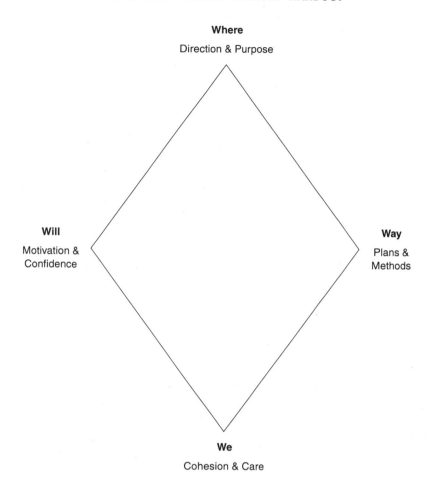

Where

Direction & Purpose

Will

Motivation &
Confidence

Way

Plans &
Methods

We

Cohesion & Care

Hope

Hope can be defined as the feeling that what one wants to happen will happen. Generally, individuals who are hopeful feel optimistic about their futures and expect positive things to occur. Hope is important for teams as well. When a work team feels hopeful about its future, members feel motivated and confident.

We can think of hope as a diamond, as shown on the diagram above. Like a diamond, it is a valuable gem. Yet, unlike the characteristics of a diamond, the quantity and quality of hope in a team can be enhanced. There are four essential parts that make up a team's sense of hopefulness about its future.

One: Where (Direction and Purpose)

Hope involves the perception that one's goals can be met. People who are higher in hope have a greater number of goals, and their goals tend to be challenging in nature. C.R. Snyder's (1994) work on hope draws heavily on the collaborative goal-setting process found in management by objectives (Drucker, 1954). This concept is represented by the "where" component of the Hope Diamond.

Two: Way (Plans and Methods)

Snyder calls this aspect of hope the "pathway" or "waypower." It involves the capacity for individuals to find one or more effective ways to reach their goals. Thus, hopeful people have mental plans or road maps that guide them toward their goals. Similarly, teams must have methods and plans to help them in reaching their goals.

Three: We (Cohesion and Care)

Although Snyder's conceptualization of hope does not include this component, it has been included here because numerous scholars of team development have noted that both task and process (or relationship) components of team functioning are important. The "where" and "way" components seem to cover task-related aspects of team functioning, and the "we" component assesses the interpersonal dynamics and relationships on the team. As Lynch (1974) notes, "Hope cannot be achieved alone. It must in some way be an act of community."

Four: Will (Motivation and Confidence)

Snyder calls this fourth component "agency" or "willpower," as it involves the determination and commitment that individuals call on to move them in the direction of their goals. The Hope Diamond retains this important motivational component and labels it the "will."

The 2000 Annual: Volume 2, Consulting/© 2000 Jossey-Bass/Pfeiffer

References

Coleridge, E.H. (Ed.). (1912). *The complete works of Samuel Taylor Coleridge* (Vol. 1). Oxford, England, United Kingdom: Clarendon.

Drucker, P. (1954). *The practice of management.* New York: Harper & Row.

Lynch, W. (1974). *Images of hope.* Notre Dame, IN: University of Notre Dame Press.

Snyder, C.R. (1994). *The psychology of hope: You can get there from here.* New York: The Free Press.

Snyder, C.R., Harris, C., Anderson, J.R., Holleran, S.A., Irving, L.M., Sigmon, S.T., Yoshinobu, L.R., Gibb, J., Langelle, C., & Harney, P. (1991). The will and the ways: Development and validation of an individual differences measure of hope. *Journal of Personality and Social Psychology, 60,* 570–585.

TEAM HOPE SURVEY

Susan B. Wilkes, Terry L. Hight, John D. DelCarmen, and Melissa I. Figueiredo

Directions: Read each item carefully. Using the scale below, determine the degree to which each item is true for your team. Select the number that best describes your response.

| 1 = Definitely False | 2 = Mostly False | 3 = Slightly False |
| 4 = Slightly True | 5 = Mostly True | 6 = Definitely True |

1. We understand the purpose of our team.   1 2 3 4 5 6

2. We have effective procedures to guide our group functioning.   1 2 3 4 5 6

3. We listen to and hear one another.   1 2 3 4 5 6

4. We energetically pursue our goals.   1 2 3 4 5 6

5. We have shared goals.   1 2 3 4 5 6

6. We have well-established and agreed-on approaches to solving problems and making decisions.   1 2 3 4 5 6

7. Our communications among members are open and participative.   1 2 3 4 5 6

8. Our past experiences have prepared us well for the future.   1 2 3 4 5 6

9. We cooperate as a unit, moving toward common goals for the good of the organization.   1 2 3 4 5 6

10. We clearly understand the roles and responsibilities of team members.   1 2 3 4 5 6

11. We have a high level of trust among members.   1 2 3 4 5 6

12. We have been successful as a team.   1 2 3 4 5 6

13. We regularly develop plans, set goals, and establish a "game plan."   1 2 3 4 5 6

| 1 = Definitely False | 2 = Mostly False | 3 = Slightly False |
| 4 = Slightly True | 5 = Mostly True | 6 = Definitely True |

14. We agree on how the team should accomplish its mission.

    1   2   3   4   5   6

15. We have a feeling of camaraderie among team members.

    1   2   3   4   5   6

16. Our team reaches the goals we set.

    1   2   3   4   5   6

17. We understand how our efforts help to achieve the goals of the group.

    1   2   3   4   5   6

18. We have effective means of working through disagreements.

    1   2   3   4   5   6

19. We are genuinely concerned for one another.

    1   2   3   4   5   6

20. We are highly motivated to work toward common goals.

    1   2   3   4   5   6

TEAM HOPE SURVEY SCORING SHEET

Directions: Transfer your responses for each question to the appropriate blank below. Then, total the numbers in each column and put your totals in the blanks at the bottom of the columns.

1._____   2._____   3._____   4._____

5._____   6._____   7._____   8._____

9._____   10._____   11._____   12._____

13._____   14._____   15._____   16._____

17._____   18._____   19._____   20._____

TOTALS = _____   _____   _____   _____

        Where   Way   We   Will

TEAM HOPE SURVEY COMPILATION SHEET

Directions: Copy the total scores from your Scoring Sheet below. For example, write the total score for "where" in the top blank. When you have put down your scores in all four categories, tear or cut your page into strips and give each strip to the facilitator or to a designated scoring person.

My Score for Where: _____

My Score for Way: _____

My Score for We: _____

My Score for Will: _____

TEAM HOPE SURVEY INTERPRETATION SHEET

Directions: When the facilitator gives you the team's average scores for each of the four areas, plot them along the corresponding axes below.

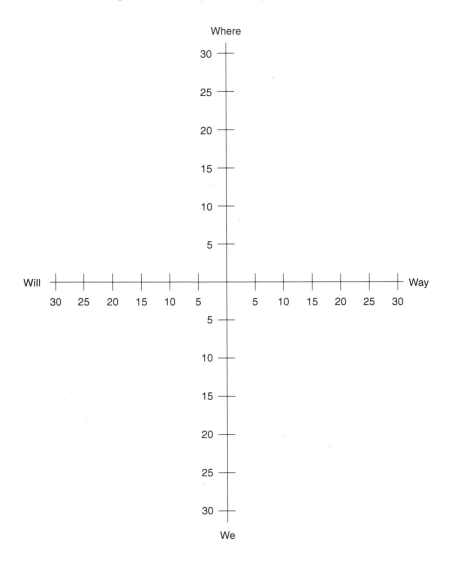

Now connect your dots with straight lines. Notice the shape of the diamond you make. Note the overall size. Is it a large diamond (that is, all sides are close to 30) or is it a smaller gem? Is it symmetrical (that is, all sides are similar) or are some sides larger than others?

How might the diamond be improved? Would you want to focus on enhancing brilliance in one facet of the diamond? Or would you want to work toward increased symmetry by improving one weaker facet? Keep these questions in mind as you complete the Team Hope Survey Individual Work Sheet.

TEAM HOPE SURVEY INDIVIDUAL WORK SHEET

Directions: Answer the following questions individually based on the team average that has been posted. Prepare to discuss your answers in the large group.

■ Is the diamond for your team large (that is, are all sides close to 30) or is the diamond small?

■ Is it symmetrical (that is, are all sides similar in size) or are some sides larger than others?

■ How could the team's diamond be improved?

■ Which strong facet do you think the team should focus on enhancing?

■ Would you prefer to increase the diamond's symmetry by improving one or two weaker facets? Why or why not?

- Which of the four areas is this team strongest in (which has the highest group average)? Are you satisfied with this score or could it be even higher? What specific strengths do you perceive that your team has in this area? What in this area might the team still improve?

- What is the second highest score? What is the team doing well in this category? Where would you like to see improvement?

- Note the third highest score. What strengths does the team have in this area? What areas can you identify that could be enhanced?

- What is the team's lowest score? Even though it is the lowest score, are there areas within it on which the team is performing well? If so, which? What one specific aspect of this category would you want to see targeted for improvement?

The Organizational Readiness Inventory (ORI): Diagnosing Your Organization's Ability to Adapt to the Future

James L. Moseley and Douglas J. Swiatkowski

Abstract: Models for business abound today. Most business people can probably name two or three off the top of their heads. These models serve a valuable purpose—to help an organization paint a picture of its future, its optimum state. As any person concerned with performance knows, however, this portrait is only half the picture. A clear snapshot of what the organization looks like now is necessary in order to have something to compare with the optimum future. The Organizational Readiness Inventory (ORI) is a means of doing this.

The authors use the 7S Model developed by Peters and Waterman (1988) and Pascale (1991) and embraced by McKinsey and Company. The model provides seven categories by which an organization can measure its current state and define an optimal future state. The ORI provides the means to measure how the members see the organization currently.

$\mathbf{T}$he 7S Model—the basis of this instrument—establishes seven key categories or areas of concentration that an organization should have a handle on in order to be successful. These categories are *strategy, structure, systems, staff, style, shared values,* and *skills,* which are defined in Figure 1. These categories were recognized and brought together by Tom Peters and Robert Waterman of McKinsey and Company with the assistance of Robert Pascale and Anthony Athos. The work of Harold Leavitt (the "Leavitt Diamond") was also influential in our thinking. The model concentrates not on technology skills or hard skills, but on those that often are considered "soft." As noted by Peters and Waterman (1988), "All the stuff you have been dismissing for so long as the intractable, irrational, intuitive, informal organization can be managed—soft is hard."

The ORI provides a systematic way to find out how the organization assesses itself based on the seven categories. The "voice" of the organization, for our purposes, refers to the amalgam of the thoughts and opinions of the members of the organization. These do not necessarily reflect the open ver-

Category	Definition
Strategy	Plan or course of action leading to the allocation of a firm's scarce resources, over time, to reach identified goals.
Structure	Salient features of the organizational chart (i.e., functional, decentralized, etc.) and how the separate entities of an organization are tied together.
Systems	Reports that are a matter of procedure and routine processes, such as meetings.
Staffing	Demographic descriptions of important personnel categories within the organization.
Style	How key managers behave in achieving the organization's goals; also, the cultural style of an organization.
Skills	Distinctive capabilities of key personnel and the organization as a whole.
Shared Values	The significant meanings or guiding concepts that an organization imbues in its members.

Figure 1. Definitions of the 7S Categories

bal opinions expressed by the individuals, which are often shaded by fear, politics, and "groupthink." The "voice" of the organization reflects what the individuals feel and believe internally. If administered properly and in an environment of anonymity and trust, the ORI helps to bring out the internal voice of the organization.

The shell of the ORI instrument is based on the Inventory of Self-Actualizing Characteristics (ISAC) (Banet, 1976). The five-point scale and the data-collection method remain much like the ISAC, but the data-reporting method has been modified to produce data in the aggregate, as opposed to the ISAC, which is an individual inventory with the data intended to be used by the person completing it.

The seventy-seven statements (eleven for each of the seven categories) were derived through a literature and Internet search of the seven topics. The authors looked for themes and common threads and framed statements to reflect them.

DESCRIPTION OF THE INSTRUMENT

The ORI consists of a seventy-seven statement inventory, eleven for each of the seven categories of the 7S Model; a Scoring Sheet; and an Interpretation Sheet. Individuals completing the inventory simply read each statement, reflect on how it pertains to their organization, and choose which of the five responses best fits the organization's current way of doing things. See Figure 2 below for a listing of the responses and their corresponding meanings.

N = The organization has *not recognized the issue yet.*

S = The organization has *begun speaking about the issue.*

I = The organization has *initiated plans of action and goals around the issue.*

W = *Work is being done* toward goals around the issue.

R = *Results are being realized* on work being done around this issue.

Figure 2. ORI Rating Scale

The individuals completing the survey do not score their own results. Because the data is intended to be viewed in the aggregate and has no real value to the individual, the administrator does the scoring. Although scoring in this way does require quite a bit of time and effort, it was deemed the better method. In testing the instrument, it was found that it took about thirty minutes to complete the scoring, and the individuals who reviewed the instrument thought that this was too cumbersome for individuals.

The administrator uses the ORI Profile Sheet to obtain a composite score for each of the categories by simply averaging the numeric values of all respondents. This information is then plotted on the ORI Profile Sheet to reflect the rating of the group that completed the survey. The Profile Sheet shows how each of the five categories was scored by the group. The ORI Interpretation Sheet helps to clarify what each of the five ratings indicates about the organization.

ADMINISTRATION OF THE INSTRUMENT

It is highly recommended that this instrument be administered in a facilitated session, as opposed to simply handing them out and requesting that people complete them, for three reasons:

- Using a facilitated session greatly increases the number of respondents who actually complete the instrument.

- A facilitated session allows for a standard explanation to be given to participants about what the instrument is intended to do.

- Questions can be immediately addressed in a facilitated session. Although this is not a guarantee of sounder data, the facilitator may be able to help an individual who otherwise may give up or provide incorrect data.

Anonymity is critical for obtaining unbiased data from the participants. All respondents should receive unmarked envelopes to use for returning the entire instrument when they are done. These should be collected in a receptacle near the exit. One person should be responsible for compiling the scores and recording the data. This person should not be a member of upper management. Great care should go into selecting an individual who is viewed as trustworthy by respondents.

Once the data are compiled, bring the members of the organization together and go over the results both verbally and visually. Allow time for some questions and answers about what the data show and what can be learned. Be sure that everyone hears the same message, and also provide an opportunity to discuss next steps based on the results. Focus groups can also be formed around each of the 7S categories to further explore the results and examine possible courses of action.

Based on the trials with this instrument, a thirty-five to forty-five minute time period should be sufficient to provide some background and have respondents complete the instrument.

PRESENTATION OF THEORY

The theory behind the instrument (the 7S Model), some background on performance improvement, and information about optimum and desired states should be presented to the respondents *after* they have completed the instrument so that results will not be biased. Some possible ways to share this information follow:

- Because a facilitator is already present, he or she could explain the theory after everyone has completed the instrument. The facilitator can provide some background on the 7S Model, explaining the categories and why are they important. The facilitator could also explain why the data are being gathered and what is going to be done with the results. A downside to this method is that people tend to finish filling out instruments at various paces. If you require people to stay after they are finished, those who finish quickly will probably be bored, while those who are moving more slowly will be likely to feel rushed.

- A small job aid could be handed out to respondents as they leave, giving the necessary information on the theory and what will be done with the data. Add the name of a contact person for additional questions people might have.

Regardless of the way that a presentation of the theory is handled, the respondents must have this information to provide a context for the results when they are shared later with the rest of the organization. Good practice is founded on solid theory.

Scoring the Instrument

It should be noted that the value-added output of this instrument is the aggregate data. Individual scores are of no value. However, if an individual is interested in doing so, he or she can be given a Profile Sheet and an Interpretation Sheet to chart out his or her own scores and interpret them.

Posting the Data

The results can be posted and compared with previous evaluations to show progress for the entire organization. The scores can be presented in a number of ways, either showing:

- Scores for the entire organization, or
- Breakdowns of scores by functional unit (human resources, accounting, marketing, etc.).

Care must be taken that each group contains at least five people to assure anonymity of respondents.

Suggested Uses for the Instrument

The ORI is designed to collect the opinions of organization members in order to find the "voice" of the organization. However, there are other possible uses. The ORI provides an extensive list of diagnostic questions that performance improvement specialists could use to guide an audit. Evidence could be sought in support for each statement, and a decision about what was needed could be made on the basis of the evidence. The ORI could also be used first with the organization's management team as a self-audit. The scores derived from this self-audit could then be compared with organization-wide results.

RELIABILITY AND VALIDITY

The instrument is an informal diagnostic tool, as opposed to a formal data-gathering instrument. There were no formal studies conducted; hence, no data exists to demonstrate reliability or validity. This instrument, however, was piloted with instructional and performance technology professionals and revised based on their feedback.

References

Banet, A.G., Jr. (1976). Inventory of self-actualizing characteristics (ISAC). In J.W. Pfeiffer & J.E. Jones (Eds.), *The 1976 annual handbook for group facilitators* (pp. 70–77). San Francisco, CA: Jossey-Bass/Pfeiffer.

Pascale, R. (1991). *Managing on the edge.* New York: Simon and Schuster.

Peters, T., & Waterman, R. (1988). *In search of excellence: Lessons from America's best-run companies.* New York: Warner Books.

James L. Moseley, Ed.D., L.P.C., is an associate professor of community medicine in the School of Medicine at Wayne State University, Detroit, Michigan. He also holds full faculty status in the College of Education, where he teaches performance technology and program evaluation. He consults with all levels of management. He is the recipient of teaching awards and service awards, the author of a variety of articles and book chapters, and a member of both ISPI and ASTD.

Douglas J. Swiatkowski, M.Ed., is an instructional designer for MSX International. He designs and develops training interventions for Ford Motor Company at the Fairlane Training and Development Center in Dearborn, Michigan. He holds a master's degree in instructional technology from Wayne State University, Detroit, Michigan, where he was awarded the 1998 Outstanding Instructional Technology Master's Student Award. He is a member of both the ISPI and ASTD and has written for both organizations' publications, as well as spoken at local functions.

Organizational Readiness Inventory (ORI)

James L. Moseley and Douglas J. Swiatkowski

Instructions: The following instrument has been designed to help give you information about your organization's readiness to adapt to the future. It has a selection of seventy-seven statements you are asked to respond to by indicating the *present* state of your organization. When responding to the statements, be sure to describe your organization's state *at this time, not what you think it should be or will be in the future.* Do not spend too much time selecting your responses. Your initial reaction to the statements is best.

Read each item and circle the letter to the right of the statement that most accurately describes your organization at this time.

N = The organization has *not recognized the issue yet.*
S = The organization has *begun speaking about the issue.*
I = The organization has *initiated plans of action and goals around the issue.*
W = *Work is being done* toward goals around the issue.
R = *Results are being realized* on work being done around this issue.

1. The organization values diversity in personnel.	N	S	I	W	R
2. The organization must stand apart from its competition.	N	S	I	W	R
3. Managers are involved in coaching and providing feedback to employees.	N	S	I	W	R
4. Potential for career development is realized.	N	S	I	W	R
5. Organizational vision is consistent with organizational action.	N	S	I	W	R
6. Educational activities are linked to business goals.	N	S	I	W	R
7. There is a drastic shortage of skilled labor.	N	S	I	W	R
8. The organization cannot be held captive to key people; there must be processes that other people could step up and use.	N	S	I	W	R
9. Skill requirements today change quickly.	N	S	I	W	R

10. Employees are empowered to make decisions. N S I W R

11. Fewer managers, more teams is the trend. N S I W R

12. The organization views itself as a part of the
surrounding community. N S I W R

13. Information is utilized, managed, practiced,
and disseminated. N S I W R

14. Employee input is encouraged and listened to. N S I W R

15. Our employees' performance must stand
apart from the competition. N S I W R

16. Development is linked to strategies of the
organization. N S I W R

17. Processes exist to ensure that things are
done right the first time. N S I W R

18. Performance is valued more than placement. N S I W R

19. People who are hired possess necessary
skill sets. N S I W R

20. Resources are allocated for employee
development. N S I W R

21. Interviews are structured to produce
information needed to make sound hiring
decisions. N S I W R

22. Laughter and having fun while working are
encouraged. N S I W R

23. The organization is able to adapt its core
skills to a rapidly changing environment. N S I W R

24. This is an organization that identifies levels
of resistance, recognizes the source(s), and
takes a proactive approach. N S I W R

N = The organization has *not recognized the issue yet*.
S = The organization has *begun speaking about the issue*.
I = The organization has *initiated plans of action and goals around the issue*.
W = *Work is being done* toward goals around the issue.
R = *Results are being realized* on work being done around this issue.

25. Retaining employees is beneficial.	N	S	I	W	R
26. Rites and rituals of the organization are integrated into employees' lives.	N	S	I	W	R
27. A collaborative versus a competitive atmosphere exists within the organization.	N	S	I	W	R
28. At the heart of the company values lies company spirit.	N	S	I	W	R
29. Internal and external scanning reveals the organization's strengths, weaknesses, opportunities, and threats.	N	S	I	W	R
30. A mutual and inspiring trust, nurtured by honest and open communication and equal opportunity, exists.	N	S	I	W	R
31. Activities are benchmarked and measured over time.	N	S	I	W	R
32. Reward and recognition systems credit skill development.	N	S	I	W	R
33. An organization needs a consistent plan of action.	N	S	I	W	R
34. Performance improvement specialists need to possess cultural self-awareness.	N	S	I	W	R
35. The organization pursues its business with honor, fairness, and respect.	N	S	I	W	R
36. When change occurs, the organization enters into a destabilization process.	N	S	I	W	R
37. Opportunities for advancement exist.	N	S	I	W	R
38. The educational/skills background of its people reflects the organization's needs.	N	S	I	W	R

N = The organization has *not recognized the issue yet.*
S = The organization has *begun speaking about the issue.*
I = The organization has *initiated plans of action and goals around the issue.*
W = *Work is being done* toward goals around the issue.
R = *Results are being realized* on work being done around this issue.

39. A performance consultant should view
    systems work as an exercise in forecasting.   N   S   I   W   R

40. Gut feelings and hunches should not be
    immediately dismissed, but considered
    based on the experience of the individual
    asserting them.   N   S   I   W   R

41. Alternative sources of human capital are
    valued (outsourcing, interns, co-ops, etc.).   N   S   I   W   R

42. Training partnerships allow the organiza-
    tion to obtain different insights on internal
    organizational issues.   N   S   I   W   R

43. In order to be successful, employee devel-
    opment systems should promote personal
    growth, enrichment, and self-learning.   N   S   I   W   R

44. Positions do not remain vacant for an
    extended period of time.   N   S   I   W   R

45. The organization recognizes that develop-
    mental activities will pay off over time on
    the bottom line.   N   S   I   W   R

46. Congruence exists between the organiza-
    tion's beliefs and actions.   N   S   I   W   R

47. Managing a training function requires
    familiarization with the instructional systems
    design (ISD) process.   N   S   I   W   R

48. Repositioning evaluation as an integral part
    of performance improvement can increase
    its credibility, utility, and institutionalization. N   S   I   W   R

49. Experience levels are recognized and valued.   N   S   I   W   R

50. The organization provides needed "tools" for
    employees to perform at their optimum best.   N   S   I   W   R

N = The organization has *not recognized the issue yet.*
S = The organization has *begun speaking about the issue.*
I = The organization has *initiated plans of action and goals around the issue.*
W = *Work is being done* toward goals around the issue.
R = *Results are being realized* on work being done around this issue.

51. Inputs and outputs of all processes must be
    identified.   N   S   I   W   R

52. The organization is aware of its position in
    the global marketplace.   N   S   I   W   R

53. A competency driven process is used to
    fill vacancies.   N   S   I   W   R

54. Assessment centers identify management
    and executive candidates and observe and
    assess their behavior.   N   S   I   W   R

55. Employee strengths and areas of expertise
    are routinely inventoried, documented, and
    shared with all so other employees know
    where to turn for information and assistance.   N   S   I   W   R

56. Beliefs, values, and wishes drive the way stake-
    holders address the strategic planning process.   N   S   I   W   R

57. Deming's Fourteen Points philosophy pro-
    vides the guidelines for creating an environ-
    ment for a TQM system.   N   S   I   W   R

58. Common visions and common purposes
    contribute to successful market positions.   N   S   I   W   R

59. Obvious trappings of position, reserved
    parking, separate facilities, should not exist.   N   S   I   W   R

60. Managing performance is a way to build
    synergy within organizations.   N   S   I   W   R

61. A climate of supportiveness rather than being
    judgmental fosters an atmosphere conducive
    to learning.   N   S   I   W   R

62. Success depends on an organization's ability
    to deliver a level of excellence respected by
    all who rely on it.   N   S   I   W   R

63. Organizations in tune with their employees
    maintain fairness and ethical standards.   N   S   I   W   R

64. The organization supports organizational
    scanning efforts through analysis of the
    organization, people, and work facts.   N   S   I   W   R

65. Processes in the organization are identified
    and represented in some way (policies, flow
    charts, etc.).   N   S   I   W   R

66. Management should regularly receive frank
    and honest feedback from those they supervise.   N   S   I   W   R

67. Fiscally sound decisions are made to support
    organizational goals.   N   S   I   W   R

68. The organization helps its members establish
    personal development plans.   N   S   I   W   R

69. Staffing needs are integrated with key busi-
    ness systems.   N   S   I   W   R

70. Outsourcing or "right sizing" is an issue of
    competency.   N   S   I   W   R

71. Human resource development policies and
    procedures shape the manner in which work
    is accomplished.   N   S   I   W   R

72. Mistakes are expected and are viewed as
    excellent opportunities to learn.   N   S   I   W   R

73. Employees are hired to ensure competitive
    vision.   N   S   I   W   R

74. The organization commits to the delivery of
    outputs that have a positive and desired im-
    pact on what it contributes to the community.   N   S   I   W   R

N = The organization has *not recognized the issue yet.*
S = The organization has *begun speaking about the issue.*
I = The organization has *initiated plans of action and goals around the issue.*
W = *Work is being done* toward goals around the issue.
R = *Results are being realized* on work being done around this issue.

75. An organization's ideal vision forms a framework through partnership with clients, stakeholders, and sponsoring and regulatory agencies. N S I W R

76. Employees want to perform tasks with pride and want to participate in the organization's survival and improvement. N S I W R

77. Employees and managers understand the impact that their decisions have on the organization's processes. N S I W R

ORI Scoring Sheet

Directions: In each of the charts below find the question numbers from the survey and place your letter score for that item in the box beneath the item number. Once you have done this for all seven charts, assign the appropriate numerical value to each letter using the following scale:

$$N = -2$$
$$S = -1$$
$$I = \ \ 0$$
$$W = \ \ 1$$
$$R = \ \ 2$$

Finally, add the values for each chart and place the number you obtain in the box below the chart. For example:

Sample Chart

Question	1	18	25	33	38	46	52	63	68	71	77
Letter	N	W	W	R	S	I	N	S	S	R	W
Value	-2	1	1	2	-1	0	-2	-1	-1	2	1
										Score	0

Strategy

Question	6	16	20	24	31	33	45	52	62	67	75
Letter											
Value											
										Score	

Structure

Question	2	11	18	29	36	42	48	57	64	70	71
Letter											
Value											
										Score	

Systems

Question	8	13	17	21	39	43	47	51	55	65	77
Letter											
Value											
										Score	

Staffing

Question	1	7	19	25	37	38	41	44	53	69	73
Letter											
Value											
										Score	

Style

Question	3	10	14	22	27	34	40	46	59	66	72
Letter											
Value											
										Score	

Skills

Question	4	9	15	23	32	49	50	54	60	68	76
Letter											
Value											
									Score		

Shared Values

Question	5	12	26	28	30	35	56	58	61	63	74
Letter											
Value											
									Score		

ORI Profile Sheet

Directions: Compute the average score in each category by totaling all scores and dividing by the number of respondents. Then plot the results on the following graph.

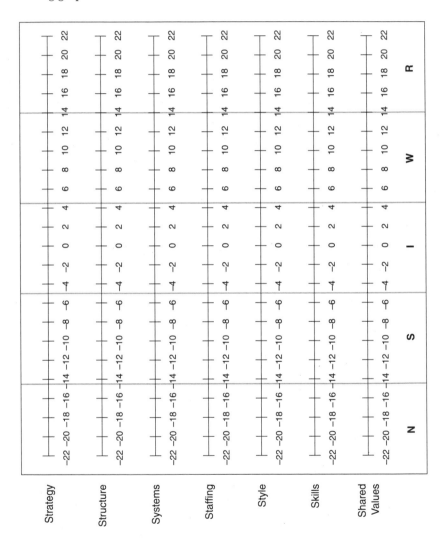

ORI INTERPRETATION SHEET

The following are short explanations of what each answer may mean for your organization. This is not intended as an item analysis, but you may draw your own conclusions about your organization's scores on each category mean.

If Your Score Is N for a Category

The organization has *not recognized the issue yet*. The employees perceive that the organization has not yet even addressed this category of the 7S Model. This could point to many problems and an equal number of solutions. It may be that the organization has not seen the category as significant. It may also be that work is being done in the category, but this has not been clearly communicated to the rest of the organization. Regardless of the cause, receiving an N in any of the seven categories should be a red flag for management.

If Your Score Is S for a Category

The organization has *begun speaking about the issue*. An S rating tells the organization that the employees' perception is that something is at least being discussed. However, an S also could mean that the employees believe talk and only talk is taking place and that there have been no actions to back up the philosophizing. Again, communication could be an issue if the organization has actually put something into practice but done a poor job of informing organization members. Receiving an S should also serve as a warning flag in that the perception of "all talk and no action" on the part of the organization can have negative effects on the employees' willingness to commit to an initiative.

If Your Score Is I for a Category

The organization has *initiated plans of action and goals around the issue*. The employees recognize that the organization is on its way to doing something regarding the category. Plans of action and goals entail allocations of people and time, and in some cases, actual monetary budgets. Receiving an I may also indicate good lines of communication in that the employees are aware of what the organization's plans are. Although receiving an I is better than receiving an N or S on a category, an organization must not allow itself to be complacent and satisfied with an I. Actual activities need to be undertaken and evident to maintain momentum and employee support.

If Your Score Is W for a Category

Work is being done toward goals around the issue. Receiving a W in a category means the employees of the organization see tasks taking place that are designed to help the organization achieve its goals in that particular category. The score tells an organization that the employees see that management is beyond the talking and philosophizing phase and has rolled up its collective sleeves. Again, if employees are aware of the work being done, it may be an indication of a good communication system.

If Your Score Is R for a Category

Results are being realized on work being done around this issue. Receiving an R in a category means that employees of the organization not only have heard the organization speak about an effort, but they have seen the plan and observed the work, and now can see results. This rating not only reveals successful efforts but a strong communication system that celebrates success and is able to help employees make the connections among plans, efforts, and results.

ORGANIZATIONAL PROFILE: DETERMINING A MATCH

Scott B. Parry

Abstract: This instrument helps employees determine whether they work in an innovative, bureaucratic, or supportive organization and determine their own needs for power and control, achievement, and affiliation. A high match between organizational type and personal needs leads to higher job satisfaction.

$\mathbf{A}$s old hierarchical structures give way to team-based environments, many people feel out of place in their own organizations. This instrument was designed to help employees see what type of organization theirs is and to match their own needs with the climate of the organization.

Managers also can control to some extent the type of company they are helping to run, at least in terms of employee affiliation needs. This is because the degree to which employees see their organizations as supportive depends primarily on the degree to which their managers show a personal interest in them, their growth and development, and their feelings. When the work is routine and lacking in challenge and opportunity to achieve, management should welcome employees with high affiliation needs and provide the supportive climate that will nurture and meet these needs.

DESCRIPTION OF THE PROFILE

The Organizational Profile presents twenty-four phrases that could be used to describe an organization. Respondents are asked to rate each phrase according to how well it fits the organization, from "never true" to "always true." Respondents then score their profiles to determine the degree to which their organization is bureaucratic, innovative, or supportive. They then display their results on a bar graph to show to what degree each applies. Five questions provide topics for discussion when the assessment is used as part of a group learning experience.

TYPES OF ORGANIZATIONS

Organizations have "personalities" that have been formed in response to many factors, such as the management style of their leaders, the nature of the work, the economic environment, the culture of the country, and so on.

Participants' responses to the list of twenty-four phrases indicates the degree to which their organization is bureaucratic, innovative, or supportive. Typically, an organization displays characteristics of all three, although one is usually dominant. Help the respondents to look at each of the types described below:

Bureaucratic

Bureaucratic organizations have lots of rules, regulations, policies, systems, and procedures. There are many controls on what employees can and cannot do. Static rather than dynamic phrases such as "We've never done anything like this before" are spoken as a warning, rather than as an exciting challenge.

In situations in which the work is well-defined and not subject to much change, the bureaucratic organization has many advantages. It is stable; decisions are predictable; and people know where they stand. For employees who are most comfortable working for a paternalistic organization (that is, management-worker relationships are similar to parent-child relationships), the bureaucracy provides comfort. Examples of such organizations are public utilities (electric, gas, telephone companies), the military, and government at all levels.

Innovative

Innovative organizations are dynamic, creative, progressive, exciting, and ambitious. Risk taking and entrepreneurial activities are encouraged. Such organizations attract high achievers, who welcome the opportunity to excel and move at their own pace. Innovative organizations tend to be at the cutting edge of their fields.

Taken to the extreme, an innovative organization can become an "ulcer factory," as high expectations and the demand to produce are too stressful for many. One's personal lifestyle and need for time with one's family may be more important than the need to achieve. Examples of this type of organization include advertising agencies, marketing firms, TV production, and technology industries (both hardware and software design).

Supportive

Supportive organizations promote friendly, nurturing, warm, helping relationships among employees. People with a strong need to develop friendships and have close ties with other employees are attracted to this kind of organization. "We're one big happy family" is the motto of a supportive organization.

How bureaucratic or innovative an organization is lies outside the control of most managers. This is influenced in large part by the nature of the work. However, all managers can strongly influence how supportive the organization is for employees. Thus, supportiveness can be seen as high or low in a bureaucratic organization and high or low in an innovative organization.

ORGANIZATIONAL TRENDS IN CORPORATE AMERICA

The past decade has seen a lot of downsizing, reorganizing, and flattening of organizations. Self-directed teams, empowerment, and fewer levels of management attest to the move away from bureaucratic organizations in favor of flatter, more innovative and supportive organizations.

Many factors explain this shift from the hierarchical organization to a flatter, more flexible one. Some of them are listed below:

- Leaner organizations are more profitable;
- Change can take place more rapidly when fewer people are involved;
- Technology makes it possible to produce more with fewer employees;
- A better educated workforce makes innovation and quality everyone's job;
- Increased competition from overseas forces innovation;
- Supportive organizations are more competitive in a tight labor market; and
- Employees want a greater say in decisions affecting their work.

The old hierarchical organizational structure and a new team-based structure are illustrated in Figures 1 and 2.

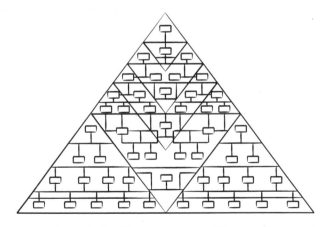

Figure 1. Traditional Hierarchical Organization

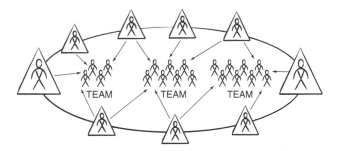

Figure 2. A Team-Based Organizational Structure

DESIGN OF THE INSTRUMENT

The twenty-four phrases that make up the Organizational Profile are divided into three groups of eight that describe each of the three types of organization. These phrases are interspersed so that the respondent does not know what type of organization is being described until the assessment is scored. Thus, the validity of the instrument depends on the respondent's agreement with the eight phrases as being truly descriptive of the organization:

- Bureaucratic organizations are seen as systematic, careful, rules-governed, stable, hierarchical, controlling, predictable, and bureaucratic.

- Innovative organizations are seen as progressive, exciting, creative, entrepreneurial, dynamic, leading-edge, ambitious, and innovative.

- Supportive organizations are seen as friendly, fair, open in terms of relationships, warm, encouraging, harmonious, helpful, and supportive.

Interpreting the Results

The Organizational Profile can be completed and self-scored in ten to fifteen minutes. When the instrument is filled out as part of a group session (for example, a training class or staff meeting), you can ask the participants to write their scores on a sheet of paper and turn them in (anonymously). You can then calculate the group's average so that (1) individuals can compare their scores with the norm, and (2) participants can discuss the implications of organizational style in response to the five questions at the end of the Organizational Profile Interpretation Sheet.

References

McClelland, D.C. (1961). *The achievement society.* New York: Van Nostrand.

Scott B. Parry *is a psychologist, consultant, trainer, and chairman of Training House, Inc., creators of instructional programs and assessments. His* Managerial Assessment of Proficiency *(MAP) has been translated into five languages. He has published numerous articles and is the author of four books and dozens of published training courses. He has conducted more than four hundred "Train the Trainer" workshops and has addressed HRD conferences in several dozen countries.*

ORGANIZATIONAL PROFILE

Scott B. Parry

Directions: The list below contains twenty-four phrases that could be used to describe an organization. Circle the letters in the column after each phrase that indicates how well that phrase fits your organization, using the following continuum:

Never True   Somewhat True   Frequently True   Always True

My organization is:	Never True	Somewhat True	Frequently True	Always True
1. Systematic, with well-established systems and procedures.	NT	ST	FT	AT
2. Progressive and forward-looking.	NT	ST	FT	AT
3. Friendly and supportive of my work.	NT	ST	FT	AT
4. Careful and avoids taking risks.	NT	ST	FT	AT
5. Exciting, as new things are often happening.	NT	ST	FT	AT
6. Fair, in that employees are treated with respect.	NT	ST	FT	AT
7. Rule-oriented, and regulations and policies govern behavior.	NT	ST	FT	AT
8. Creative with lots of fresh, new ideas.	NT	ST	FT	AT
9. Open with a healthy level of trust in relationships.	NT	ST	FT	AT
10. Stable with infrequent and slow change.	NT	ST	FT	AT
11. Entrepreneurial with new ideas and services.	NT	ST	FT	AT
12. Warm with supportive relationships.	NT	ST	FT	AT
13. Hierarchical, with many levels of management.	NT	ST	FT	AT

	Never True	Somewhat True	Frequently True	Always True
14. Dynamic, with frequent changes.	NT	ST	FT	AT
15. Encouraging of my efforts.	NT	ST	FT	AT
16. Controlling and restrictive of employee behavior.	NT	ST	FT	AT
17. Leading edge, encouraging of innovative thinking.	NT	ST	FT	AT
18. Harmonious as employees work together.	NT	ST	FT	AT
19. Predictable with few surprises.	NT	ST	FT	AT
20. Ambitious with challenging goals that require employees to stretch.	NT	ST	FT	AT
21. Made up of helpful people who are also friends.	NT	ST	FT	AT
22. Bureaucratic and heavily organized.	NT	ST	FT	AT
23. Innovative and encouraging of risk taking.	NT	ST	FT	AT
24. Supportive, with an environment that is positive and reinforcing.	NT	ST	FT	AT

ORGANIZATIONAL PROFILE SCORING SHEET

Scoring Your Profile

Directions: First circle the numbers that correspond with your answers to each question (never true, somewhat true, frequently true, or always true) on the following grid.

	NT	ST	FT	AT
1.	0	1	2	3
2.	0	1	2	3
3.	0	1	2	3
4.	0	1	2	3
5.	0	1	2	3
6.	0	1	2	3
7.	0	1	2	3
8.	0	1	2	3
9.	0	1	2	3
10.	0	1	2	3
11.	0	1	2	3
12.	0	1	2	3
13.	0	1	2	3
14.	0	1	2	3
15.	0	1	2	3
16.	0	1	2	3
17.	0	1	2	3
18.	0	1	2	3
19.	0	1	2	3
20.	0	1	2	3
21.	0	1	2	3
22.	0	1	2	3
23.	0	1	2	3
24.	0	1	2	3

Next, total your scores by first adding together the numbers in the eight rows of boxes that are *not shaded*. Put the total for these eight boxes in the box beside "Bureaucratic Total" below. Your responses to these eight phrases indicate the degree to which you regard your organization as bureaucratic.

Bureaucratic Total:

Now, add the numbers that correspond to your answers from the eight rows of boxes with the light shading and put the total in the "Innovative Total" box below.

Innovative Total:

Now, follow the same procedure for the most heavily shaded rows to obtain a total for the "Supportive" Total box below.

Supportive Total:

Profiling Your Organization

Now locate the numbers for each organizational type on the scale below and make a profile of your organization. Connect the numbers to create a line graph, or make them into a bar chart.

Bureaucratic	Innovative	Supportive
24	24	24
22	22	22
20	20	20
18	18	18
16	16	16
14	14	14
12	12	12
10	10	10
8	8	8
6	6	6
4	4	4
2	2	2
0	0	0

Organizational Profile Interpretation Sheet

Because the characteristics of bureaucratic and innovative organizations are quite different, it is not likely that your organization will have a high score on both at the same time. However, it is possible to rate your organization high on either of these scales and also to rate it high on the supportive scale.

Carefully read the three paragraphs below that describe an individual's need to achieve, to affiliate, and to have power. Decide which is your strongest need and how this need relates to the type of organization you work for.

Relating Organizational Profiles to Human Needs

David McClelland of Harvard has identified three needs that are present in all humans to a greater or lesser degree. They are described below.

Need to Achieve

Persons with a high *need to achieve* require lots of recognition and respect. Their satisfaction comes from the act of achieving rather than from external rewards (for example, money, awards). They tend to set goals that are moderately challenging, neither too easy nor too difficult. Achievers have a strong need for concrete, specific feedback on how well they are doing so that they can continually strive to be better.

Need to Affiliate

Persons with a high *need to affiliate* tend to derive greater satisfaction from the people they work with than from the work itself or the act of achieving goals. The feedback they seek is related to their attitudes, their loyalty, their importance to the organization, and the quality of the relationships they have cultivated with customers and other employees. Competition and the opportunity to achieve may actually be seen as threats to the person with high affiliation needs.

Need for Power

Persons with a high *need for power* want to influence the behavior of others. Sometimes this influence is desirable, as with teachers, ministers, lawyers, architects, and leaders in all fields. At other times their need to influence is dangerous, as with dictators, corrupt politicians, and gangsters. Persons with high power needs measure their success by the number of persons they are able to influence, either directly or through others.

These three human needs are associated with the three types of organizations in the following ways:

- People's need to *achieve* is best met in *innovative* organizations;
- Their need to *affiliate* is met best in *supportive* organizations; and
- Their need for *power* is satisfied most often in *bureaucratic* organizations.

Answer the following questions either individually or with your group to help you think about the "fit" between your personal needs and the organization for which you work.

1. Were you surprised by the three scores you gave your organization? Why or why not?

2. How do your perceptions compare with others in your group? Was there close agreement or was there a wide range of opinions about your organization?

3. Have you seen any changes in your organization's "personality" during the past five to ten years? Has it become more or less bureaucratic? Innovative? Supportive? Decide as a group.

4. What future forces and events do you anticipate that might change the personality of your organization? In what direction is it likely to go?

5. If you were running the organization, what would you regard as the ideal scores for the organization to have? Why?

Introduction

to the Presentation and Discussion Resources Section

The Presentation and Discussion Resources Section is a collection of articles of use to every facilitator—theories, background, models, and methods to challenge facilitators' thinking, enrich their professional development, and assist their clients (internal and external) with productive change. These articles may be used as a basis for lecturettes, as handouts in training sessions, or as background reading material.

This section will provide you with a variety of useful ideas, theoretical opinions, teachable models, practical strategies, and proven intervention methods. The articles will add richness and depth to your training and consulting knowledge and skills. They will challenge you to think differently, explore new concepts, and experiment with new interventions. The articles will continue to add a fresh perspective to your work.

The *2000 Annual: Volume 2, Consulting* includes thirteen articles in the following categories:

Individual Development: Developing Awareness and Understanding

Spirituality in the Workplace: Ten Things the HR Professional Needs to Know by Steven L. Phillips

Individual Development: Personal Growth

The Potent Pause: How Organizations and Individuals Learn from Experience by David R. Glaser

Communication: Communication in Organizations

Communicating Organizational Change:
Information Technology Meets the Carbon-Based Employee Unit by Joseph G. Wojtecki, Jr., and Richard G. Peters

Problem Solving: Models, Methods, and Techniques

New Applications for the Delphi Technique by Richard Phillips

Problem Solving: Change and Change Agents

Increasing Your Organization's Effectiveness
with Project Management by Michael Stanleigh

Groups and Teams: Behavior and Roles in Groups

Managing the Dynamics of "Having Nothing to Say"
in Small Groups by Gary Gemmill

Breaking Down Boundaries: Breaking Through Resistance
by Ron Ashkenas

**Consulting: Organizations: Their Characteristics
and How They Function**

Aligning Team Behavior with Organizational Values:
A Survey-Based Intervention by Marilee Crosby

Consulting: Consulting Strategies and Techniques

Strategic Planning Made Practical
by Michele Matt Yanna and Lee Towe

Causal-Utility Decision Analysis (CUDA): Quantifying SWOTs
by Doug Leigh

Consulting: Interface with Clients

Key Stakeholder Analysis: Preparing to Introduce
a New Organizational Idea by Neil J. Simon

Leadership: Theories and Models of Facilitating

The Relationship Between Leader Behavior and
Team Performance and Satisfaction by Mary Ann Burress

Leadership: Top-Management Issues and Concerns

Views of the 21st Century Organization by Elizabeth A. Smith

As with previous *Annuals,* this volume covers a wide variety of topics. The range of articles presented should encourage a good deal of thought-provoking discussion about the present and future of HRD. Other articles on specific subjects can be located by using our comprehensive *Reference Guide to Handbooks and Annuals.* This book, which is updated regularly, provides an index of the contents of all the *Annuals* and the *Handbooks of Structured Experiences.* With each revision, the *Reference Guide* becomes a complete, up-to-date, and easy-to-use resource for selecting appropriate materials from the *Annuals* and *Handbooks.*

Here and in the *Reference Guide,* we have done our best to categorize the articles for easy reference; however, many of the articles encompass a range of topics, disciplines, and applications. If you do not find what you are looking for under one category, we encourage you to look under a related category. In come cases we may place an article in the "Training" *Annual* that also has implications for "Consulting," and vice versa. As the field of HRD becomes more sophisticated, what is done in a training context is based on the needs of, and affects, the organization. Similarly, from a systemic viewpoint, anything that affects individuals in an organization has repercussions throughout the organization, and vice versa.

It is for this reason that the new "Organization" category was added to the *Annuals.* We encourage you not to limit yourself by the categorization system that we have developed, but to explore all the contents of both volumes in order to realize the full potential for learning and development that each offers.

SPIRITUALITY IN THE WORKPLACE: TEN THINGS THE HR PROFESSIONAL NEEDS TO KNOW

Steven L. Phillips

Abstract: Employers and employees alike are feeling the call for a deeper sense of purpose, a greater sense of faith, and larger legacy than simply earning a living. Human resource professionals must determine how this fits with current workplace norms (and laws) regarding religion. "Reasonable accommodation" is current workplace practice; on the productivity front, anything that creates more profit and better earnings interests management. Therefore, the HR professional must determine, often case by case, where spirituality fits in the workplace. This article explores this new trend, the fear and faith associated with its practices, and its proposed outcomes and gives some guidelines for the HR professional. Further, the implications for individuals and the consulting community in general are explored.

THE SPIRITUAL WAVE

Thousands of people are seeking a more holistic approach to life, blending the spiritual with daily work and routine. The topic of spirituality at work is showing up in best-selling books, popular Web sites, business periodicals, magazine articles, newspaper special sections, and even in the daily conversations of senior executives. What started as a personal journey for me has opened my eyes to the oncoming tidal wave of spirituality at work.

Many authors start with the assumption that the majority of working Americans are currently "unfulfilled" at work. Headlines in *The Los Angeles Times* (1998) flash such intriguing questions as: "Does your job offer you personal fulfillment or merely a paycheck?" "Are you looking for more but are not sure what?" Another article points to a more specific calling: "Across America, employees and employers are exploring the concept of the Soul at Work." *HR Magazine* reported in 1996 about a workplace trend of spirituality. Its headline read "Corporate Pioneers Explore Workplace Spirituality." It is also not unusual to find practical hands-on tools and tips. There are even spiritual questionnaires on which people can assess their current level of spirituality.

Surfing this wave are many of the popular publishing houses. *Publishers' Weekly* (Billitteri, 1997) reports there are seventy-eight million baby boomers running corporate America—many desiring to reconcile their spiritual lives with their current job demands. Boomers seem to be asking, "Why am I doing what I am doing?" Consequently, sales of the so-called "S" books (spirit and soul) are brisk, and publishing houses are clamoring for more titles on every niche of the topic.

Even corporations are starting to employ spiritual practices. *HR Magazine* has reported that Tom Chappell, CEO of Tom's of Maine, offers creative and easy ways to initiate ideas for making Tom's a more spiritually satisfying place. *Business Week* (Galen & West, 1995) detailed spirituality as a management tool that could potentially impact the bottom line. Citing practices at Boeing, AT&T, Lotus Development, and Medtronic, the authors concluded that many spiritual practices show some intangible results, as measured by other employees. They state, "Even though mainstream companies are using spirituality to prod workers and inspire managers, they are still squeamish about admitting it."

ORGANIZATIONS FEAR THE TOPIC

Organizations are leery of allowing spirituality in the workplace for several reasons. First, they fear the connection of spirituality to religion, religious dogma, and labor laws. There is a fear that practicing spirituality at work will somehow lead to unfair labor practices and/or hostile work environments.

Second, although the fear about allowing the practice of religion is overt, there is a covert fear about spirituality, perhaps stemming from ignorance or an ambiguous definition of "spirituality."

A third fear is that there is no direct connection to increasing overall business results. Human resource professionals are slow to promote indirect human development strategies for fear of losing what small amounts of credibility they already enjoy. A brief discussion of each of these three fears follows.

Fear of Promoting Religion in the Workplace

Religion in the workplace is a very challenging topic. The bottom line, and probably the point from which most employers' fears emanate, is the cost of accommodation. As it stands today, charges of religious discrimination in the workplace have jumped 43 percent since 1990 and increased over 9 percent in the last year alone (Digh, 1998). The increasing claims of religious discrimination have not gone unnoticed. Last year the Clinton administration introduced the Workplace Religious Freedom Act to amend Title VII of the Civil Rights Act of 1964. This act would increase employers' responsibility to accommodate workers' religious beliefs. Even without the proposed act, organizations have to be careful how they treat employees who bring their religion to work. The norm today is to follow a "reasonable accommodation" philosophy (Digh, 1998). Religion in the workplace can be a costly and potentially volatile issue, and the perception of its connection to spirituality is widespread.

Lack of Knowledge About Spirituality

In a search of hundreds of books, Web pages, and articles, the author did not find a common definition of "spirituality," let alone "spirituality at work." Its broad interpretation makes it difficult to establish acceptable workplace practices. Employers face the costly risk that disgruntled employees will choose to connect spirituality with religion, for which the laws are clear.

No Connection with the Bottom Line

Over the past two decades human resource professionals have been severely criticized for not adding significant value to organizations' ongoing operations. Although we may think we understand how human resources as a function can impact hard dollars in a corporation, many of us still have to justify our existence. There is no proof that spirituality at work increases an organization's bottom line, so advancing "spirituality at work" to a number-crunching CEO does not work well. HR professionals are not encouraged (and at times are blatantly discouraged) from promoting intangibles.

DEFINITION OF SPIRITUALITY

As mentioned earlier, there are many ways to define spirituality. Some of the more popular definitions include the following:

- "Spirituality is a quest for meaning in a sea of confusion and a world of emptiness."

- "Spirituality is a connection to the sacred, the belief in some higher power, and the sacredness that goes along with that."

- "Spirituality brings a sense of God into everyday life by looking beyond an individual reality."

- "Spirituality is the recognition and connection to the life force within us."

Some say it is easier to define what spirituality is *not*. According to the *Personnel Journal* (Laabs, 1995), spirituality is not about religion nor converting people. It is not about following a system or dogma of beliefs. It is not about telling others how to be.

Others suggest that it is better not to define the word but simply to engage in the values and practices (also undefined), often described as truth, integrity, caring, cooperation, trust, morality, balance, harmony, communication, service, respect, partnership, flexibility, energy, and vision.

Another way to define spirituality is to consider what spiritual practices are acceptable and which are not. Following are some of the unofficial "rules" present in the workplace today:

Acceptable	Not Acceptable
Prayer notes in cubicles, on lunch trays, on automated parking tickets	Talking about your own religion and the religions of others
Wearing a cross, a star, a crystal, or other spiritual objects	Praying in public
Saying "God bless you" when someone sneezes	Publicly speaking about God
Sharing personal experiences	Sharing spiritual experiences
Bible study and yoga at work (on personal time)	Chanting or verbalizing
Quietly practicing spirituality	Verbalizing spirituality
Creating a deep and personal leadership vision	Creating a deep and personal spiritual vision
Faith and private prayer	Religion
Celebration	Spiritual ceremony or ritual
Intuition	Being psychic or having a sixth sense
Quoting from the Bible during conversation	A supervisor quoting from the Bible during an employee review
Quiet, uninterrupted time	Meditation

Although this list is anecdotal, it highlights the difficulty of determining what is spiritual in the workplace. It also illustrates the ambiguity about what is acceptable and what is not acceptable. This ambiguity is often a result of subconscious feelings and practices. With the advent of a more openly spiritual culture, it is predicted that many of these "unacceptable" practices will become common and therefore more acceptable.

At the core of most explanations of spirituality is the fact that people are more than just mind and body—that they are spiritual beings with unique and individual gifts. No definition of spirituality was given at the 1998 Spirituality in the Workplace Conference in Toronto. It was simply acknowledged that people were spiritual beings. The mission for the conference was "to explore and discover together, as a community of spiritual beings who work, how to further our own journeys and positively affect our broader communities of workplace stakeholders." The conference organizers then described several guiding principles:

- Spirituality was seen as practical and actionable information, wisdom, and ideas that are transferable to work.

- Spirituality was described as shaped by faith and vision of the future, whereas values determine our choices and decisions.

- Healthy spirituality was described as seeking to "attain a balance in meeting the needs of self, family, and all people, based on mutual respect and our recognition of differing values and concerns."

In the end, there may not be a single definition of spirituality or what spirituality in the workplace really means. It can encompass all of the definitions and descriptions above. For example, Rutte (1996), a leader of the spirituality at work movement, suggests that spirituality at work should be considered more a question than an answer.

CURRENT PRACTICES

In the past few years, many spiritual practices at work have emerged and been widely written about. Some of the more popular include Bible and spiritual study sessions, company sponsored yoga and meditation, and wellness programs. As cited in *Business Week* (Galen & West, 1995), Boeing had managers listen to poet David Whyte three times a month for a year with the goal of helping people think differently about their company and their lives. AT&T hired a values coach to help leaders more clearly define their personal values. Lotus Development created a "soul" committee to reexamine the company's management practices. Medtronic uses its mission statement as a way to help workers feel as though they are a part of something greater than themselves. *Entrepreneur* magazine (Lynn, 1999) notes that more and more companies are using the services of workplace chaplains to incorporate spirituality into employee counseling. Tom's of Maine incorporates spirituality into many of its daily activities, using an eleven-step program to becoming a more spiritual company (*HR Magazine,* 1996). *Working Woman* (Jidoun, 1999) lists Feng Shui, aroma therapy, and Native American smudging as common "corporate soul" practices.

The author has personally experienced three eye-opening spiritual experiences at work. The events allowed participants to speak authentically about their spiritual natures and transformed each of these executive work groups. The first instance was at a retreat of a volunteer advisory board consisting of successful entrepreneurs. As pre-work we answered the single question, "What are you living for?" We shared answers and had a dialogue about the process.

My answer was simple, immediate, and one I have known intuitively for many years: "At work, my purpose is to help humankind evolve through the way people are treated at work." My assumption was that others would also be very clear about their answers. As the ten of us took turns answering the question and then sharing our experiences of how we came to our answers, I was transformed as I realized many people have never truly thought about this question. Of the ten of us, no two were living for the same thing. I also found an explanation for why, at times, I feel so alienated from others. Others on the board had different lessons to learn, but we all shared a very special evening together. Finding the answer to this question was nothing less than a profound experience. As a group, willing to be open and honest, we were transported to a place that could only be described as spiritual. In individual and group debriefing sessions that followed, we all agreed that the "purpose in life" dialogue had deepened our relationships with one another and increased our self-awareness. This experience built a deeper community and offered life lessons to everyone.

The second experience came several months later at a senior management retreat I was co-facilitating at Lake Arrowhead, California. Among the critical issues blocking high performance was an incomplete understanding of the CEO's vision. One night, using David Bohm's (1990) dialogue process, the group members decided to share their personal visions in life. Again, amazing realizations were shared. The CEO, a visionary, spiritual man, clear on his purpose, realized that not everyone has even pondered his or her personal vision. The group members gained a much deeper respect for one another as they listened to one another's stories. The team came to understand the CEO's corporate vision in a way that embodied its truest meaning, and the evening was the most memorable event of the off-site.

Finally, at a committee meeting for a professional business association, I learned that Ken Blanchard (the renowned co-creator of *Situational Leadership* and co-author of *The One-Minute Manager*) holds the official company title of "chief spiritual officer" of the Ken Blanchard Companies. At lunch that day, Ken led a prayer of thanks and also told us several stories about how he leads a volunteer prayer session for his employees every morning. Anyone in his company can ask for a prayer and then participate in response. Ken was emphatic about how powerful this was in creating a positive and caring culture.

As these examples illustrate, spiritual practices at work are on the rise. Whether company sponsored, employee organized, or individually practiced, there is no escaping the trend. Whether it is a deep philosophical discussion about values or company purpose, an invitation to a prayer or Bible study group, or simply a co-worker speaking of karma, energy, and crystals, chances are you have already been exposed to a practice that ten years ago was probably unacceptable in the workplace.

Such spiritual practices are not completely sanctioned nor are they proven to show any significant business results. Nevertheless, people seem to be becoming bolder with their personal practices. Any spiritual practice, seen individually, is not all that surprising. What is amazing is the magnitude of the collective movement. The spirituality in the workplace wave is clearly building.

EXPECTED OUTCOMES IN THE WORKPLACE

Some studies connect meditation to less stress and better decision making, but other than that—zip! Given the nature of spirituality, it is predictable that most effects would likely be intangible and nonquantifiable. Nevertheless, the literature suggests a number of possible outcomes, including greater motivation; increased self-esteem; spiritual fulfillment; integrity; a more heart-centered work environment; the creation of a caring and humanistic organizational culture; fewer harassment and discrimination claims and costs; increased awareness on the part of management; a community feeling at work; a cooperative, prosperous, and peaceful work community; better teamwork, creativity, and innovation; deep personal fulfillment; a shift from an environment of fear to one of cooperation; better, more honest, and authentic communication; renewal; resilience; and increased ethical and moral behavior.

Although the specific outcomes of more spirituality at work have not yet been proven quantitatively, it can be predicted that as people come into their spiritual selves they will be happier, more balanced, and more compassionate. This should, in turn, affect all of the variables listed above. The anecdotal and qualitative evidence so far is strong. Once the topic is raised and people perceive a safe environment, almost everyone has a story to tell. People seem to be looking for outlets to talk about spirituality, and the stories they tell suggest that spirituality is already coming to the workplace.

It is not a question of "if" this will happen. It is more a question of "when and how" this new movement will become accepted within the business arena. Key questions yet unanswered include: "What is the relationship of spirituality at work to productivity or profit?" and "If organizations are going to spend money on this trend, what should they expect as a return?"

The movement, like many before it, will no doubt be corrupted and turned into a fad as American enterprise scrambles for Neptune's treasure. However, many trends and fads of the past have significantly advanced the bottom line: A good organizational culture can help a company attract and retain great people; the intelligent use of teams can help a company reduce cycle time and waste; knowledge management allows for easy access to best practices and overall time savings; and because of the quality movement we can once again thrive in a global marketplace.

What will spirituality do for us? Will it truly change the American business landscape? Will it impact people in a profound way? Should spirituality in the workplace be put in a different category and just grouped with that "touchy-feely" stuff? Only time will tell.

WHAT HR PROFESSIONALS NEED TO KNOW

Ten points for HR professionals to ponder for the future are given below.

1. The Wave Is Cresting. It may not have crashed onto our beaches yet, but it soon will. Some say it is a trend or a movement; others suggest it is a paradigm shift. In any case, most agree that spirituality in the workplace will be big in the next few years.

2. Many People Are Afraid or Cynical. The link between spirituality and religion (and thus religious dogma) is commonly assumed. This scares people. One book critic warned his readers that the spirituality at work movement was chock full of untested cliches and empty platitudes. He put everyone on a "psychobabble alert" (Zack, 1993). A report on American spiritualism in *The New York Times* (Zaleski, 1997) calls the movement solipsistic, optimistic, and banal.

3. Many Employee Practices Are Associated with the Movement. Prayer, meditation, personal development workshops, organizational ritual ceremonies, storytelling, and many other practices are associated with spirituality. These are manifest in any number of ways that are sure to impact organizational structure, strategy, and culture. Our work in these and related areas will inevitably be affected. As practitioners, and often as agents and facilitators of change, we must make a choice. Do we want to lead this change, follow and support the movement, let whatever happens happen, or argue against the movement. Each of us will have to make this choice.

4. Organizations Are About to Evolve Spiritually. Just as organizations have advanced technologically in the past decade, they are now about to undertake a spiritual evolution. This may call for personal development on our part. When was the last time you took note of your spiritual development? It may be time to focus on ourselves. It may be time to explore our own personal journey. If we are to have any part in this movement, we must explore our own paths before helping others to explore theirs.

5. We Must Be Practical. For the spirituality movement to really catch on, it must be practical for businesses. It must not only show results that improve the human condition, but also show quantitative results for business—increases in profit, earnings, and return on investment. Disciplined studies are needed to connect spirituality at work to the bottom line. As active HR professionals, we are perfectly positioned to take on this research.

6. A Common Definition Is Needed. To some extent ambiguity is good. People can define spirituality as they choose, or they can literally say whatever they want about religion and/or spirituality. Eventually, however, we will need a more focused definition and less emotionally charged language. To help this process along, practitioners can take note of the language and definitions that seem to be acceptable to business types. Keep an ear open, publish what works, and be flexible. It may take some time for a clear definition and an appropriate language to emerge.

7. Information Is Out There. Because of the Internet and the ease with which it allows us to collect information from all over the world, we have means to contact those who are already informed and writing about this topic. The Internet allows like-minded souls to find one another, to work together, and to spread the word with unparalleled speed. If you want to keep up with the fast-moving current, then surf the Web. When the wave hits, it will most likely hit there first.

8. Be Careful. Not everyone buys into spirituality, but most people do have strong opinions about the topic. Be careful about how and what you say. The topic, although appealing to many, repulses others. By forwarding the concept, you may be labeled as a "fruits and nuts" person, and it may also be career-limiting. Choose your approach wisely. Remember, preaching does not help anyone.

9. You May Already Be a Believer. If you have read this article through to this point, you may already be a believer. Ask yourself, "What do I need to do next?" Do you need to check out your own purpose in life? Do you need to think about God? Do you need to learn how to meditate (or resume the practice)? Do you need to go to a retreat and discover your deeper, higher, greater self? Whatever you need to do, start doing it. Knowing what others have done or are doing can be very helpful. For that purpose, a readings list is at the end of this article.

10. Communicate with Others. During your journey, start communicating with others. Open up. Share your exploration. Speak authentically. Make connections with others. The personal experiences you gain along the way will inform your work with others in the future. Talk your walk and stay open to the experience it brings. You never know where it may lead, and you may be pleasantly surprised.

CONCLUSION

Spirituality at work appears to be the next great phenomenon and promises an amazing array of changes. It will touch all of us. It will be pervasive. People are confused by and afraid of the topic, although the concept is very compelling because many people believe that our human soul is lost or ignored at work. As Hillary Rodham Clinton (Hudson, 1993) noted, we are in a crisis of meaning and spirituality, and one of our challenges is overcoming the alienation, despair, and hopelessness of the American people.

Is it right to bring spirituality into our work? Is it acceptable to be a spiritual person on company time? The old answer was no. The current answer is maybe. People are now more often seen as resources or assets. They are encouraged to think and add value beyond what their hands can produce. The future answer is unknown. But in our prospering, high-tech, high-touch world, business is booming, money is flowing, technology is driving constant white water and, at least in American companies, high involvement strategies are "in." What is missing from these good times is the development of our soul, our core, our spirit. Spirituality in the workplace would seem to be a great fit for our future. It may not provide all of the answers or easy solutions, but is an avenue for exploration. Just as a lighthouse acts as a beacon to ships, we as organizational and human specialists can also act as harbingers, helping people and companies explore spirituality at work and modeling the fun and enlightenment of surfing this new wave as it crests, curls, and crashes onto our shores.

References

Billitteri, T. (1997, May 19). Finding the spirit at work. *Publishers' Weekly,* pp. 46–53.

Bohm, D. (1990). *On dialogue.* Ojai, CA: David Bohm.

Corporate Pioneers Explore Spirituality. (1996, April). *HR Magazine.* [Online: http://www.shrm.org/hrmagazine/articles/0496read.html.]

Digh, P. (1998, December). Religion in the workplace: Make a good faith effort to accommodate. *HR Magazine,* pp. 84–91.

Galen, M., & West, K. (1995, June 5). Companies hit the road less traveled. *Business Week,* pp. 82–85.

Hudson, E. (1993, April 7). First lady calls for "caring." *The Washington Post,* A1, D13.

Jidoun, G. (1999, May). Spirituality inc. *Working Woman,* p. 16.

Laabs, J.J. (1995, September). Balancing spirituality and work. *Personnel Journal,* pp. 60–69.

Los Angeles Times Business Section, Part II: Careers. (1998, April 6). *Los Angeles Times,* D2; 3–31.

Lynn, J. (1999, February). Higher power. *Entrepreneur,* p. 98.

Rutte, M. (1996). Spirituality in the workplace. [Online: http://www.cop.com/info/rutte01.html].

Zack, J. (1993, Summer). Inner excellence: Spiritual principles of life-driven business. *Business and Society Review,* pp. 62–64.

Zaleski, P. (1997, March 23). Channel U. *New York Times,* p. 24.

Readings

Barrett, R. (1998, August). The new spirit of work. *Fast Company,* [Online: http://www.fastcompany.com/online/156/barett.html].

Bedolla, B., & Gaines, D. (1998, April 6). Feeling euphoric or used-up? *Los Angeles Times,* D2; 22, 26.

Belis, G. (1993, June 28). Inner excellence: Spiritual principles of life-driven business. *Fortune,* p. 148.

Brandt, J. (1995, May 1). Spirituality-business: An enduring link. *Industry Week,* p. 6.

Briskin, A. (1996). *The stirring of soul in the workplace.* San Francisco, CA: Jossey-Bass.

Brown, T. (1995, March 6). Jesus, CEO? *Industry Week,* pp. 14–20.

Bruzzese, A. (1997, May 20). Divine intervention. *Human Resource Executive, 1,* 22–25.

Chappell, T. (1993). *The soul of a business: Managing for profit and the common good.* Toronto, Ontario, Canada: Bantam Books.

Colby, A. (1998, April 6). The missing link. *Los Angeles Times,* D2; 6, 28.

Conger, J.A. (1994). *Spirit at work: Discovering the spirituality in leadership.* San Francisco, CA: Jossey-Bass.

Dick, R. (1995). *Artful work: Awakening joy, meaning, and commitment in the workplace.* San Francisco, CA: Berrett-Koehler.

Dickerson, M. (1998, April 6). Higher power lunches. *Los Angeles Times,* D2; 5.

Dorsey, D. (1998, August). The new spirit of work. *Fast Company,* pp. 124–134.

Fulmer, M. (1998, April 6). Workplace guideposts. *Los Angeles Times,* D2; 13–15.

Groves, M. (1998, April 6). It comes naturally. *Los Angeles Times,* D2; 10, 24–25, 28.

Groves, M. (1998, April 6). Look inward, employee. *Los Angeles Times,* D2; 8, 20.

Handy, C.B. (1998). *The hungry spirit: Beyond capitalism: A quest for purpose in the modern world.* New York: Broadway Books.

Hotz, R.J. (1998, April 26). Seeking the biology of spirituality. *Los Angeles Times,* pp. A1, A32.

Jacobson, B., & Kaye, B. (1993, February). Balancing act. *Training & Development,* pp. 24–27.

La Ganga, M. (1998, April 6). A profession of faith. *Los Angeles Times,* D2; 3–4.

Lane, P. (1992, May 5). Spiritual bottom line: Work less for success. *The Seattle Times,* p. C1.

Lee, D. (1998, April 6). Feel the burn? *Los Angeles Times,* D2; 18–19, 23.

Leigh, P. (1997, March). The new spirit at work. *Training & Development,* pp. 26–33.

Liebig, J.E. (1994). *Merchants of vision: People bringing new purpose and values to business.* San Francisco, CA: Berrett-Koehler.

Maltais, M. (1998, April 6). Setting "prophet margins." *Los Angeles Times,* D2; 12, 32–33.

Manz, C.C. (1998). *The leadership wisdom of Jesus: Practical lessons of today.* San Francisco, CA: Berrett-Koehler.

McLaughlin, A. (1998, March 16). Seeking spirituality at work. *The Christian Science Monitor,* pp. 1, 4.

Mitroff, I.I., Mason, R.O., & Pearson, C.M. (1994). *Framebreak: The radical redesign of American business.* San Francisco, CA: Jossey-Bass.

Neal, J. (1997). *Work as nourishment.* [Online: http://www.prosperityplace.com/articles/jneal.html].

Newman, P.C. (1993, April 12). A spiritual link in the workplace. *Maclean's*, p. 28.

Oldham, J. (1998, April 6). Amen at the top. *Los Angeles Times*, D2; 7.

Rainbows & miracles, etc. *Bringing spirituality into the workplace.* [Online: http://www.itstime.com/rainbow.htm].

Rifkin, G. (1996). *Finding meaning at work.* [Online: http://www.strategy-business.com/briefs/96495/].

Rosebush, J. (1996, August 4). Don't miss the moral in Reagan's story. *The Washington Post*, p. A3.

Ulin, D. (1996, December 25). Soul concern. *Los Angeles Times*, pp. E1, E4.

Whittaker, S. (1998, August 29). Spirituality in the workplace: Consultant isn't calling for religion on the job, just a new set of values. *The Gazette*, p. 11.

Wilber, K. (1996). *A spirituality that transforms.* Boston, MA: Shambhala Publications.

Steven L. Phillips, Ph.D., *is well-known for his seminars, presentations, and consulting on organizational transformation, executive leadership, and the art of developing high-performance teams. He is a keynote speaker for conferences and organizations worldwide. Dr. Phillips is also well-known for behind-the-scenes executive coaching. He works one-on-one with presidents and CEOs, helping them strategize for powerful and successful leadership. His clients have included senior executives at Microsoft, PepsiCo, Disney, and Mattel.*

THE POTENT PAUSE: HOW ORGANIZATIONS AND INDIVIDUALS LEARN FROM EXPERIENCE

David R. Glaser

Abstract: A "potent pause" provides an opportunity for learning. It can occur in action research, for the organization, and, in meditation, for the organizational consultant. This article explains the analogies between action research and meditation and why turning toward experiences and problems, rather than away from them, can teach us about them and ourselves and reduce the pain and difficulties that they might cause. It defines the ancient aspects of meditation: mindfulness, equanimity, insight, and purification, and relates them to the levels of understanding that consultants help clients to go through in trying to learn profound truths about their organizations. Finally, it describes the benefits of thinking rather than planning and the implications for individual consultants and organizations.

$\mathbf{M}$any OD consultants have explored Eastern wisdom and learned how to meditate. Some of us have found such exploration to be a great source of calmness, concentration, peace, comfort, and relief from stress. We may also have found that meditation can provide insight, wisdom, and a refinement of consciousness. This article proposes that there is a strong parallel between many forms of meditation and the core technology of the OD profession: action research. Both produce opportunities for learning in what can be called the "potent pause."

THE POTENT PAUSE

For organizations, the potent pause is action research. Based on the seminal work of Kurt Lewin (1946) and refined by countless organization development consultants since the 1940s, action research is a powerful set of intervention techniques designed to assist leaders and members to learn about their organizations and to change them in planned and participative ways. The ultimate goals of action research are extremely ambitious; they include improving the levels of productivity, creativity, learning, and empowerment; adjusting the balance of authority and responsibility; raising morale; and facilitating a strong commitment on the part of all employees to the organization and its objectives. Obviously, these goals are not always fully met, but they serve as valuable ideals and guide the activities of consultants.

Action research requires clients to make fundamental shifts in their approaches to data and in their relationships to their work on a temporary basis. Rather than engaging with their work directly, as they do every day, we ask them to set aside a period of time and to step back from their experience in order to learn about its process. We help them to create a shift from content to contour; we help them to concentrate on the shape of the work—the "how" rather than the "what." Making this shift is often difficult because the organizational culture's task orientation is so pervasive. This is the reason that consultants say, "If you want to understand water, don't ask a fish!" Because the fish and most organizational members take their environments for granted, they do not have much understanding of them. But once the shift is made, new perspectives and new behaviors can emerge. The pausing and reflecting that are part of action research help to catalyze insights that can guide planned change.

For individuals, the potent pause is meditation, a variety of practices that have been used for centuries to shed light on the mysteries of life. The ultimate goals of meditation, like those of action research, are extremely ambitious; they include a greater capacity for wisdom and compassion and an ability to be calm and happy regardless of the circumstances in which we find ourselves. As with action research, these goals are often only partially met, but they guide our efforts as meditators.

Meditation is analogous to action research in a variety of ways:

- A shift in focus from content to contour or process;
- An emphasis on using life experiences to generate insight and to create learning;
- The dynamic tension between being a participant in and being an observer of the system;
- The strategic use of ambiguity, paradox, and confusion;
- The importance of calibrating learning to the readiness level of the learner; and
- The importance of maintaining a calm presence in the midst of change.

THE ORIGINS OF MEDITATION

In prehistoric times life was very simple and very mysterious. Human beings had no explanation for forest fires, eclipses, and a host of other natural, painful events. Meditation evolved to help people cope with their ignorance. When all else failed, one could always sit very still or beat a drum to attain a calm, meditative state and, in turn, achieve insight that could lead to survival, as well as greater ease in a difficult world. The meditative disciplines that are available to us today have developed over many centuries.

Like action research, meditation is based on a fundamental shift in the way we relate to our experience. Rather than focusing on our goals and working to achieve them, as we do in many domains of our lives, in meditation we work at understanding our experience. We watch what happens in our minds and our bodies and we try not to judge ourselves, especially if what we find is unpleasant. This requires a significant shift in our attitudes toward the inevitable difficulties of life. The First Noble Truth of the Buddha tells us that life is painful and unsatisfying by its very nature, because it is always changing (His Holiness the Dalai Lama, 1998). Because we have minds, bodies, and relationships with others, we will have occasional difficulties and pain. Our usual response is to tighten up and turn away from our troubles. In meditation, however, we try to open up and turn toward them so that they can teach us about themselves and about ourselves. The remarkable result of our inquiry is the spontaneous release of the very feelings that are so burdensome. A simple formula explains the process:

$$\text{Suffering} = \text{Pain} \times \text{Resistance}$$

Pain is the natural result of having a mind and a body and living in a changing world. There are many forms of *resistance*, such as avoidance, rejection, and distraction. Some subtle, insidious forms of resistance are stress-related illness, addictions, and materialism. In the Western world, we tend to view the unpleasant experiences of life as challenges to be overcome, hidden, or actively ignored, lest they be seen as evidence of our inadequacy. These forms of resistance magnify our pain (including physical and emotional pain), thus creating unnecessary suffering.

Meditation is a way of reducing or eliminating suffering by reducing our resistance to pain. As the mystic Thomas Merton said, "I didn't become a monk so I could suffer more than other people—I became a monk so I could suffer more effectively."

How Meditation Works

According to ancient meditation practices, we pay attention to our experiences in special ways, explained by the following formula:

$$\text{Mindfulness} + \text{Equanimity} = \text{Insight and Purification}$$

Mindfulness is a precise, continuous, and focused awareness, which we try to maintain as we meditate. The object of our attention can be any aspect of our ordinary experience, including our breath or what we feel, think, see, or hear. *Equanimity* is a profound permission to feel exactly what we feel, without any interest in having it change in any way.

When we apply mindfulness and equanimity to our experiences, we generate *insights* about life that help us to feel happy and calm regardless of circumstances. For example, we may experience deep insights about the ways that we turn our pain into suffering or about the constantly changing nature of all phenomena or about the inadequacy of our language to describe the delicacy of our experiences. We may discover that what we call "feelings" are actually combinations of thoughts and sensations in the body. This precision helps us to be more aware and more alive.

Purification is the spontaneous release of limiting forces from the past.

Mindfulness and equanimity reinforce one another as we develop greater concentration and acceptance of what is. The more we can accept our experience as we meditate, the more aware we can be. And the more aware we are of our experience, the easier it is to accept. As our practice deepens, we see that our capacity for becoming more conscious and more appreciative of the realities of life seems to be unlimited.

LEVELS OF UNDERSTANDING

When we are helping organizational leaders to discover paradigms that are completely new to them, to cope with radical changes in their markets, or to respond appropriately to unforeseen data from within their organizations, we must help them first to be comfortable with their confusion. Engaging with complicated, unfamiliar problems may cause even very smart people to flounder for awhile. In fact, there are several levels of understanding all human beings may go through when trying to learn a profound truth:

Level 1: I think I may have read it, but I have no recollection of it.

Level 2: I remember hearing about it, but only vaguely.

Level 3: I remember the words, but it doesn't make a lot of sense to me.

Level 4: I can explain it clearly, but I've never experienced it.

Level 5: I see how it works in my own organization. Now I know it.

Because this is an additive learning process, we must assure our clients that the work is more productive than it may seem, that feeling confused is to be expected, and that significant change takes time. This iterative process of individual learning makes it possible for leaders to champion organizational change. It is analogous to the aspects of meditation described above.

"Thinking, Thinking," Rather than Compulsive Planning

Often we find ourselves planning for the future in ways that feel like being on "automatic pilot." We may be driving or washing dishes and, rather than enjoying the moment, our minds are busy planning. There may not be a particularly important issue to decide about; we just plan because planning is familiar. Our planning often turns into worrying: "What if I get lost or have a flat tire?" This kind of unconscious mental activity keeps the mind whirling, wasting precious energy and interfering with our enjoyment of the moment. So how can we re-ground ourselves in the present moment? When we find our minds spinning like this, we can simply say, "Thinking, thinking" and free ourselves from this familiar trap. We can take a potent pause, a moment of quiet reflection, renewal, and rest. If we slow down our unintentional mental activity enough, we receive a wonderful reward: Wisdom arises unbidden when the mind is no longer driven to find answers. The answers we need will find their way to us.

Implications for Organizations

In retreat centers throughout the world, a bell is rung to signal the beginning and ending of the meditation period. The bell is used because it automatically creates mindfulness; as the sound fades, people's minds remain focused on the diminishing sound. Their attention is then concentrated and ready for meditation. Nothing else matters for the next period of time. They all know why they are there, and they're ready to work.

What can organizations do to send such a signal? Most people would agree that smooth, efficient work carried out by people who are "in the loop," clear about their objectives, and committed to fulfilling the mission are important goals. Eliminating obstacles to these goals takes time, energy, and attention that could be focused on the work itself. A clear signal (like the bell) is required to help people to focus on process issues.

Implications for Consultants

If you understand action research and have had good results with your clients using it, then (whether you know it or not) you understand a lot about meditation and can experiment by sitting quietly, gathering some data, and feeding it back to yourself.

Summary

Action research represents a potent pause for organizations. It enables them to become smarter, more productive, and happier places for their members to work. Like any other important skill, it requires time, effort, patience, and persistence to bring about the profound benefits of planned organizational change.

Meditation also requires time, effort, patience, and persistence. It represents a potent pause for individuals in their efforts to become more insightful, more clear about their values, and more efficient and happy in their lives, regardless of their particular circumstances.

Reference

Lewin, K. (1946). Action research and minority problems. *Journal of Social Issues, 2*(4), 34–46.

David R. Glaser is a partner in Vogel/Glaser & Associates, Inc., an organization development consulting firm located in Columbia, Maryland. Since 1982, Mr. Glaser has consulted with a variety of organizations that are planning and implementing change efforts that challenge leaders and members to learn, innovate, and collaborate with mutual respect. He specializes in teamwork interventions and executive coaching. He is a co-author of Renewing Organizations in a Time of Change, published in Volume 2 of The 1995 Annual. Mr. Glaser is an active member of the OD Network and is a professional member of the NTL Institute. He has practiced meditation for twenty-three years.

COMMUNICATING ORGANIZATIONAL CHANGE: INFORMATION TECHNOLOGY MEETS THE CARBON-BASED EMPLOYEE UNIT

Joseph G. Wojtecki, Jr., and Richard G. Peters

Abstract: Change is a constant reality in today's workplace, causing substantial psychological stress within a workforce concerned about its livelihood and quality of life. Against this backdrop is the information technology (IT) explosion, bringing its unprecedented capacity for disseminating information. Many managers are embracing e-mail, intranets, and other technological innovations as efficient solutions to the high communication demands during times of change. However, simply making information available is not the same as communication. People under stress can lose as much as 80 percent of their ability to process information. Situations in which concerns are high and trust is low call for as much attention to the methods of communicating as to the messages.

This article offers insights into why human resources need more low-tech communication during times of change. The research on risk communication provides nontraditional and sometimes counterintuitive principles for avoiding some familiar pitfalls to effective internal communication.

Two powerful forces are surging through American enterprises with accelerating velocity: organizational change and information technology (IT). In the wake of organizational change often lies a workforce in turmoil, shaken by loss of employment security and loss of loyalty to seemingly uncaring employers. For all its capacity, information technology provides only limited relief for the anxieties and frustrations of human resources burdened by change.

There are costs in productivity and competitiveness, often hidden, caused by the psychological drag of constant change in the organization and uncertainty in the workforce. The question is whether effective internal communication can lessen the negative impacts of change on the workforce. If so, what part can information technology play in this?

INTERNAL COMMUNICATION: FORM AND SUBSTANCE

The constant pressure to do more with less as organizations downsize naturally drives a quest for efficiency in all processes and activities—including communication. Under such pressure, the efficiencies inherent in new information technology (IT) applications, as high-tech means for disseminating information, appear seductively attractive to busy managers. Vast amounts of information can be disseminated to most of the workforce almost instantaneously.

"This is good," the busy manager reasons, "so long as we are disseminating the right messages." The underlying premise is that simply making information available is communicating. If the substance of the message is right, and it is efficiently disseminated, then the manager assumes that he or she has communicated. However, the form of communication is critically important for meeting the needs of people experiencing the stressful effects of change. While IT capabilities have evolved exponentially, psychologists question whether the human brain has kept pace. In fact, research suggests that our minds remain hard-wired essentially as they were in the Stone Age and we cope with the world and its threats much as our early ancestors did (Nicholson, 1998).

It is in this "human" dimension that the efficiencies of IT applications become mired and fall short of meeting the workforce's crucial communication needs during change. Research by Covello (1991) and others has found that people under stress, that is, those who feel threatened or put at risk by some force beyond their control, experience "mental noise" that can cause them to lose up to 80 percent of their ability to process information. Furthermore, the remaining 20 percent of processing capacity most often will be focused on issues of high personal concern to the employee, rather than on issues deemed important by management. These principles explain why employee responses to information sometimes seem irrational.

This reality has clear implications regarding over-reliance on IT for communicating change: *Because people under stress can process a normal load of information at only 20 percent efficiency, little is gained by increasing the efficiency at which information is disseminated.* To achieve more successful outcomes during periods of change, a company's management must focus on low-tech communication—especially face-to-face dialogue—about high concern issues in order to overcome mental noise.

ADAPTING RISK COMMUNICATION TO ORGANIZATIONAL CHANGE

The Power of Perception

The foremost principle of risk communication is that "perception equals reality." In other words, what is perceived as real is real in terms of consequences. Employees react to perceived threats, rather than to "reality." Their level of stress during times of change is proportional to their perception of threat. From management's perspective, employees may appear to overreact—even to act in an irrational manner. However, from the employee's perspective the behavior is perfectly rational, given the perceived magnitude of the threat.

Thus, when workforce response to information seems irrational, management must check its own premise and seek to understand the perceptions they have somehow created. Risk communication research has identified more than twenty factors affecting perceptions of threat (Covello, 1991). Knowledge of these factors can help managers anticipate and adjust for them, especially in the way they communicate information.

Trust and Credibility

Perception of threat is a powerful source of mental noise—psychological barriers—impeding communication. Trust and credibility—the goals of all communication—can overcome these barriers. The determinants of trust are discussed in greater detail a bit later. First, it is useful to examine how organizations create credibility that leads to that employee trust.

Within every organization, as within any segment of society, there exists a credibility hierarchy. In terms of employees' preferred sources of information, that hierarchy is as follows, according to research by Foehrenback and Rosenberg (1983):

- *Supervisors:* More than 90 percent of employees surveyed named their first-line supervisor as the preferred source of information.

- *Top Executives:* Just over half of those surveyed named top executives of the organization as a preferred source of information.

- *Union Representatives:* Fewer than 30 percent named union representatives as a preferred source of information.[1]

To the extent that a preference for a particular source for information is a measure of that source's credibility, this research provides some guidance. However, only research specific to an organization can determine the actual hierarchy, so it is important to know and consider an organization's credibility hierarchy when considering which communication strategy is best. There are two reasons for this, according to Covello (1991):

- *The Rule of Credibility Transference:* A message will take on the credibility of the highest credible source that will publicly state or agree to it. (This is the basis of celebrity endorsements in advertising and marketing.)

- *The Rule of Credibility Reversal:* When a lower credible source challenges or attacks a higher credible source, the lower credible source further loses credibility. Ignoring this second rule and counter-attacking when one's position is challenged by someone with more credibility may produce a result that is exactly opposite from what is desired.

The conclusion for higher level managers, who are often perceived as less credible than first-line supervisors in high concern situations, is that they may need to bring in more credible third-party allies to communicate effectively with the workforce. Attempts to "go it alone" could well boomerang.

Within this context of trust and credibility, the dynamics of threat perception can be examined.

---

[1]Note that respondents were permitted more than one response.

FACTORS IN THREAT PERCEPTION

Of the various factors of threat perception studied, three of the most powerful, trust, control, and benefit, are examined below to illustrate how they collectively impact the processing of information.

Trust

Trust is the single most powerful factor in perception of threat. Research shows that a risk managed or communicated by a trusted source is perceived as less threatening than one represented by an untrustworthy source (Covello, 1991; Fessenden-Raden, Fitchen, & Heath, 1987; Slovic, 1993). The trust factor can alter the perception of a threat two thousand times. An example can be used to illustrate the point: A quantifiable risk, such as a health risk from poor indoor air quality, may be objectively determined to pose one chance in one million of causing cancer. When the source of information about that risk is not trusted, those who feel threatened perceive the chances as one chance in five hundred. Remember, what is perceived as real is real in its consequences.

Perceptions based on trust are similarly altered when risks cannot be so precisely quantified, for example, the risk of losing one's livelihood as the result of organizational change.

Control

Control is one tier below trust in its power over perception of threat. Research shows that when we have some control over a risk it is less threatening than if the risk is imposed involuntarily (Covello, 1991; Fischhoff et al., 1978; Slovic, 1987). The control factor can bias the perception of a risk one thousand-fold.

To continue with the same illustration: If the same indoor air quality risk of a million to one is imposed on a group that has no voice in the decision and no means of affecting the risk, the perception of this risk assumes the proportions of one in one thousand. Predictably, the group's reactions will be more consistent with the greater risk. This, in part, explains why people willingly accept a higher risk that is voluntary, such as a one in sixty-seven risk of a fatal traffic accident, yet become outraged over a much lower risk that is imposed on them, such as a one in one million increased risk of cancer.

In the same way, the perception of threat associated with management decisions during change will be skewed if these decisions are imposed and lack meaningful input from the people they impact.

Benefit

Benefit carries the same threat-perception weight as control (one thousand-fold), that is, a risk that provides some balancing benefit is less threatening than a risk with no associated benefit (Covello, 1991; Fessenden-Raden, Fitchen, & Heath, 1987; Slovic, 1987). Using the example of indoor air quality, lack of benefit can increase the perception of a one in a million risk to an apparent one in a thousand risk, with a correspondingly intensified reaction.

To lessen the perception of risk, it is important that those who benefit from a risk be the same as those who will face its consequences. When the risks faced by some yield benefits only for others, an additional perception of threat factor is invoked—fairness—and causes further negative reactions.

Cumulative Effects

Individually, the power of these three threat-perception factors is very strong, but they are overwhelming when seen as cumulative (Fischhoff et al., 1978).

Consider again the example of indoor air quality. In two simple steps, withholding both control and benefit, a calculated risk of one in one million becomes a perceptual certainty of one in one! Add to this the effect of mistrust of the messenger, and employee reactions quickly can become extreme.

Once managers know the effects of these threat-perception factors, they should not be surprised at the workforce reactions to decisions they make over which the workforce has no control and sees no perceived benefit. What might seem irrational is very rational in a workforce that does not trust those who are communicating with them.

Managing Threat Perceptions

Because *perceptions*, not reality, determine the direction and intensity of employees' reactions and behavior, organizations must learn to manage the perceptions they give. The risk communication research provides some useful principles for effective, though often nontraditional and counter-intuitive, approaches managers can follow for communicating with their workforce.

Managing the Trust Factor

To gain the advantages of trust, managers must understand the basis of trust. Research shows that when people are asked how they decide whether or not to trust someone in a high concern situation, their responses fall into these broad categories (Covello, 1993).

- Honesty and openness;
- Competence and expertise;
- Dedication and commitment; and
- Caring and empathy.

Most managers would wish to have these characteristics ascribed to them, but are not sure how to exhibit the characteristics for employees. Managers are often shocked to learn how the factors relate to one another in terms of earning employee trust. As Figure 1 shows, caring and empathy are equal to all the other characteristics combined for earning employee trust in high concern situations.

Trust is the most powerful threat-perception factor, and in high concern situations people seek assurance first that a manager cares about their well-being. Will Rogers once observed, "People want to know that you care,

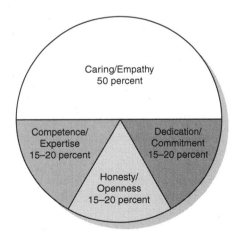

Figure 1. Relative Weight of Elements of Trust

before they care what you know." Caring and empathy are best communicated by direct, face-to-face, two-way dialogue. The importance of two-way communication cannot be overemphasized in high concern situations.

The simple act of listening to an employee's concerns is one of the most compelling gestures a manager can make to demonstrate caring and empathy. Seeing employee concerns as real—that is, real in the employee's perception—further establishes the manager's caring and empathy, and in turn establishes employee trust. Generally, information technology-based channels of communication are too one-way and impersonal to allow managers the opportunity to convey empathy and caring.

Managing the Control Factor

People in a democracy generally have the right to participate in decisions that affect their lives, their property, and the things they value. By participating in the decision-making process, people gain the satisfaction of knowing that they have exerted some measure of control over what will happen to them.

Employees, as products of a democratic society, bring definite expectations to the workplace about whether or not decisions made by those in authority are acceptable to them. Their judgment often hinges on whether or not they had a voice in the decision.

Many organizations at least tacitly acknowledge the value of employee involvement in the decision process. Even the Malcolm Baldrige Award criteria recognize the value of employee involvement. However, organizations often fall short of the goal. What often substitutes for legitimate employee involvement is the more familiar model of decide-announce-defend (DAD).

In the DAD model, employee input usually is sought, if at all, during the "announce" phase—after the decision has been made. Employees are offered the opportunity to respond to a decision that has been reached, and then management defends the decision by explaining all of the compelling facts and rationale that led to the decision.

The DAD model does not qualify as employee involvement. Because the dialogue is after the fact, the decision is seen as imposed, and employees are denied an opportunity to influence it. High concern decisions reached without employee involvement trigger the threat-perception factor of control, increasing the perception of any risk associated with the decision one thousand-fold.

Management is often reluctant to accede legitimate employee involvement in the decision process because they fear the results of relinquishing control. This is not necessarily something to fear. Granting the workforce a voice in decisions, through an appropriate forum, is just that—a voice. It does not constitute a vote or a veto. All that employees need, and in most cases expect, is assurance that their point of view has been heard, reasonably considered, and responded to before the decision is made. Outrage is a common consequence of denying employees a voice in decisions that impact them in high concern situations.

The expectation of employees to have a voice in decisions is a reflection of our democratic society and of management trends, such as the participatory decision making stressed in total quality management (TQM) programs. The reality for managers is that this expectation has become a part of the culture, and it's very much like the genie that once out of the lamp refuses to go back inside.

Managing the Benefit Factor

Communicating the benefits associated with a perceived threat that employees are asked can be extremely difficult. In most cases, there either is an offsetting benefit to employees or there is not. Whichever is true, managers must be mindful of the impact of the perception of benefit factor (one thousandfold) when communicating with employees. They must consider:

- If there is a benefit for accepting a risk, that benefit must be clearly defined and communicated to the employees. This is especially important for "survivors" of an organizational change, who ultimately will determine the success of the post-change organization.

- In the same way, benefits that derive to the organization (senior management, stockholders, and others), but not to the employees themselves, must be judiciously avoided. Benefits act as a positive threat-perception factor only when the same people who bear the risks gain the benefits, whereas benefits that accrue to others can increase outrage.

This second point is particularly sensitive in an era of widely reported instances of CEO bonuses linked to massive workforce reductions. In this context, some workforce cynicism is understandable.

Reducing Other Threat-Perception Factors

Although it is beyond the scope of this article to discuss in detail other prominent threat-perception factors, managers also may encounter one or more of the following points:

- *Fairness:* Are the consequences of the perceived risk fairly distributed among all members of the organization?

- *Alternatives:* Are viable alternative courses of action available? Have these been fully considered?

- *Natural:* Is the perceived risk the result of powerful, external business forces, or was it generated arbitrarily within the organization?

Recognizing and understanding these threat-perception factors can better prepare managers to communicate effectively with employees during times of change. This knowledge can help managers to understand, and even predict, workforce reactions that otherwise might seem irrational.

This may involve nothing more than respecting the employees' point of view on issues of high concern to them. Genuine caring and empathy translate to demonstrating respect and communicating one-on-one.

COMMUNICATION OF RISK DURING CHANGE

Each organization's situation is unique, and there is no one way to communicate to reduce employees' perception of risk. However, some typical methods are described below. Because two-way communication is so critical for lowering employees' perceptions of risk during change, one general option for improving upward communication and one for improving downward communication are given below.

Upward Communication

As discussed earlier, research shows that employees' most preferred source of information about an organization is their first-line supervisor. This is not surprising, because immediate supervisors have the most opportunity for direct two-way communication with employees, and they most closely understand and relate to the employees' perspective. First-line supervisors seldom are isolated or insulated from the day-to-day realities of the workplace.

Employee preference for first-line supervisors as the source of information can be interpreted at least partly as a reflection of the employees' trust and the supervisors' credibility. This has obvious implications for the downward dissemination of information, but also has important implications for credible upward communication and employee feedback.

Depending on the size of the organization, the difficulties of large spans of control can limit meaningful dialogue between the top and bottom tiers. One good way to overcome bottle necks in communication and establish an open two-way channel is to form an employee advisory forum (EAF) comprising representative first-line supervisors. An EAF should conform closely to the following specifications:

- Forums should be established at each geographic or organizational location and, as appropriate, at headquarters.

- Membership of each EAF should be limited to twelve to eighteen people to permit quality dialogue. One or two members should be management representatives positioned high enough to make decisions on routine issues and to have influence at the highest levels for addressing larger issues. The remaining members should be first-line supervisors.

- Membership should represent a cross section of the workforce, including union members if applicable.

- Membership should be selected by the forum itself, rather than be appointed by management. This preserves the objective credibility of the forum in the view of the workforce. The membership process could begin with a selection committee made up of two initial members and then expand to involve new members.

- The forum should be self-directed, that is, it should set its own agenda and select its own issues for discussion with management. Management can place issues on the agenda, but should not be able to exclude any workforce issues.

- The forum should collaboratively explore potential resolutions to high concern workforce issues. Management should commit to listen fully to EAF concerns and recommendations and provide open, well-considered responses.

- The forum should exercise no approval authority regarding management decisions. However, management should offer full explanations of how decisions were reached, including why any forum suggestions were not adopted.

- Responsibilities of forum membership should include a commitment to ongoing dialogue with workforce "constituents" to sustain an awareness of the forum's proceedings.

Properly constituted, an EAF can build trust and increase employee involvement in addressing high concern issues. At the same time, it fully preserves management's authority and responsibility for directing the business of the organization. While an EAF might begin as an ad hoc measure for navigating a difficult period of change, its upward communication value may be sufficient to continue its function indefinitely.

Downward Communication

One mechanism for effective downward communication works particularly well in tandem with the EAF. This mechanism is the InfoEx (information exchange). An InfoEx is based on the "poster station" format and provides an effective alternative to the mass employee meeting, a familiar technique used in many organizations. These meetings fail to achieve the benefits of face-to-face dialogue. Among the limitations of mass meetings for employees are these:

- Most attendees are too intimidated by the large group to stand up and express their personal concerns, even when invited to do so.

- A vocal minority can dominate the meeting and not necessarily represent the majority views.

- The necessary logistics of large group meetings impose physical barriers between the speakers and the audience (lecterns, tables, and stages). These become perceptual barriers to communication.

- The balance of time between management presentations and open discussion commonly tips heavily in favor of the presentations, although the opposite is more appropriate.

- Employees often leave large group meetings further frustrated that their concerns are not being addressed.

In contrast, the InfoEx format presents a greatly enhanced opportunity for two-way dialogue. The InfoEx can be conceptualized as a trade show in which the product is communication. It consists of an open-house arrangement of informational poster stations at a location convenient for employees and spanning a longer duration than most traditional meetings. (See Figure 2.) Logistically, the InfoEx consists of the following elements:

- A general theme or message that is relevant and addresses workforce concerns about which management wants to communicate. (Themes and messages could come, for example, from the proceedings of an EAF.)

- A convenient location large enough to accommodate numerous simultaneous small group discussions without interference.

- Up to six exhibits or poster stations, each one addressing some aspect of the theme or message with text and graphic information on display panels. Exhibits should be simple and judiciously avoid a glitzy or expensive appearance.

- Tables at each station with takeaways of all information on the poster panels, plus more detailed information and background documents supporting the messages.

- A team of presenters at each station (a minimum of two) with expertise in the subject matter of that station and training in risk communication presentation skills. Presenters should include first-line supervisors active in EAFs.

- Comment cards and collection boxes at each station and other convenient locations for employees to leave comments "on the record" for later management response.

- Representatives of senior management present at all times—not attending any particular station—to circulate with employees who may engage them individually to make any comments or ask any questions they desire.

The dynamic of the InfoEx is one-on-one or small group discussions, in contrast to the large group dynamics typical of mass employee meetings. The advantages include:

- Employees have the option of coming and going at their convenience.

- They can stand back twenty feet from a properly designed poster station and obtain the key messages related to that topic.

- They can approach closer as interest warrants and obtain more detailed information on a topic.

- They can step up to the station presenters (trained in the importance of listening effectively and conveying caring and empathy) and discuss personal concerns in relative privacy.

- They can take away information for later consideration and leave comments or questions on the record for management's response.

- They can meet senior managers under less intimidating circumstances than would otherwise be possible.

Figure 2. InfoEx Exhibit and Discussion Groups

An InfoEx can run for a day, from before a workday begins until after it ends, or for selected periods over several workdays. The objective is to make it as convenient as possible for employees to attend and to allow enough time that the number in attendance at any one time is likely to be relatively small. Although the InfoEx consumes more time than mass meetings for managers and presenters, it yields far more effective communication for the time invested.

The InfoEx is solidly rooted in the principles of risk communication, providing an excellent venue for managing important threat-perception factors and gaining trust and credibility with the workforce.

Both the EAF and the InfoEx present management with opportunities for solid return on its investment in communication. However, successful implementation requires precise application of critical risk communication principles and is best approached with a solid grounding in research.

SUMMARY

When concern is high and trust is low, conditions consistent with organizational change, a departure from the traditional communication model becomes necessary. Research studies on risk communication explain why this is so and suggest how to change the communication model for more effective results during difficult times.

In recognition of human nature, the approaches suggested by risk communication principles are low-tech rather than high-tech. They are often nontraditional and counter-intuitive, and sometimes uncomfortable to adopt. However, successful application of risk communication techniques can enhance the workforce's trust and the credibility of management and go far toward overcoming the perceptual barriers that otherwise impede communication.

Trust and credibility are the greatest assets a manager can have to lead the workforce through the throes of change, emerging intact and motivated to contribute to the success of the new organization.

Reliance on the efficient but impersonal techniques developed through information technology for disseminating information might suffice for the theoretical "carbon-based employee unit." However, human resources comprise real people, and real people require real communication—especially during times of organizational change.

References

Covello, V. (1991). Risk comparisons and risk communication: Issues and problems in comparing health and environmental risks (pp. 79–124). In R. Kasperson & P. Stallen (Eds.), *Communicating risks to the public*. Boston, MA: Kluwer Academic Publishers.

Covello, V. (1992). Trust and credibility in risk communication. *Health & Environment Digest, 6*(1), 1–3.

Covello, V. (1993). Risk communication and occupational medicine. *Journal of Occupational Medicine, 35*(1), 18–19.

Fessenden-Raden, J., Fitchen, J.M., & Heath, J.S. (1987). Providing risk information in communities: Factors influencing what is heard and accepted. *Science, Technology and Human Values, 12*(3/4), 94–101.

Fischhoff, B., Slovic, P., Lichtenstein, S., Read, S., & Combs, B. (1978). How safe is safe enough? A psychometric study of attitudes toward technological risks and benefits. *Policy Sciences, 9*, 127–152.

Foehrenbach, J., & Rosenberg, K. (1983). How are we doing? *Journal of Communication Management* (cited in Larkin & Larkin, *Communicating change: Winning employee support for new business goals*. New York: McGraw-Hill, 1994).

Nicholson, N. (1998, July/August). How hardwired is human behavior? *Harvard Business Review*, pp. 134–147.

Slovic, P. (1987, April 17). Perception of risk. *Science, 236*, 280–285.

Slovic, P. (1993). Perceived risk, trust and democracy. *Risk Analysis, 13*(6), 675–682.

Joseph G. Wojtecki, Jr., joined in forming Covello, Peters & Wojtecki, LLC, to specialize in risk communication practice. His thirty years' of communication experience spans senior government, corporate, and consulting positions, including the firms of Hill and Knowlton and Ruder-Finn and a career in the U.S. Air Force. He has a bachelor of science degree in mass communication from Kent State University, and a master of arts in organizational communication from the University of North Dakota.

Richard G. Peters, DrPH, MBA, MS, has more than ten years' experience directing both qualitative and quantitative research projects. He is assistant professor at William Paterson University and has conducted opinion research for the Jupiter Corporation and the Center for Risk Communication. He received his doctorate in environmental health science from Columbia University and performed postdoctoral studies at the Massachusetts Institute of Technology. He received a master of science degree in chemistry and an MBA from the University of Virginia.

NEW APPLICATIONS FOR THE DELPHI TECHNIQUE

Richard Phillips

Abstract: The Delphi Technique has been used successfully for many years to develop scenarios in situations in which objective data are lacking. It has not
been used as widely as other techniques in training
and education because of a lack of knowledge of the
technique and because of one particular drawback:
the time it takes to develop the survey instruments
and communicate with the respondents. This paper
lists some of the advantages of the Delphi Technique, tells how technology can be used to overcome
time constraints, and explains the basic steps in the
process.

$\mathbf{T}$he Delphi Technique is a method for obtaining consensus of informed opinion by soliciting the views of experts in the specific field being studied. The procedure uses a series of successive questionnaires (called rounds). In each questionnaire after the first round, the respondents receive feedback about the outcome of the preceding round and have the chance to modify their answers (Bunning, 1979). The respondents, or panel members, usually are in geographically separate locations and often are unknown to one another (McBride, 1974).

The Delphi Technique was developed during the late 1940s and early 1950s by Helmer and his associates at the Rand Corporation as a method of technological forecasting (Dalkey & Helmer, 1963; deBrigard & Helmer, 1970). Since then, it has been used to develop future scenarios and solicit expert opinions in a number of fields, especially when there is a lack of objective data about the issue under consideration. It has also been used to develop training programs and educational curricula.

Some advantages of the Delphi method are as follows:

1. The isolated generation of ideas gives all respondents time to ponder, placing introverted respondents on the same level as extroverted ones and giving all respondents time to think through the complexity of the issue or problem being considered.

2. The first round of the process forces each respondent to think about the issue independently, without hearing others' objections or reacting to others' ideas.

3. There is no pressure to conform, as each panel member is unknown to all others.

4. In the second round, the thoughts and ideas of other panel members can be evaluated and compared (without pressure) to one's own.

5. All panel members are considered equals, and the anonymity of the process eliminates influence based on power or personality.

6. The process tends to conclude with a perceived feeling of closure and accomplishment.

7. The technique allows experts from geographically remote and separate sites to contribute to the process (Delbecq, Van de Ven, & Gustafson, 1975).

The Delphi Technique is essentially a debate without the influence of dominating personalities. The participants have the advantage of nontimed reflection and are able to express their opinions anonymously (Phillips, 1984).

The disadvantages of the technique include lack of widespread knowledge of the process, which has limited its use in training and development and educational settings, and the time constraints.

OVERCOMING TIME CONSTRAINTS

The biggest drawback cited by those who are familiar with the Delphi Technique is that it takes a long time. In the past, each round had to be mailed to the experts. The experts completed their instruments and mailed them back to the monitor. The monitor tabulated each round, developing a modal response for each item and indicating to each member what his or her response was for each item in regard to the modal response. Now, by utilizing fax or e-mail, the time required to send questionnaires to the panel members and receive their responses can be substantially reduced. The monitor's preparation time also can be reduced with the aid of faster computer programs for tabulating and presenting data.

EXPLANATION OF THE PROCESS

The following are the basic steps in the Delphi process.

Step 1: Selection of the Issue. The issue or topic to be considered generally is complex, and little objective data can be gathered about it. Some examples of presenting topics are: "What are the components of a management training program that will prepare managers for the future?" and "What appliances will be in the typical American home in 2050?"

Step 2: Selection of the Expert Panel Members. You may select experts who are very familiar with the subject you are studying or you may select nominators who will select the experts. (For example, you might contact professional organizations in the field and ask each to suggest four experts. You might also contact universities, book publishers, etc.) The optimum size of the panel is seven to twelve members. If there is a possibility that some panel members may resign during the process, you may want to begin with more.

Step 3: Development of the Research Instrument. After the instrument has been developed for round one, send it (preferably by e-mail) to the experts, along with an explanation of how to complete it and how and when to return it to you.

Step 4: Tabulate the Results of Round One. Determine the modal response for each item after tabulating results. The instrument sent out for round two will show these results and will include the panel member's response for round one along with the modal response for each item. If the expert's response is different from the modal response, ask the respondent to move toward the modal response or to defend his or her initial response. Send (preferably by e-mail) the round two instrument to the panel members.

Step 5: Tabulate the Results of Round Two. Create a new instrument showing the converged responses, and send a third round to the panel members, as above. This round provides an opportunity for panel members to reach consensus or to provide reasons for not doing so. Generally, three rounds are enough to obtain consensus or be able to use the results of the study. Experience indicates little benefit, and diminishing responses, from conducting succeeding rounds (Bunning, 1979).

Step 6: Complete the Study and Send Panel Members a Final Report. Be sure to include any rankings, conclusions, etc.

SUGGESTIONS FOR USE

In addition to its typical use in product development and the forecasting of business trends, the Delphi Technique has relevance for professionals in the fields of human resource development, organization development, and education. An obvious application is organizational strategic planning. Exploration of new approaches to customer service, management styles, organizational designs, technologies, and other relevant issues can make this technique a valuable tool for organizations and consultants. It also can be used in developing topics and approaches for training programs on issues or positions that are complex and subjective. In the field of education, it can be used in developing new programs and structures. These are just a few of the possibilities.

References

Bunning, R.L. (1979). In J.E. Jones & J.W. Pfeiffer (Eds.), *The 1979 annual handbook for group facilitators.* San Francisco, CA: Jossey-Bass/Pfeiffer.

Dalkey, N.C., & Helmer, O. (1963, April). An experimental application of the Delphi method to the use of experts. *Management Science,* p. 102.

deBrigard, P., & Helmer, O. (1970). *Some potential societal developments: 1970–2000.* Middletown, CT: Institute for the Future.

Delbecq, A.L., Van de Ven, A.H., & Gustafson, D.H. (1975). *Group techniques for program planning.* Glenview, IL: Scott, Foresman.

McBride, A. (1974). Delphi technique and futures planning in Catholic education. *Religious Education Forum,* Vol. 10.

Phillips, R.I. (1984). *The development of curriculum using the Delphi technique.* Ann Arbor, MI: University Microfilms International.

Dr. Richard Phillips is division chair of the Technologies Division at Mountain Empire Community College in Big Stone Gap, Virginia. He has over twenty years' experience in implementing change initiatives, developing training and educational programs, and working with continuous improvement and team facilitation issues in both private industry and in academia.

INCREASING YOUR ORGANIZATION'S EFFECTIVENESS WITH PROJECT MANAGEMENT

Michael Stanleigh

Abstract: As we wade through yet another series of economic crises, our organizational imperatives lean toward managing our work and, in particular, our projects, on time and on budget. No longer do we have the luxury to exceed budget requirements and time constraints. Yet we must continue to meet and exceed our customer expectations and quality requirements in order to maintain our market position. This paper presents the Project Management Life Cycle, a process to increase the success of project management efforts.

PROJECT MANAGEMENT DEFINED

The successful management of projects, increasingly spoken about, is not a new fad or strategy but rather a pragmatic approach to work. As we approach the 21st Century we are seeing this method bring many organizations tremendous success.

The Project Management Institute, an organization that deals with the certification of project management professionals, has created a body of knowledge, which includes defining a project as a temporary endeavor (projects must have a beginning and end time frame) undertaken to create a unique product or service (unique in that it is different in some distinguishing way from similar products or services). Projects can have a total duration from half a day to three years and be comprised of anything from a single resource to multiple resources operating throughout the world. Project management is the application of knowledge, skills, tools, and techniques necessary to develop the project plan and to execute it successfully so that it meets or exceeds customer and stakeholder needs and expectations.

WHERE TO START

How do we involve people in developing the plans and successfully managing these plans to meet our quality and customer expectations, and, of course, to bring our projects in on time and on budget?

The management of projects is a process. The Project Management Life Cycle (see Figure 1) articulates this process. It is designed to act as a simple guide to help people responsible for the management of projects, regardless of size. When followed, the life cycle ensures that customer and quality expectations are met, successful project plan execution will occur, and that the project will be brought to a successful closure.

Stage 1: Project Definition	Stage 2: Project Planning	Stage 3: Project Execution	Stage 4: Project Close
Create project charter	Develop the work breakdown structure (WBS)	Schedule management	Presentation of report to sponsor, stakeholders, customer, team, etc.
Select project manager	Allocate resources to each activity & task	Change management	Recommendations and/or conclusions
Identify project team members	Estimate duration for each activity & task	Issues management	Final evaluation of project
Form project team	Input the WBS into project management software, if available	Quality management	Project team disbanded
Explain project planning process to project team	Develop network diagram	Documentation management	
Develop project team member roles and responsibilities	Identify dependencies (predecessors & successors)	Cost management	
Develop the scope statement	Identify milestone dates	Risk management	
Identify stakeholders and customers	Input network diagram into project software	Review planned vs. actual work progress	
	Allocate costs to the project plan	Review planned vs. actual cost progress	
	Review critical path	Project status reports	
	Baseline project		

© 2000 Business Improvement Architects

Figure 1. The Project Management Life Cycle

How to Proceed

Stage 1: Project Definition

We begin at Stage 1, which includes developing the project team, agreeing on the project deliverables, and ensuring that customer and stakeholder expectations can be met. Projects can come from anywhere—an accepted proposal, business requirements, specifications, customer request, and so forth. The individual who oversees the project is known as the "project sponsor." The sponsor will complete the final evaluation of the project and its project members. The sponsor selects the project manager and develops a project charter to present to the project manager. Alternatively, the sponsor may provide a copy of the business requirement or customer requirement. These documents outline the main purpose of the project and expected deliverables.

Once selected, the project manager will be accountable for project success. Therefore, following the Project Management Life Cycle becomes crucial. The project manager will select the appropriate people, given the size of the project, to work with him or her on the project. The project manager then brings all the key people together at a "kick-off meeting." During this meeting, time will be spent reviewing the project charter, forming what will now be the project team (including identification of team members and their roles and responsibilities), and developing the scope statement. The scope statement reiterates the project manager's understanding (as well as team members' understanding if this is a project requiring a team) of the project's mandate, its deliverables, and overall scope.

Last, the project manager and team will develop a list of customer and other stakeholder requirements. This ensures that those needs will not be overlooked. Many projects may be deemed successful but not meet the needs of the customers and/or other stakeholders for whom the project was designed. Defining their requirements at this early stage makes it easier to integrate their needs into the project plan. In the plan, specific activities will be identified that will ensure that the needs are met throughout the project.

Although this stage does not require a lot of time, it forms the foundation for project success. In my experience, most projects that I audit lack a clear scope statement, and the people involved have not identified and documented the customer requirements and have spent little, if any, time developing the project team.

Stage 2: Project Planning

Stage 2 of the Project Management Life Cycle, project planning, requires the most effort on the part of the project manager and project team—yet in a relatively short span of time.

It is at this stage that the project plan is developed. In this step, the activities and related tasks are identified, a duration of time is attached to each, and a resource allocation to each is made. It is structured as a sequential flow of activity known as a "work breakdown structure."

In my experience, the level of detail at this stage is often not sufficient to manage the project successfully and bring it in on time and on budget. I have established the following guidelines. On a project with a total duration of three months or more, the lowest level task should take no more than five days. If total duration is under three months but more than one month, the lowest level task should take no more than two days. If total duration is less than one month, the lowest level of task should take no more than one day. The amount of time allocated to each step should be reflected in the critical path, which shows the timeline for the project. To change the work breakdown structure from a "to-do list" into a full project plan, dependencies must be created. Every activity must have both a *predecessor* (what must be done before this task can be started) and a *successor* (what can begin only when this task is completed). These steps should then be recorded in a network diagram, a visual or graphic representation of the process.

Milestones are then identified. These represent the completion of key tasks that, if missed, may prevent the successful completion of the project. The final part of this stage is to allocate costs to the lowest level of task possible, whether you have been given a budget for the project or whether you have been asked to develop one.

It is during this stage in the project life cycle that control mechanisms are created that ensure success in project execution. At this point we have three control mechanisms:

- Customer requirement activities identified in the project plan to ensure that their expectations are met throughout the project.
- Start and finish times for each activity and related task.
- Costs broken down to the lowest level of activity possible.

If the mechanisms are not identified and addressed at this level of detail, the likelihood of project success will be greatly diminished. Once you have established all of the parameters of the project, you will have created the baseline. It is important to record this because it may change during execution (Stage 3) and you will need to document both the original plan as well as the changes.

Stage 3: Project Execution

The plan is now complete. All project team members and additional resources know what they should do, when they should do it, how long it should take, what costs are involved, and who they should hand off to when they have completed their task.

To ensure that commitments are met, weekly project team meetings must take place. The main objective for each meeting is to examine the tasks that were scheduled to be started and finished over the previous week compared to what was actually started and finished. The idea is not to place blame, but rather to identify the early warning signs of potential problems that can be rectified. For example, a team member may have underestimated the amount of time necessary or been pulled away to attend to other tasks. As project manager, you can offer assistance or do whatever is necessary to get the project back on track.

This is also the stage at which change management is critical. The very nature of managing projects is that there will be customer changes, sponsor changes, management changes, and so forth. In order to maintain the basic integrity of the project it is essential that a change management form be completed and signed by the sponsor. Essentially this one-page document would include what the change is, what impact it will have on the project if approved (more time/money and so on) or if not approved, and the sponsor's recommendations. When signed, the form becomes the basis on which change can be applied to the project's baseline, permitting adjustments to total duration, cost, and quality of the project.

Stage 4: Project Close

With the control mechanisms in place—weekly project meetings, use of the change management documentation, continuous quality and customer checks—you should now have a project that is on time and on budget.

The original cost and time structure, as well as customer requirements, may be different than what the final project delivered. As long as change management forms have been completed and authorized to account for these differences, then the project is considered a success. The final project should represent the original scope statement, plus all authorized change documents.

If the change forms do not exist but the end project differs from the original scope statement, the project was not successful. No excuses as to why!

As a part of closing the project, it is important to complete a final project evaluation. The sponsor leads this step. He or she should, in conjunction with the project manager, team members, and any other key resources, review the project and evaluate its success based on the original scope statement, any change documentation, and the final results.

The project plan will become a template for all future, similar projects. In this way, the next time you have a similar project, you do not need to go through the entire process in the same amount of detail. Rather, you can use the previous project plan as a template upon which to build the new plan. With the comments from the project evaluation, you will know what elements need to be adjusted.

My experience auditing many projects, managing many projects, and developing other project management skills suggests that the key is understanding that managing projects is a process—not just knowledge of the tools.

With some discipline to apply the methodology, project management can save organizations money and can increase their level of customer satisfaction.

Michael Stanleigh, president of Business Improvement Architects, is a management consultant and award-winning trainer who specializes in strategic planning, executive coaching, project management, leadership, reengineering, and process analysis. He has spoken at many conferences and has written articles that have been published in many countries on the subjects of innovation, total quality, employee motivation, management, and human resource development. He teaches at the University of Toronto in Ontario, Canada.

Managing the Dynamics of "Having Nothing to Say" in Small Groups

Gary Gemmill

Abstract: People often are unable or reluctant to express their thoughts and emotions in a group setting. This article discusses the costs of such reticence to the individual and to the group. The psychological and cultural dynamics underlying the reluctance of group members to express their thoughts, perceptions, and emotions openly are analyzed, and the inhibiting effect of language is discussed. Ways of intervening to encourage identifying experiences and expressing emotions within groups are discussed. Guidelines are presented for coping with the expression of emotions by others in the group and for establishing boundaries in regard to the emotions and experiences to be expressed within the group.

$\mathbf{I}$n the early phases of a group's development when relatively silent members are queried on what they are thinking and feeling about events taking place in the group, they often reply by stating they feel nothing and they have "nothing to say." They present themselves as having no experiences, no perceptions, no thoughts, and no emotions. Later, as the group develops, these relatively silent members—when confronted about their silence—often open up, expressing in vivid detail their incisive perceptions and emotions. Other group members are astonished at the insights and depth of feelings that these previously silent members bring to the group. The silent members themselves often discover that, although they might be quiet people, they have much to say that is of value in understanding what is happening in the group and that they have a wide range of emotions about the events taking place in the group.

THE COSTS OF SILENCE

Silent members withhold their experiences of life in the group. They may have numbed their feelings, for some reason, and/or lost touch with what they think and feel in social situations. Or, believing that their inner experiences have no meaningful value for anyone, they disconnect, trivialize, and dismiss what they feel and think while in the group. Because they believe that they feel and think nothing, and/or that their contributions are meaningless, they often feel empty. However, the paralyzing belief that they have had no pertinent experience or that they have nothing meaningful to say is a mistaken one. Everyone has an innermost experience of the world as it unfolds. We all have perceptions, thoughts, feeling, and emotional reactions to interpersonal events. We are what we experience, so discounting or denying our experience of ourselves leaves us feeling impoverished, superficial, empty, and lonely. What we need to discover and examine is the various reasons we disconnect and become distant or alienated from our experiences in interpersonal situations.

Within groups, fears of openly expressing and discussing emotions are often reflected in sarcastic comments about "touchy-feely" relationships or "trying to psychoanalyze each other." Some people fear that any open expression of their emotions would indicate that they were in need of a psychotherapist. Not having developed their ability to experience and express emotions constructively, they feel incompetent to deal with their own emotions or the emotions of others.

Emotions are always embedded within interpersonal relationships, whether or not we are aware of them or whether or not we choose to discuss them openly. Members of a group become angry with each other, they feel threatened, they become upset, they become defensive, they feel hurt, they feel sad, they feel disappointed, they feel affirmed, they feel elated, they feel passionate about something, they feel discouraged, they feel alone, they feel manipulated, they feel frustrated, they feel competitive, and they experience pain and a whole multitude of other emotions. Within the life of a group one can at one moment experience laughter and in another moment experience tears. Commitment, ownership, and passion are common emotions that occur in groups.

When we do not openly deal with the emotionality that arises in working together, we not only collude to suffer in silence but our feelings become distorted and go underground. They seep out in the form of escalating fears, mistrust, gossip, rumors, scapegoating, apathy, boredom, feelings of stagnation, alienation, and a sense of being lonely in the midst of a group. These are but a few of the forms that unexpressed emotions can take.

Inhibiting Effects of Culture and Language

Culture

Most of us live in a culture that discourages introspection and emotional closeness in relationships, particularly in the context of work. We are used to engaging in social rituals, roles, and pretense in each other's presence, rather than expressing our experiences more openly and deeply. Rituals, roles, and pretense function as social walls that keep us from knowing either ourselves or one another at a deep level.

There are many explicit and hidden cultural messages that can blunt our experience of our emotions and discourage communication of our experiences and emotions. Messages such as "suffer in silence"; "don't cry"; "don't show that you're afraid"; "don't get angry"; "don't get too close"; and "don't upset others" discourage open expression of feelings. Sometimes we receive such messages explicitly, and sometimes we infer them from observing the behavior of others. We act as if these messages are "rules," mainly because we are not aware of the extent to which we have been influenced by our culture in regard to expressing emotions. No one has intentionally created this state of affairs, but we typically assume that emotions are not discussed because there is something wrong with them or that it is dangerous to do so because things might get out of control. Most of us are fearful of our own emotions—of losing conscious control and being overpowered and controlled by them. These fears can be noted in a group setting by the absence of the expression or discussion of emotions.

Some people mistakenly conclude that because their inner experience is not "scientifically derived" and belongs to a subjective world of emotions and perceptions, it is arbitrary and without personal or social value. This belief is reinforced by the tendency in our culture to deify "scientific" knowledge as the only valid knowledge. Because most of us feel distant from scientific knowledge, it is relatively easy to feel that we have nothing of importance to say. This belief is further reinforced by a belief that everything worth knowing is to be found only in articles or books. The assumption underlying this belief is that all important knowledge can be translated into language that is exact and precise.

Language

When we attempt to communicate our interpersonal experiences to one another we search for words to describe them; often it is an imprecise, inexact, and ambiguous process. Language is simply a symbolic attempt to convey our inner experiences, which consist of sensations, intuitions, emotions, perceptions, and images that are not directly communicable. When the language we use evokes a similar inner experience in others, the clearer we are in symbolically communicating our own experience. Yet we often know more of our experience than we can express through words. Much vicarious interpersonal and social learning happens without the use of words, through social observation of the actions of other people.

Similarly, interpersonal communications have nonverbal components that are outside the context of language. For example, a smile; an angry tone of voice; a trembling lip; a cold stare; a defensive stance are all nonverbal ways to convey a message without translating it into language.

Although in a sense we are all prisoners of language in conveying our inner experience, it is a tremendous relief to realize that at best language is a changing art form that we can use imaginatively to express our inner experiences. There are usually several ways that we can express a particular experience in language. This means that we can explore several ways of expressing ourselves to discover impactful and meaningful ways of relating to one another. Being open to exploring ways of expressing ourselves to one another is often an exciting and rich experience.

LEARNING TO EXPRESS EMOTIONS

Emotions are seen as potentially dangerous and destructive, thereby needing to be avoided and controlled carefully so that they do not surface in relationships.

Emotions that arise in working together are not an illness; they are part of the human condition and tell us what matters most and what is really going on between us. They are important voices for us to listen to in order to discover the message they are giving us. In withholding these voices from one another, we not only diminish one another but we also dampen our ability to learn from one another.

The language of emotions is a fuzzy one, because there are so many ways to express our experience of them. For example, we can choose to label our experience of feeling angry by describing it as feeling angry, irritated, annoyed, "pissed off," "ticked off," or resentful, to name just a few. The experience of anger is an inner sensation, while the words to describe it are exterior to us.

People who have denied or blunted their feelings have not developed ways of expressing them. Feelings to them seem like a secret code or foreign language that is unknown and mysterious. "Silent" group members often say that they "feel naked" when they begin to explore openly expressing their emotions within the group. They feel awkward and uncomfortable in trying to find ways of expressing their emotions. With practice, however, they become more expressive and enjoy it. Expressiveness need not be simply verbal; learning to embrace people with a hug can be an awkward experience but, with practice, one develops a sense of spontaneity, stemming from what is happening in the relationship.

Coping with the expression of emotions by others can cause us to feel apprehensive and frightened. For example, if a group member feels hurt and begins to cry the other members can become apprehensive, partly because it stirs up their own hurts or sadness and partly because they are not sure how to respond. In fact, all they need to do is be with the person in a supportive way. They do not need to do anything to "fix" the person; the crying will end. At times a group uses one member to express emotions for the others. The important learning task for the group is to acknowledge their emotional pain and to learn how to express it personally. Similarly, members of a group may be apprehensive about how to respond to an angry outburst. Chances are that the angry member is not alone in having the angry feelings. The learning task for the group is for the other members to acknowledge and express their angry feelings, rather than pretend that only one member is angry. Group members can support both the angry member and the member who becomes the target for the anger. When they are able to acknowledge and discuss their reaction openly, they discover that the expression of anger brings them closer together, that they can all handle it in a constructive way, and that they can learn from it in a meaningful way.

Sometimes the process is quite uncomfortable, awkward, confusing, and messy. It takes courage to learn. For members of a group to make the most of the opportunity, they must have an intent to learn from one another in a constructive way. This may mean that, when heated exchanges take place, the members wait until things cool down so that they can examine what happened in a less impassioned way and heal whatever wounds occurred.

When group members begin to acknowledge and express their emotions, they learn how to manage the emotional life of the group more creatively. They begin to realize that when the energy level is low and members are restless and apathetic, there is an emotional logjam that needs to be surfaced and explored. They learn they can disentangle the emotional logjam in a constructive manner. They become skillful in disentangling emotional logjams that previously would not have been discussable.

When fears stifle our expression of emotions, we are not able to develop our capacity to handle them in a meaningful way and we are unable to confront our fears to discover how we have exaggerated them. Like an unused muscle, our capacity to express emotions can atrophy with the passage of time. The awkwardness and discomfort we feel in learning a new skill can be a relatively small cost for the benefits we can gain by developing our ability to acknowledge and express our experience. We can authorize ourselves to experience, express, and discuss our perceptions and emotions. With awareness and practice, we can become more complete in the way we create meaningfulness in our lives within groups.

The awkwardness and power of becoming more skilled in identifying and expressing emotions is shown in the example of a young engineer. He was in a group of scientists and engineers that I was consulting with on the dynamics of group development. At one session I provided them with a list of feelings to aid in identifying what they were feeling in the group. At the end of the consultation, the young engineer thanked me for helping him with his home life.

He indicated he had always felt at a loss when his wife would ask him what he was feeling. He would almost automatically say, "Nothing." She would then become frustrated with him. During the consulting sessions, he put the list of feelings I had distributed on their refrigerator. Each day he would select two or three feelings he was aware of experiencing and express these to his wife. She was delighted. Rather than being a prisoner of his existence he became a pioneer of his existence.

ESTABLISHING EMOTIONAL BOUNDARIES

A central issue for any group is establishing boundaries in regard to what emotions and experiences to express within the group. Probably the most important experiences and emotions to express are the immediate ones engendered by life in the group itself. This consists of the emotions members hold about what is happening in the group and what is happening in their relationships with other members of the group. It is directly relevant to the work they are doing together. The issue of how to relate the past experiences that members bring with them to the group is often cloudy. Probably the most important experiences are the memories that are triggered by being in the group. For example, a member who angrily walks out of the group and slams the door may have memories of similar times when he or she had similar feelings. The strong expression of emotions by one member can also trigger the memories of other members, and it may be quite productive to discuss these memories with the purpose of understanding their implications for the development and management of the life of the group.

When group members are looking for guidance outside themselves, they can look at what they might want a leader to do, or what they feel needs to be done, and than do it themselves. When members of a group do this, they become a "leader-full" group rather than a "leaderless" group or a group with a designated leader. We are what we experience and what we express; we are the ones who determine what work is meaningful for us; and we have a lot to say to one another. Each of us needs to take personal responsibility for making life in the group real and meaningful by speaking as best we can from our heart and our mind. When we do this, we are more apt to spend our time together in a way that strengthens our ability to deal creatively and constructively with issues that are of importance to us.

Gary Gemmill, Ph.D. *is a professor emeritus of organizational behavior in the School of Management at Syracuse University, as well as a faculty mentor for doctoral students in applied management at Walden University. He has published several articles on the psychodynamics of groups that have appeared in such journals as* Small Group Research *and* Human Relations. *He consults with the top management of several organizations on group dynamics.*

BREAKING DOWN BOUNDARIES: BREAKING THROUGH RESISTANCE

Ron Ashkenas

Abstract: As the 21st Century dawns, the new drivers of competitive success are speed, flexibility, integration, and innovation. Gaining ground in any of these areas almost always requires making organizational boundaries more permeable. Boundaryless organizations are those which have loosened up the vertical boundaries between levels of the hierarchy, horizontal walls between functional areas, external barriers between members of the value chain, and geographic boundaries between home and abroad.

Boundaryless behavior is the art of the fluid. Consultants, external and internal, are challenged to help their clients break away from rigid thinking, old categories, and habitual patterns of behavior. To meet this challenge, they must break out of their own boxes and design learning experiences that are innovative and responsive to changing needs.

For much of the 20th Century, the success of organizations has been a function of their ability to grow in size, achieve role clarity, specialization, and control. Sears, IBM, General Motors, Digital Equipment Corporation, Eastman Kodak, and other respected companies have prospered. However, as the century draws to a close, the advent of the microprocessor, the dizzying speed of information processing and communications, and the arrival of the global economy have conspired to shift the basis of competitive success radically. Faced with a rate of change that in many cases has exceeded their ability to respond, these organizations have faltered and their profitability has suffered. But other companies, included Wal-Mart, GE Capital, and Microsoft, have been able to capitalize on these forces of change. Instead of relying on size, role clarity, specialization, and control to ensure their success, these companies offered a superior level of speed, flexibility, integration and innovation.

These four factors have emerged as the new success drivers that organizations must master to survive. The key to developing these capabilities is the extent to which businesses can ensure that ideas, resources, expertise, talent, and technical advances flow to where they are needed rapidly and easily.

The effectiveness of this resource flow is in turn determined by the presence or absence of organizational boundaries. Vertical boundaries divide one level in an organizational hierarchy from other levels and impede the communication from one to another. Horizontal boundaries trap information and ideas in functional silos. External boundaries separate one organization from another, preventing partners in a value chain from cooperating to solve problems or make better use of resources. Geographic boundaries created by distance and cultural difference make it difficult to transfer resources and learning from one place to another. But companies that have mastered the new drivers of success have been able to lower these boundaries, work across them, make them more permeable.

These companies can be termed "boundaryless." Tearing down the walls has not happened quickly or easily, but iteratively and cumulatively. The learning and confidence gained from taking the first steps have been the foundation for taking bigger and bolder steps.

Boundary breaking feels scary because boundaries have traditionally defined organizations. Rearranging the lines of demarcation—between managers and employees, between departments, between the company and its customers, between home and abroad—hits people where they live. They no longer have the safety of knowing who's who and what's what, and often a kind of organizational immune response kicks in. Resistance, both overt and covert, emerges.

Some years ago, a senior manager at a manufacturing company decided that the workers in a newly acquired machine-building plant should be reshaped into a "high performance" workforce. He brought in a new plant manager who believed in empowerment and set out immediately to make it happen. The plant manager removed all time cards from the factory and put the employees on salary. This was meant to be a gesture of goodwill, but the employees did not see it that way. They strenuously objected to having the time cards removed, seeing the gesture as a ploy to keep them from earning overtime pay.

This story has an unhappy ending. A union campaign was launched. Within months the plant manager was gone. The employees were deeply mistrustful of management. The dream of a model, high-performance plant went down in flames. The immune system did its work, and the boundaries, instead of becoming permeable, were more fortified than before.

Success at boundary busting does not often come from abstract concepts like "empowerment" or grand designs for creating "high performance work forces." Rather, the process is driven by concrete business needs. Something has to be done soon, and it can't be done using the old structures and processes. To achieve a measurable result, something has to give, and that something is often a traditional boundary.

Those of us in consulting, training, and developmental roles are often in a position to cut through the resistance, get the ball rolling, and jump in with the particular learning experiences that enable people to work in fast and integrated ways. We, too, must be flexible and innovative in our designs for developing the competencies that our organizations need to be competitive now. We need to be both creative and responsive in deciding when and where some specific skills training, a "stretch" challenge, a retreat, or boot camp experience will make a meaningful, measurable difference. Here we offer many examples of steps that companies have taken to become more boundaryless.

In our experience, it is unwise, even impossible, to tackle vertical, horizontal, external, and geographic barriers all at once. Boundaryless behavior tends to spread because success breeds success, so the best place to start is wherever will make the most positive difference in the bottom line.

Toward a Healthy Hierarchy

Everyone knows the downside of traditional command-and-control hierarchies. It takes too long to make decisions, respond to customer requests and complaints, and adapt to changing market conditions. Progress is difficult because so much is invested in the way things have always been done. Creative people are viewed as subversive, and new ideas rarely see the light of day. Employees often feel unappreciated and unrewarded and don't put forth the effort and loyalty they are capable of. Ultimately, customers don't like dealing with the organization either.

Although everyone knows that the military hierarchical model is no longer in any company's best interests, changing it is a slow and difficult process. By now it has become clear that lopping out layers doesn't automatically create a healthy organization, nor does sharing information, decisions, and rewards necessarily mean that employees are happy and productive. Many companies have also learned through experience that not all employees want to be "empowered" and that not all middle managers resist spreading the authority and control around.

It has always been evident that training is essential for changing people's attitudes. If people at all the levels below the executive suite are going to have more responsibility and more authority, they need a much better understanding of the company's overall direction and strategy, and they need to acquire and develop new skills. But training alone cannot dispel the old patterns of top-down decision making and central control.

Chase Manhattan Bank, for example, spent enormous amounts of money training corporate lending professionals in the mid-1980s around a shift from standard commercial products, such as loans, to sophisticated investment banking products, such as advisory services and financial engineering. Chase Manhattan then had a group of relationship managers who knew all about investment banking products. Unfortunately, they had no information system to support the new products, and they were still measured and rewarded on the basis of corporate loans and still subject to a decision-making process that required deals to be evaluated on the same credit-risk parameters they had always used.

When employees are trained and competent to act in new ways, but not allowed to act on that competence, frustration flares up, but walls don't come down.

Training is necessary *but not sufficient* for rewiring hierarchies. It's also necessary to have a two-way flow of information, authority to act close to where decisions need to be made, and rewards that reinforce performance. The St. Louis branch of Farm Credit Bank mustered all those elements when it hit a rough spot. At one point, Farm Credit's loan portfolio was greater than the value of the farm land on which the loans were based. Instead of blaming the loan agents, the bank gave them what they needed to work in the best interests of both the bank and the customers. The loan agents were provided with detailed information about the status of each farmer's loan, so they could work with the farmers to meet their obligations. They were given special training in how to work with customers in a cooperative way during a crisis. They were given the authority to devise individual plans to help each farmer work his or her way out of financial trouble, and they had the authority to foreclose, if that was the only option. The loan agents were rewarded not only on how quickly they resolved loan issues, but also on the quality of their relationships with the farmers. The upshot was that farmer morale around St. Louis was much higher than in the bank's other branches; the branch solidified its relationship with its customers and paved the way to future business.

GOING BEYOND TURF AND TERRITORY

Horizontal boundaries are almost as ingrained in our minds as vertical boundaries. Specialties and subspecialties have been proliferating in organizations for decades and, to a point, dividing up tasks this way promotes efficiency and prevents redundancy. Functional groupings also appeal to the natural tendency of people to want to congregate and bond with their own kind and make it easier for employees of large organizations to feel a sense of belonging.

But when horizontal boundaries are too rigid, the process of handing a project from one department to the next, all down the line, takes too long. Employees become caught up in protecting and defending their own turf. Organizational goals become subordinated to departmental goals. And when a company has many divisions and products, a customer may wind up dealing with a dozen different representatives and receiving conflicting advice and information.

When horizontal boundaries are this haywire, the biggest obstacle to change is usually employee mind-set. Words such as "not my department" and "those guys" linger on, even when cross-functional teams and task forces are established.

A good first step for overcoming resistance to horizontal change is to create new mental models to replace the old. For example, executives at World Bank, as part of a major change effort in 1994, recognized that the human resource function had to be aligned better with operations. Human resources was going to have to be much more flexible and able to pull together a variety of disciplines and tools to meet changing needs of operations managers and staff. Because the basic HR approach had been in place for years, this idea was met with skepticism and confusion. The HR people could not visualize what the management group had in mind. To create a new mental model, groups of HR professionals and their internal clients at the bank visited Chase Manhattan Bank, Northern Telecom, Hewlett-Packard, and other organizations that were already using flexible HR teams in the ways envisioned by World Bank's management. These site visits, and subsequent discussions about them, helped management refine its thinking and generated enough support to move the new structure along.

It is vitally important to teach teamwork, to set up measures of shared success, to reward people for sharing resources, and to restructure smoothly across functions, but conceptual learning is a good first step. Most people need a new vision before they can drive out old, reflexive ideas and habits.

Toward Partnership with Customers and Suppliers

The idea of cozying up to suppliers and customers is new and, to many people, strange. Every-company-for-itself is the time-honored attitude, and the weight of legal tradition supports this, as each piece of the value chain looks out for itself and tries to maximize its own profits, even at the expense of suppliers and customers.

This attitude in untenable in the fast-paced modern world. As product life cycles shrink, global competition heats up, the cost of product development shoots up, customers demand more, and everything moves faster, companies see that they can no longer work alone. They need to join forces to drive new technologies, expand distribution, enter new markets, ensure sources of supply, and match end-user expectations.

Obviously, sharing information with potential partners—who may well be your competitors in other arenas—is not easy. Partnerships are increasingly necessary, but they are also fraught with peril; horror stories abound. But when companies coordinate their operational planning and accounting and measurement systems, when they solve common problems together, and when they can share resources, enormous gains in speed, flexibility, integration, and innovation can be made.

At the individual employee's level, the main obstacle to this kind of cooperation is simply ignorance. Most employees don't get out much. Suppliers and customers are, at best, voices on the phone. Strengthening the value chain begins with getting acquainted with those outside the company.

A very easy first step is to bring in speakers from the companies in the value chain. Ask a supplier or customer representative to organize a talk around these questions:

- How does my business work?

- Who are our customers and competitors?

- What are our goals?

- What do we need to do differently?

- What changes in the market are we losing sleep over? What are the risks and problems?

- How can we do business together in more effective ways?

- If we were one company instead of two, what would we do differently?

- What could we do to reduce transaction costs, eliminate paperwork, or speed up cycle time?

Another way to begin the process is to take employees to visit some of the other companies. Allied Chemical Fibers (now AlliedSignal Fibers) took this approach in connection with a plant-wide quality effort. Two bus loads of hourly and middle-management people from the company's plant in Columbia, South Carolina, went to visit a customer's carpet mill. The mill workers showed them how certain fiber quality defects shut down their knitting machines. Until then the Allied employees had not thought about how their work affected other people. Once they got back, they immediately went to work on reducing defects, without a lot of prodding from management. Everyone pitched in with suggestions, and defect levels began dropping in a matter of weeks. Over the next year, the company visited other customers and reduced costs by eliminating several recurring quality problems—also boosting customer satisfaction.

When employees hear from the customers themselves and actually see the impact of their work, the value chain becomes real to them. Whether or not members of the chain become formal or strategic partners, "getting to know you" experiences like this pay off powerfully.

Toward the Global Corporation

Global reach has quickly become a new business standard. For many companies, "going global" is a matter of competitive survival. Newer technologies such as videoconferencing and e-mail have made this kind of expansion easier and more compelling. The challenges for breaking through global boundaries include establishing a workable global structure, hiring global supermanagers, designing unifying mechanisms to create a global mind-set, and overcoming a whole new level of complexity.

It is crucial to lay the groundwork, beginning with HR practices, the most basic of which is to sensitize people to the world beyond their doors. Foreign language training is also necessary, although English is the international language of business. Employees who will be working with people in other countries need at least enough proficiency in the language of the country to get along in social situations.

A second basic requirement is cultural awareness. Attitudes and values, business practices, etiquette, and social customs vary greatly from one part of the world to another. Violating the rules and rituals of another country, however unknowingly, can have disastrous repercussions.

Travel is usually the next step, usually fact-finding missions and discussions, and living abroad. Consider what Samsung, South Korea's largest company, did. The company sent about four hundred of its brightest young employees to "goof off" in other countries for a year. Those who came to the United States were encouraged to hang out at malls, watch television, observe consumer behavior, and travel around the country.

SUMMARY

Many innovative individuals and companies are moving a step at a time to overcome boundaries and to increase the flow of ideas, resources, and expertise within organizations. Each example presented here has demonstrated an openness to new ideas and the courage to challenge long-held assumptions about what success is, who can learn from whom, and how change occurs. Each has shown willingness to give up some control and certainty for the sake of achieving a faster, more flexible, more innovative organization.

All of us who are instrumental in moving our clients toward boundaryless behavior must confront our own walls and boxes. To lead the journey we need not only to overcome the natural resistance in our organizations, but also to overcome our own needs for control, clarity, and certainty.

Ron Ashkenas is the managing partner of Robert H. Schaffer & Associates, Stamford, Connecticut, and a well-known consultant on organizational transformation. His articles on change have appeared in the Harvard Business Review, The New York Times, *and many other publications. This article is based on his book,* The Boundaryless Organization *(co-authored with Dave Ulrich, Todd Jick, and Steve Kerr), published by Jossey-Bass, San Francisco, in 1995 and reissued in soft cover in 1998, together with a workbook,* The Boundaryless Organization Field Guide.

ALIGNING TEAM BEHAVIOR WITH ORGANIZATIONAL VALUES: A SURVEY-BASED INTERVENTION

Marilee Crosby

Abstract: Organizational value statements describe the ideal workplace: an environment of respect, trust, cooperation, individual responsibility, and well-serviced customers. We desire these characteristics, but sometimes fall grossly short of them.

One methodical way to determine the correlation between stated organizational values and actual behaviors is to design and conduct a survey. The steps in creating such a survey are: (1) Write behavioral descriptions of the organizational values; (2) Quantify the behavioral descriptions and have the team members respond to them; (3) Make wall charts and track the responses; (4) Discuss the charts with the team; and (5) Have the team plan the steps needed for improvement. This article tells how to interpret survey scores and presents six strategies for teams to use to plan and implement any required improvements.

The value statements we write for our organizations convey beliefs about how people should act toward one another, toward customers, and toward our products. If we listen carefully, our organizational values send out a homing signal that can guide us when we make decisions and interact with people. The further removed our behavior is from our stated values, the more likely it is that we are creating a negative work environment and the less likely that we are satisfying our employees and our customers.

Deming (1982) wrote that organizations are perfectly aligned to yield the results they are yielding. If organizational values describe a good work environment and good customer relationships, then not aligning with the values yields a negative work environment. Some characteristics of such an environment are confusion, disillusionment, dissatisfaction, anger, and apathy.

When organizations are well-aligned, we should recognize behaviors that create a positive, productive environment. We should see growth of individual responsibility, mutual respect, and team support. This should lead to healthy partnerships. We should see people committed to meeting the needs of others, and employee and customer loyalty should blossom.

One way to help people tune in to the signal and realign is to ask them to complete a survey that measures a team's behaviors to see how closely those behaviors align with the organization's values. Through a facilitated discussion of the results, team members should recognize behaviors that need to be changed. The team can then take steps to make those changes possible.

The following is one way to design a survey that takes a team through this process.

STEP 1: WRITE BEHAVORIAL DESCRIPTIONS OF VALUES

Because values are beliefs, and beliefs cannot be quantified, a team will not be able to evaluate itself until someone translates the organization's value statement into tangible behaviors. By comparing the desired behaviors with the actual, current behaviors, the team can assess what its values actually are. The following are suggestions for writing behavioral descriptions:

- Read through the values one at a time and ask, "What behavior would we see if this value were being lived out? What evidence would there be?"

- Write several behavioral descriptions for each value. Be specific enough that examination of actual behaviors will indicate whether team members' actions align with the value.

- Each behavioral description should be a simple sentence or phrase. Complex sentences should be avoided, as they can describe more than one behavior and can be confusing.

The following are examples of behavioral descriptions for the value, "We show respect for one another."

- Team members listen to one another's ideas.

- Team members accept feedback from one another.

- Team members treat each other with an appropriate level of patience.

- Team members speak favorably about other team members to persons outside the team.

- Team members ask questions of other team members when they do not understand them or disagree with them.

- Team members consider conflicts normal and resolve them quickly and openly.

Once you are satisfied that your behavioral descriptions will provide the information you need, then you are ready to place them on a scale.

STEP 2: QUANTIFY THE BEHAVORIAL DESCRIPTIONS AND HAVE THE TEAM MEMBERS RESPOND TO THEM

Place the behavioral descriptions on a Likert-type scale, so team members can quantify the level of each behavior that is apparent in the team. A scale with six possible responses may work best. Because people tend to avoid the top and bottom scale scores, the distinctions may not be clear on a scale with fewer options. Odd-numbered scales allow respondents to select "middle-of-the-road" answers, while even-numbered scales force an opinion.

The following example places the behavioral descriptions from above on a six-point scale. Team members are asked to answer the question, "How accurately does each statement describe the normal behavior of your team?"

1 = very inaccurate	2 = inaccurate	3 = somewhat inaccurate
4 = somewhat accurate	5 = accurate	6 = very accurate

1. Team members listen to one another's
   ideas.   1   2   3   4   5   6

2. Team members accept feedback from
   one another.   1   2   3   4   5   6

3. Team members treat each other with an
   appropriate level of patience.   1   2   3   4   5   6

4. Team members speak favorably about
   other team members to persons outside
   the team.   1   2   3   4   5   6

5. Team members ask questions of other team
   members when they do not understand
   them or disagree with them.   1   2   3   4   5   6

6. Team members consider conflicts normal
   and resolve them quickly and openly.   1   2   3   4   5   6

Total Score = _____

The behavioral descriptions may be organized by value or may be in-termixed. Either way, it is helpful to create a way for the team member to total the score for each value.

STEP 3: MAKE WALL CHARTS AND TRACK THE RESPONSES

Make a wall chart for each value, with a scale that ranges from the lowest possible total score to the highest possible total score for the value.

For instance, in the example above, there are six statements on a scale with six possible responses, so the lowest score is 6 and the highest score is 36. The wall chart for this value would contain the following scale:

6 8 10 12 14 16 18 20 22 24 26 28 30 32 34 36

Each team member should go to each value chart and mark his or her score for that value with an "X" or a Post-it® Note. At the end of this step, the charts should display each team member's response to each value.

Step 4: Discuss the Charts with the Team

The marks on the wall charts will show patterns of behaviors. The team members' responses may be polarized around the high and low ranges, clustered together, or scattered across the scale.

Polarized Scores

Polarized scores can generate a discussion of differences. If the scores show clusters at both ends of the scale, the chart confronts the team with conflicting interpretations. Members can try to answer the question, "Why do you suppose some members of our team interpret our behavior as not showing much respect while others believe that we do great in this area? What might different people be considering?"

It may be best to help team members keep the anonymity of their scores. Probing questions can be phrased like the ones above. Do not ask team members to justify their responses; ask, in general, why someone may have given a particular response.

If team members begin dismissing others' interpretations with phrases such as "They're overly sensitive," or "Their view of what it should be is unrealistic," an analogy about marital conflict can reopen the discussion. Most people can draw the conclusion that a marital relationship is in trouble if one member is sharing a concern and the other responds, "You're too sensitive," or "Your view of marriage is unrealistic." It is clear that saying that the problem exists only in the mind of the other person does not keep the problem from hurting the relationship. It only gives it hot air in which to incubate. Relating that to the team, members may more readily agree that even if the behavior is not of personal concern, they will work through it together to foster healthy work relationships.

Once the team is back on track and the members recognize the need for change, they should move toward a plan for development.

Clustered Scores

Scores may be clustered on the high, middle, or low parts of the scale. If they are high, affirm the group and celebrate its success in aligning with the organization's values. If they are mid-range or low, the team and its leader should decide whether to target that area for improvement.

Sometimes low scores discourage team members, who may view the problems as insurmountable. One way to help the team past those feelings is to connect their scores to Tuckman's (Tuckman & Jensen, 1977) first four stages of group development. On the scale of 6 to 36 used in the example above, the following connection could be made:

- A score of 6 to 13 could be interpreted to mean that the group is "forming" regarding that value (for example, defining it, forming impressions about it, orienting toward it, and so on).

- A score of 14 to 21 could be interpreted as showing that the group is "storming" regarding that value (for example, experiencing conflict in regard to the interpretation of it or scope of it; clarifying conflicting opinions of it; and asking questions about commitment, accountability, authority, evaluation, and rewards in relation to it).

- A score of 22 to 29 could be interpreted to mean that the group is "norming" regarding that value (for example, sharing ideas and feelings, acknowledging members' input and resolving issues, feeling that all members know what the behavioral norms are).

- A score of 30 to 36 could be interpreted as showing that the group is "performing" regarding that value (for example, taking responsibility for acting out the value, individually and as a group).

Teams move sequentially through these stages of development. Some basic intervention strategies can be suggested or initiated as techniques to move the group from one stage to the next.

Discussion questions could focus on influences that are causing the team to be in its current stage. Relating team members' behavior to a stage of group development helps to create the feeling that it is possible to move past unproductive behavior into behavior that is more aligned with the organizational value.

Scattered Scores

Scattered scores may be the result of an unclear or complex behavioral statement that is understood differently by team members. It may be useful to ask some probing questions to find out why the scores are so diverse. The techniques used for polarized scores also can be used.

Step 5: Have the Team Plan the Steps Needed for Improvement

If team members are not familiar with their choices for interventions, the six strategies (Bens, 1998) that follow may help them sort through the options:

1. *Reform the Team.* Clarify goals, work objectives, and results indicators; identify the team's customers; create group norms; clarify roles and responsibilities; create skills profiles, training plans, and a team communication plan.

2. *Train the Team.* Get needed training in team concepts, meeting skills, facilitation skills, personal and interpersonal skills, and business knowledge.

3. *Identify and Methodically Solve Problems.* Learn tools for problem identification and sorting, generating ideas, evaluating ideas, creating action plans, and following up.

4. *Share Feedback and Information.* Become regular givers and receivers of feedback and information. Learn simple techniques for sharing feedback and information with team members, peers, leaders, and other teams. Also share feedback about meetings.

5. *Provide Individual Coaching.* If individuals on the team are having or causing problems, individual coaching can help them to assess the problems and take responsibility for personal changes.

6. *Mediate Conflict.* The team should learn a method for identifying and discussing conflicts. This method should be used whenever conflict is creating a problem in the team.

Conclusion

After the team's scores are discussed and improvements are planned, the team should take the necessary steps to improve its alignment with the organization's values. Team members may be energized as they realize that they are making changes that will actually move them toward the ideal workplace described in the values. Employee and customer satisfaction will follow if team members continue aligning their behaviors with the homing signal of organizational values.

References

Bens, I. (1998). *Teams in trouble.* Sarasota, FL: Participative Dynamics. Self-published.
    Deming, W. E. *Out of the crisis.* (1982, 1986). Cambridge, MA: Massachusetts
    Institute of Technology.

Tuckman, B.W., & Jensen, M.A.C. (1977, December). Stages of small-group devel-
    opment revisited. *Group & Organization Studies, 2*(4), 419–427.

*Marilee Crosby manages organizational development for Cardinal FG in Portage,
Wisconsin. She is devoted to projects that help align the organization to its values.
She has designed 360-degree feedback inventories, team surveys, and employee satisfaction surveys; she has started a customer partnership program, helped leaders
create development plans, mediated conflicts, and facilitated problem-solving discussions. Ms. Crosby has published course material in business communication
and public speaking and has spoken nationally on the topic of industry/education
partnerships.*

STRATEGIC PLANNING MADE PRACTICAL

Michele Matt Yanna and Lee Towe

Abstract: Organizations do not plan to fail; more
often, they fail to plan. Strategic planning is one of
the best ways for an organization or team to evaluate
its current situation and position itself for changes in
the future. Changes in products, technology, locations, and so forth are inevitable. Strategic planning
allows planning teams to anticipate circumstances,
make thoughtful decisions, and chart a course of action, rather than reacting in haste. This article explains how to develop and implement a strategic
plan successfully. It describes a six-step process for
creating a strategic plan and presents tools and techniques to use during each step.

Strategic Planning Defined

Strategic planning is the proactive process of assessing an organization's current condition, determining a desired future state, and identifying actions that will achieve that future (Pfeiffer, Goodstein, & Nolan, 1989). It answers these questions:

- Where are we now?
- Where are we going?
- How do we get there?
- How are we doing?

Why Do Strategic Planning?

Strategic planning allows an organization's key decision makers to step back from the daily operations and evaluate the big picture. Threats that could destroy an organization, if not detected, are identified and managed. Opportunities outside the range of normal operations are recognized and seized.

A solid strategic plan also improves the motivation and daily decision making of employees by clarifying the organization's goals and values.

Organizations that conduct effective strategic planning are like lawns that are fertilized regularly. One does not see the effects right away, but the long-term difference is clear.

When Does One Start?

Strategic planning can be done on an annual basis or whenever an organization undergoes a significant change. Ideally, the strategic plan should be completed prior to starting the budget process so that financial provisions can be made for the actions identified within the plan. Strategic planning is not a one-time occurrence. To be most effective, organizations need to commit to making strategic planning an ongoing process that is incorporated into the way they do business.

Who Does It?

Many key people are involved with the strategic-planning process. Most organizations designate a planning team to be responsible for initiating and monitoring the process. A typical strategic-planning team consists of twelve to thirteen people from top management, plus a facilitator. For instance, team members may include the president; board members; and the directors of marketing, operations, finance, information systems, human resources, and other key areas.

Senior management needs to be actively involved for strategic planning to be successful. Other key people and groups (e.g., employees, customers, stakeholders) may also be involved in the process by providing input and/or by validating the planning team's decisions. Using an internal or external facilitator will keep the group on track and allow everyone to participate fully.

An Overview of the Process

The following six-step process can be used to help a planning team to assess an organization's current condition, identify desired future goals, and establish plans to accomplish the goals. The process describes four important aspects of each step.

- The objectives;
- Key questions the planning team will answer during each step;
- The process and tools used; and
- Key people to involve.

Step One: Organize the Strategic-Planning Process

The first step in the strategic-planning process is to make a conscious decision to begin the process and involve the appropriate players. The objectives of Step One are:

- To decide why you are doing strategic planning;
- To determine who will serve on the planning team;

- To identify information that must be collected;
- To decide when the planning and implementation will take place;
- To make a formal commitment to start or continue the strategic-planning process; and
- To identify the timetable and critical players of the process.

Questions That Are Answered by Step One:

1. Why does the organization need strategic planning?
2. Who will be involved in the strategic-planning process?
3. When will you initiate and implement the strategic planning?
4. What information will be important to consider?
5. How will you facilitate, monitor, and evaluate the process?
6. When and where will the strategic-planning team meet?

Process to Accomplish Step One:

- Obtain approval from your board of directors and senior management to pursue the strategic-planning process.
- Clarify the roles and responsibilities of the key players in the process.
- Identify an internal or external facilitator to assist the organization with this step.
- Establish a timetable for initiating and implementing the process.

The strategic-planning process can take from one to six months, depending on the size and complexity of the organization and the amount of information that already exists. Exhibit 1 shows a typical timetable required to complete the six steps (Yanna & Towe, 1977).

People Involved in Step One

The president, chief executive officer, or a board member should initiate and lead the strategic-planning team. The use of an internal or external facilitator who has expertise in the process allows everyone else to participate fully. Ideally, the planning team should consist of ten to thirteen key decision makers.

Step One:

Week 1   Distribute information about strategic planning. Select a facilitator and a planning team.

Week 3   The planning team and facilitator set the timetable.

Week 4   Customer surveys, employee focus groups, and other forms of data collection are compiled.

Week 8   The collected data is distributed to the planning team. Findings are communicated to employees.

Step Two:

Week 9   The planning team meets for one day to conduct a SWOT analysis and determine the most critical factors.

The facilitator gives instructions for the next meeting.

Step Three:

Week 10   The planning team meets for one day to revise the mission statement, prioritize values, and create a vision.

Three people are appointed to finalize the statements.

Step Four:

Week 10   The planning team meets for one day to determine strategic issues and create long-term objectives for the strategic profile. Individuals add rationale statements later, based on notes from the meeting.

Step Five:

Week 11   The planning-team members meet with managers individually over a one-week period to explain the strategic profile. The managers then have two weeks to develop their action plans.

Week 15   Over a one-week period, the managers present their plans to the planning-team members and receive feedback.

Week 16   The managers have one week to make modifications.

Week 17   The facilitator collects and compiles the written plans.

Week 17   The compiled plans are distributed to the planning team. The team members scan the compiled plans and meet individually as needed to work out interdepartmental issues before the next meeting.

Week 18   The planning team meets for three hours to finalize plan. The facilitator creates a one-year progress chart.

Step Six:

Week 23   The planning team begins monthly meetings to review progress. The team modifies the plans as needed.

Exhibit 1. Timetable for Completing the Six-Step Process

Step Two: Determine the Critical Factors

The best decisions are made with good information. The second step provides this information. The team collects and analyzes information both internal and external to an organization that may impact the business. Exhibit 2 is an example of a pre-planning questionnaire that may be used to collect this information. The objectives of Step Two are:

- To identify customers, stakeholders, and their needs;

- To list and analyze critical factors within the organization that will affect its success;

- To list and analyze critical factors outside the organization that will affect its success;

- To assess the organization's strengths, weaknesses, opportunities, and threats (SWOT); and

- To gather all information and determine the most critical factors that will influence the organization's success.

Questions That Are Answered by Step Two

1. Who are the organization's customers and stakeholders?

2. What are the customers' and stakeholders' needs and concerns?

3. What are the internal factors that affect the organization's future success?

Typical Internal Factors Include:

- Product and service quality,

- Product and organizational life cycles,

- Organizational structure,

- Operations and communications,

- Financial information,

- Information management,

- Technology,

- Distribution channels, and

- Human resources and training.

4. What are the external factors that affect the organization's future success?

Date: _____

To: _____

From: _____

Subject: _____

Prior to our strategic-planning session, we would like you to evaluate and describe our organization's current condition and future opportunities. Your feedback will be an important contribution to the success of our strategic-planning process.

Please return this questionnaire to _____ by _____.

Thank you for sharing your thoughts.

1. What is the basic purpose of the organization?

2. What are the organization's most important strategic issues or problems?

3. What are the critical areas of performance in order to be successful in this business?

4. What are the organization's major strengths?

5. What are the organization's major weaknesses?

6. What are the organization's major opportunities?

7. What are the organization's major threats?

Exhibit 2. Sample Pre-Planning Questionnaire

Typical Categories of External Factors Include:

- Customers,

- Market demand,

- Competitors,

- Suppliers,

- Economy,

- Technology,

- Demographics,

- Social changes, and

- Government policies.

  5. Which internal factors are the most critical strengths and weaknesses?

  6. Which external factors present the greatest opportunities and threats in the future?

Process to Accomplish Step Two

- Identify sources and collect the necessary data.

- Identify the customers and their needs, significant stakeholders, competition, internal strengths and weaknesses, and external opportunities and threats (SWOT).

- From the SWOT analysis, prioritize the ten to twenty most critical factors.

- Whenever possible, distribute information to the planning-team members before meetings.

People Involved in Step Two

The planning team identifies the primary stakeholders and customers. Other key employees may be involved in identifying stakeholders and customers as well as the organization's internal strengths and weaknesses. The external analysis of opportunities and threats is best done by the planning team. Many organizations use consulting firms to conduct internal organizational assessments, identify external trends, obtain industry statistics, collect marketplace data, and so on.

Step Three: Formulate Mission, Values, and Vision

Step Three lays the foundation for an organization by creating and/or refining its guiding statements. These statements crystallize the organization's purpose, beliefs, and vision. The objectives of Step Three are:

- To affirm, modify, or develop the organization's mission statement;
- To identify the organization's values; and
- To create or revise the organization's long-term vision.

Questions That Are Answered by Step Three

1. What does your organization do?
2. Whom do you want to serve?
3. What makes you unique?
4. What beliefs, ethics, and priorities do you hold for your organization?
5. What relationships are important to you?
6. How will you manage these relationships?
7. What will your organization be doing in three to five years?
8. How will you be doing it?

Process to Accomplish Step Three

- *Mission:* The planning team consolidates the most important aspects of its answers to the key questions mentioned above into a single sentence of no more than twenty-five to thirty words. It puts these thoughts into a purpose statement that is easy for everyone to understand and remember. The format for most mission statements is: "We provide [what product or service] to [target customer base] for [end-user benefits]."

- *Values:* The planning-team members begin by identifying their own beliefs and desired interactions with key stakeholders. After they share their values with one another, they create a list of three to fifteen common values, then consolidate and prioritize them. Examples of common values are: honesty, security, compassion, quality, integrity, respect, and flexibility.

- *Vision:* The planning team uses its creativity to describe the organization as it would like it to be in a few years. It summarizes the preferred future in areas such as products, services, customers, workforce, competition, locations, distribution, revenues, expenses, technology, and reputation. The format for most visions is: "We are [description of long-term goal] in [field in which you will be known]."

■ These guiding statements are then communicated to the organization's key stakeholders in a variety of ways. Some examples are the employee handbook, company newsletter, plaques in common areas, business cards, company stationery, payroll stuffers, marketing pieces, annual reports, or meetings.

People Involved in Step Three

Determining an organization's mission is the job of top management and/or board members (the planning team). Once consensus is reached on the basic concept of the mission, two or three people can draft the actual mission statement for approval by the entire team.

The organization's values should also be determined by the planning team. The team may, however, want to gather input from key stakeholders. The planning team may create the vision by itself or use this as an opportunity to involve other board members and key employees.

Remember to identify ways to inform employees about the mission, values, and vision, including employee handbooks, annual reports, display areas, and others listed earlier.

STEP FOUR: DEVELOP A STRATEGIC PROFILE

The heart of a strategic plan is its strategic profile. All critical information and valuable ideas are summarized into a focused strategic profile. The objectives of Step Four are:

■ To determine three to twelve strategic issues;

■ To develop one to five long-term objectives for each strategic issue; and

■ To state a rationale for each long-term objective.

Questions That Are Answered by Step Four

1. Considering the information prepared to this point, what are the top three to twelve strategic issues facing the organization over the next few years?

2. What long-term (three to five years) objectives will address each strategic issue?

3. What is the rationale behind each long-term objective?

Process to Accomplish Step Four

- Based on the critical factors identified in Step Two, the strategic-planning team identifies and prioritizes the top three to twelve strategic issues facing the organization.

- For each strategic issue, the planning team and key department heads identify one to five long-term objectives to assist the organization in achieving its vision.

- For each long-term objective, it writes a paragraph that clarifies the rationale behind the objective. The paragraph includes key information, assumptions, and relationships to other objectives.

People Involved in Step Four

The selection of strategic issues is best done by the planning team. It is possible to involve large groups with various brainstorming and voting techniques, but the disadvantage is that complex relationships among the issues can be overlooked. The planning team can obtain input at this step by developing a first draft of the strategic issues and circulating it to other key managers and staff for feedback.

STEP FIVE: CREATE THE STRATEGIC PLAN

In order to accomplish an organization's long-term objectives, it is important to develop an action plan that defines who, what, and when. The objectives of Step Five are:

- To develop one to five short-term goals for each long-term objective; and

- To list action steps, completion dates, and the people responsible for each goal.

Questions That Are Answered by Step Five

1. What short-term (within one year) goals are needed to meet each long-term objective?

2. What action steps are needed to achieve the short-term goals?

3. Who is responsible for completing each step?

4. What are the target dates for completing each step?

5. What resources (e.g., people, materials, equipment, funds) are needed?

Process to Accomplish Step Five

- The planning team assigns individuals and/or groups to develop an action plan for each long-term objective. (A format for a strategic action plan is displayed in Exhibit 3.)

- The individuals and/or groups identify several short-term goals and the steps for accomplishing each objective.

- The individuals and/or groups present their action plans to the planning team for approval and resource allocations.

People Involved in Step Five

The planning team decides who will create the short-term goals for each long-term objective. Planning-team members develop any short-term goals appropriate at their level. Planning-team members then meet with key people to explain the strategic profile. This can be done in a large-group meeting or one-on-one. The assigned individuals or groups develop the remaining short-term goals and action plans.

   The individuals or groups present their goals and action plans to the planning team for approval. The planning team determines the resources required to accomplish the goals.

STEP SIX: IMPLEMENT, MONITOR, AND MODIFY THE PLAN

The last step in the strategic-planning process is the single most important step to making strategic planning a process instead of just an event. The objectives of Step Six are:

- To identify obstacles and ways to overcome them;

- To begin implementing the strategic plan; and

- To evaluate progress and make appropriate modifications to the plan.

**Strategic Action Plan for
[Team/Department Name]:**

_____

Strategic Issue: _____

Long-Term Objective: _____

Rationale: _____

Short-Term Team/Department Goal: _____

Action Steps	**Responsible Party**	**Due Date**
_____	_____	_____
_____	_____	_____
_____	_____	_____
_____	_____	_____
_____	_____	_____
_____	_____	_____
_____	_____	_____
_____	_____	_____
_____	_____	_____

Resources Needed

People   Equipment

_____   _____

_____   _____

Materials/Supplies   Budget

_____   _____

_____   _____

Other

_____

_____

Exhibit 3. Sample Strategic Action Plan

Questions That Are Answered by Step Six

1. What obstacles might hinder the successful implementation of the strategic plan?

2. How can these obstacles be overcome?

3. Who will monitor the plan? When and how?

4. Who will revisit the plan? When and how?

Process to Accomplish Step Six

- The strategic-planning team identifies potential obstacles and strategies for dealing with them in order to implement the strategic plan.

- The president of the organization, along with senior management, communicates the plan to employees and other stakeholders through speeches, memos, newsletters, meetings, and displays.

- The planning team establishes ways to measure progress toward the goals identified in the action plans.

- The planning team schedules specific times to evaluate and modify the overall strategic plan.

People Involved in Step Six

As managers and teams throughout the organization develop action plans for each goal, the planning team keeps a record of the obstacles that are identified. The obstacles usually can be addressed by small groups of people from the planning team or by other managers.

The planning team is responsible for communicating an overview of the plan to the employees. This communication is critical because most, if not all, of the people in the organization will be involved in the action steps required to accomplish the plan's goals.

The president or chief executive officer needs to play an active role in overseeing the plan's progress. The planning team meets monthly to monitor and modify the plan as needed.

Plan Size and Length

Strategic plans vary in length and format. The list on the next page provides guidelines about the number and length of some of the components (Yanna & Towe, 1997). These guidelines provide an initial starting point only; each organization has different needs. Each plan will vary according to the size, complexity, and needs of an organization. (*Note:* Length refers to an individual component. For example, each value is one sentence in length.)

Component	Quantity	Length
Mission Statement	1	1 to 3 sentences
Values	3 to 15	1 sentence each
Vision	1	Varies; short and easy to remember
SWOT Analysis	10 to 40 items in each category	1 phrase or sentence for each
Critical Factors	10 to 20	1 phrase or sentence for each
Strategic Issues	3 to 12	1 phrase or sentence for each
Long-Term Objectives	1 to 5 per issue	1 sentence each (5 to 15 suggested)
Rationale	1 per objective	1 paragraph
Short-Term Goals	1 to 5 per objective	1 sentence each (5 to 30 suggested)
Action Plans	1 per goal	Several steps

GLOSSARY OF TERMS

Many of the terms used in the strategic-planning process are defined below. The step number after some of the entries refers to the primary place in the process during which the term is used.

Action Plan. A list of specific steps that need to be accomplished to achieve the short-term goals. Each step includes the person responsible, the action to be taken, and a completion date. The resources required also may be included. (Step 5)

Assumptions. Beliefs thought to be true but that are too obvious, costly, time-consuming, or impossible to prove. The word "assumption" may refer to past, present, or future events. Some assumptions probably will be part of the rationale statements. (Step 4)

Competitor. Anyone offering products or services that can reduce the demand for the organization's products or services. A *direct* competitor offers similar products to the same customers. An *indirect* competitor offers products that meet customers' needs in a different way, reducing the demand for an organization's product. An *economic* competitor offers products that cause customers to spend their money in a different way, reducing the amount of money available to spend on the needs that the organization meets.

Although direct competitors are the most immediate concern, strategic planning is the proper time to consider the potentially devastating affects of indirect and economic competitors. (Step 2)

Critical Factors. A summary of the most important information identified in the internal and external analysis. Most critical factors will be identified by the SWOT analysis. (Step 2)

Customers. People who purchase or use an organization's products or services. (This definition refers to external customers. Internal customers are the people being served, supported, or supplied by other employees within the same organization. Although it is possible for issues regarding internal customers to be critical factors, external customers are usually the primary focus of strategic planning.) (Step 2)

Demographics. Population statistics and characteristics, such as the age, income, education, and ethnic background of primary customers, that are appropriate for consideration. (Step 2)

Distribution Channels. The methods and locations used to get the organization's products and services to its customers. (Step 2)

Economy. The external financial factors that affect customers' buying power, demand for product, supply costs, and value of the organization. Some examples of economic factors are interest rates, inflation, international commerce, retail sales, job growth, and unemployment figures. (Step 2)

External Analysis. The positive and negative influences over which the organization has little or no direct control. The strategic-planning team uses these influences to identify opportunities and threats. (Step 2)

Facilitator. A person who is knowledgeable about strategic planning and group dynamics who assists the planning team.

Financial Condition. Current and trend information in areas such as profitability, cash flow, debt, and equity for the organization. (Step 2)

Government. The actions and requirements of local, state, and national governments. Areas to consider include changing tax laws and incentives, new regulations, and the addition or elimination of programs and agencies. Government actions can affect an organization in many ways, such as creating a market need, affecting the decisions that some customers may make, or requiring the organization to keep additional reports. (Step 2)

History. The organization's record and trends from the past few years, especially those events that help explain the organization's present situation. (Step 2)

Information Management. The storage and communication of data and documents within an organization, typically involving computers. (Step 2)

Internal Analysis. An assessment of the conditions within and largely controlled by the organization. The strategic-planning team uses these conditions to identify strengths and weaknesses. (Step 2)

Life Cycle Four stages that an organization, product, or service goes through during its existence: (1) start up, (2) growth, (3) maturity, and (4) decline. (Step 2)

Long-Term Objective. A desired result to be achieved within three to five years. At least one long-term objective is developed to address each strategic issue as part of the strategic profile. (Step 4)

Marketplace. All of the physical and mental characteristics of the exchanges between buyers and sellers for particular products or services. (Step 2)

Mission Statement. A concise summary of an organization's reason for existence that everyone can understand and remember. It explains what an organization does and for whom in a way that differentiates the organization from its competitors. (Step 3)

Opportunities. Circumstances, usually outside an organization, that have potential benefit for an organization. Most of the opportunities will stem from the external-analysis information. (Step 2)

Organizational Structure. The reporting relationships among all the employees of an organization, usually depicted by a chart. (Step 2)

Planning. A systematic process of preparing for the future that answers the question, "Who does what by when?"

Quality of Products or Services. The degree to which customers are satisfied. Accuracy, consistency, reliability, and efficiency are frequent indicators of quality. (Step 2)

Rationale. A statement of facts, assumptions, and reasons that lead to a decision. For the strategic plan outlined here, the planning team includes one paragraph of rationale for each long-term objective. (Step 4)

Resources. The time, money, equipment, people, materials, or facilities required to accomplish the steps in the plan. (Step 5)

Short-Term Goal. A specific, measurable outcome to be achieved within one year. The achievement of short-term goals leads to the accomplishment of long-term objectives. (Step 5)

Social Changes. The broad shifts in attitudes, behaviors, and norms among large segments of the population. Some examples of social changes are perceptions regarding household composition, forms of housing, eating habits, approaches to education, perceptions regarding retirement, and migration patterns. (Step 2)

Stakeholders. Any person or group significantly and directly affected by an organization's outcomes. *Primary* stakeholders usually include all levels of employees, board members, owners, creditors, customers, and suppliers. *Secondary* stakeholders might include community groups, neighbors, organization retirees, or others. (Step 2)

Strategic Issue. An important area stemming from the analysis of critical factors that requires direction from top management. The top three to twelve strategic issues, and their corresponding long-term objectives, become the main thrust of the strategic plan. (Step 4)

Strategic Plan. The written analysis, objectives, goals, and steps that explain how an organization chooses to carry out its mission and fulfill its vision. For a strategic plan to have any value, implementation and follow-up also need to be part of the process.

Strategic-Planning Team. A group of three to seven people (sometimes more) who develop and monitor the strategic plan. Although many people may have input into the plan, the planning team should consist of the organization's top management and/or board members.

Strategic Profile. A summary of the top three to twelve strategic issues, with the related long-term objectives and rationale shown for each issue. (Step 4)

Strengths. An organization's internal capabilities or resources that are better than those of its competitors. (Step 2)

Suppliers. People who provide resources for an organization. (Step 2)

SWOT. An acronym for strengths, weaknesses, opportunities, and threats. These categories of information are traditional bases for determining strategy. (Step 2)

Technology. The application of new information and methods, especially related to computers and electronics. (Step 2)

Threats. Circumstances, usually outside an organization, that could harm the organization. Most of the threats will stem from the external-analysis information. (Step 2)

Trends. New phenomena and the direction of changes that are significant to the organization. (Step 2)

Values. The collective set of deeply ingrained beliefs, ethics, and priorities that guide an organization's behavior. (Step 3)

Vision. A vivid description of what an organization would like to become in the future. (Step 3)

Weaknesses. An organization's internal capabilities or resources that are worse than those of its competitors. (Step 2)

References

Folger, J. (1990, April). Strategic plans provide lasting solutions to rural crisis. *Healthcare Financial Management, 44*, 24–26.

Goodstein, L.D., Pfeiffer, J.W., & Nolan, T.M. (1985). Applied strategic planning: A new model for organizational growth and vitality. In L.D. Goodstein & J.W. Pfeiffer (Eds.), *The 1985 annual: Developing human resources.* San Francisco, CA: Jossey-Bass/Pfeiffer.

Pfeiffer, J.W., Goodstein, L.D., & Nolan, T.M. (1985). *Applied strategic planning.* San Francisco, CA: Jossey-Bass/Pfeiffer.

Pfeiffer, J.W., Goodstein, L.D., & Nolan, T.M. (1989). *Shaping strategic planning: Frogs, dragons, bees, and turkey tails.* San Francisco, CA: Jossey-Bass/Pfeiffer.

Yanna, M.M., & Towe, L. (1997). *Strategic planning handbook.* Des Moines, IA: The TRAINERS Group, Inc., and Innovators International, Inc.

Michele Matt Yanna is the founder and president of The TRAINERS Group, Inc. She has developed and facilitated a strategic planning process for both organizations and professional associations. In addition to conducting workshops on topics such as time management, team building, and communication skills, she has authored Attitude: The Choice Is Yours *to help people gain control of their lives by gaining control of their attitudes.*

Lee Towe is the founder and president of Innovators International, Inc. He facilitates organizational processes such as strategic planning, scenario development, vision creation, team communication, and quality improvement. Mr. Towe's book Why Didn't I Think of That? *shows individuals and teams how to apply creative thinking at work. He also has an online newsletter,* The Big Picture. *He zaps buzzwords, tracks trends, and predicts consequences at* www.innovatorsinc.com.

CAUSAL-UTILITY DECISION ANALYSIS (CUDA): QUANTIFYING SWOTS[1]

Doug Leigh

Abstract: Traditionally, SWOT (strengths, weaknesses, opportunities, threats) analysis has been used as an organizational brainstorming activity in which stakeholders identify environmental issues affecting an organization. However, conventional SWOT analysis does not provide HRD practitioners with the means to gauge the relative costs and consequences of given SWOT factors in relation to all other factors generated. In an era of performance accountability, such useful impact data is required to make successful, responsible decisions. This article presents an expansion to traditional SWOT analysis to measure internal strengths and weaknesses, as well as external opportunities and threats, according to two dimensions: the perceived causality and the associated costs and consequences of those factors (utility). With this data, policy makers can make more informed decisions regarding the assets, liabilities, and other factors affecting their organizations.

[1]Thanks to the following individuals for their reviews and formative feedback regarding earlier drafts of this manuscript: Dr. Roger Kaufman, Dr. Ryan Watkins, Dr. Vic Williams, Chuck Georgo, Scott Schaffer, John Parker, Leon Sims, and Don Triner.

Human resource development (HRD) practitioners, much like all managers of contemporary organizations, are tasked with adding value to organizations through the development of human capital. In addition to being able to deliver training and education interventions, HRD practitioners are expected to be familiar with contemporary models of performance improvement. These models stress the importance of defining the individual and organizational results to be achieved and demonstrating how those results will be useful to external customers and the surrounding communities (Kaufman, 1992, 1998; Leigh, 1998).

This shift in focus is supported by the literature. Triner, Greenberry, and Watkins (1996) conclude that at least 80 per cent of performance problems in the workplace are organizational in nature and frequently require nontraining interventions. Similarly, Dean, Dean, and Rebalsky (1996) found that two-thirds of employees identify environmental, not individual, factors as those most likely to improve their on-the-job performance. It is thus becoming increasingly important to identify, rank, and prioritize the potential consequences of factors both internal and external to the organization in order to succeed in an organizational climate increasingly dominated by information and data.

Some suggest that the external environment is the most practical area from which to develop an understanding of an organization's context (Capon & Disbury, 1999; Kaufman, 1992, 1998). Needs assessment is a popular data-based tool for ensuring that an organization's resources and methods deliver useful results both internally and externally. The process involves formally identifying gaps between current and desired results, placing those needs in priority order, and selecting the most important needs for reduction or elimination. Needs assessment justifies organizational planning and certifies the value added to the organization by selected interventions.

RELATIONSHIP OF INTERNAL AND EXTERNAL FACTORS TO PLANNING

Kaufman's "Strategic Planning Plus" framework incorporates needs assessment as a tool for defining an organization's direction and developing criteria for knowing when it has achieved its goals and objectives (Kaufman 1992, 1998; Leigh, Watkins, Platt, & Kaufman, 1999). Figure 1 presents this frame-

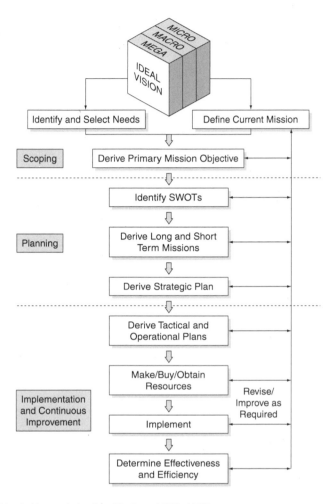

Used with permission from Kaufman (1992, 1998).

Figure 1. The Strategic Planning Plus Framework

work in terms of three interrelated activities: scoping, planning, and implementation and continuous improvement.

In the first phase, "scoping," an organization's primary mission objective is derived from the current mission statement and the data collected in the needs assessment regarding individual employees and departments (micro), the organization as a whole (macro), and external clients and the surrounding environment (mega). An ideal vision—a statement describing the kind of world one wants to create for future generations and the measurable results—guides this process.

In the second phase, "planning," the organization's internal strengths and weaknesses are identified, as well as external opportunities and threats. This often is referred to as a SWOT analysis. From these data, long-term and short-term missions are derived. These products are then used in creating a strategic plan.

In the "implementation and continuous improvement" phase, tactical (organizational) and operational (departmental) plans are deduced from the strategic plan. Resources and interventions are made, bought, or otherwise obtained, then implemented and assessed in terms of the degree to which they move the organization closer to the requirements specified in its strategic, operational, and tactical plans. Based on these findings, interventions are maintained, modified and/or replaced as required.

Although this "rolling down" process may be unconventional, by first identifying the results to be achieved and then (and only then) determining the interventions and processes for accomplishing those results, organizations can best ensure success.

Needs assessment and SWOT analysis are used as the driving force behind planning (Balamuralikrishna & Dugger, 1995; Kaufman 1992, 1998). Needs assessment involves three empirical issues at the mega, macro, and micro level:

- The results an organization and its departments are currently accomplishing;
- The required results that should be achieved; and
- The costs and consequences of the discrepancy between current and required results.

Whereas needs assessment is useful for the identification and costing of these gaps in results, SWOT analysis provides a means for HRD practitioners to assess the organization's assets and liabilities in terms of both the internal and external environment.

Traditional SWOT analysis does not provide the ability to rank and prioritize factors generated in relation to one another (Marshall, 1997). The capacity to identify, rank, and prioritize SWOTs would change the process from a brainstorming activity to a more pragmatic and effective tool for planing and decision making.

Quantifying SWOTs

Pseudonyms for SWOT analysis such as "environmental scanning," "external needs assessment," and "competitive analysis" underscore the importance of first examining opportunities and threats external to an organization, then considering their effects on the strengths and weaknesses internal to the organization (Capon & Disbury, 1999). Such an emphasis has led some writers to refer to the process as "TOWS analysis" or "WOTS analysis" (Arnold, Porterfield, & Smith, 1996; Balamuralikrishna & Dugger, 1995; Capon & Disbury, 1999; Weihrich, 1982;). Regardless, the vast majority of SWOT analysis models do not provide practitioners a method for determining the degree to which a given SWOT factor is an asset or liability to their organization or department. Additionally, most models provide little assistance in measuring how much internal and external environments regulate these factors, nor do they usually propose decision rules regarding how various SWOT factors should be addressed.[2]

Most SWOT analysis models ask two questions regarding any factors influencing an organization: "Is this factor a benefit or cost?" and "Is this factor occurring within or outside this organization?" Figure 2 displays a common format for classifying factors according to a "nominal" scale (one in which each factor is simply labeled a strength, weakness, opportunity, or threat without regard for its relative impact).

A greater degree of measurability can be added by ranking each factor according to its perceived importance, that is, by sorting the factors within each quadrant by importance or by the impact they may have on the organization. This is often called "ordinal" scale measurement. While slightly more information can be obtained in this manner, policy makers still cannot determine the degree to which each factor is more or less "important" than the others. Additionally, the criteria by which importance is determined leaves much to be desired, because different stakeholders will rank SWOTs differently due to their own definitions of "importance."

A more useful method for quantifying SWOT factors involves supporting each strength, weakness, opportunity, or threat with independently verifiable data such as fiscal resources, market share, external impact on the

---

[2]A notable exception is the "Environmental Option Assessment" co-developed by the Association of the Dutch Chemical Industry, the Netherlands' Ministries of Environment and Economic Affairs, and McKinsey & Company, which quantifies the environmental yield and economic impact of potential interventions (Crosbie & Knight, 1995).

Strengths	Weaknesses
•	•
•	•
•	•
•	•
•	•
Opportunities	Threats
•	•
•	•
•	•
•	•
•	•

Figure 2. A Traditional SWOT Matrix

surrounding communities, measures of legislative support and the like (Kaufman, 1992). This process involves asking more questions related to the cost and causality of each SWOT factor, namely:

- How much is each factor currently and potentially costing us?
- How much control do we have over each factor?

Although these questions obviously require stakeholders to make inferences regarding the cost and causality of SWOTs, they quantify strengths, weaknesses, opportunities, and threats according to higher levels of measurement. More precisely, the control question quantifies causality on an "interval" scale of measurement in which factors have equal scale differences, but an arbitrary zero point. The first question quantifies cost on a "ratio" scale that acts like an interval scale, except that the zero point is genuine and really means "zero." Interval and ratio scales are commonly recognized as being best suited for providing criteria regarding the status of factors such as SWOTs (Kaufman & Grise, 1995; Kaufman, 1998).[3]

---

[3]For a more detailed discussion of scales of measurement, see S.S. Stevens (1951) Mathematics, Measurement, and Psychophysic. In S.S. Stevens (Ed.), the *Handbook of Experimental Psychology*, New York: John Wiley.

Causal-Utility Decision Analysis (CUDA)

Causal-utility decision analysis (CUDA) is an enhancement of the traditional SWOT analysis. It quantifies assets and liabilities according to their relative costs and benefits, and displays this data in relation to each factor's locus of causality. Commonly referred to as locus of control (Rotter, 1966), locus of causality is the degree to which the control of various factors is perceived as being governed by attributes internal or external to an organization. The advantage of this approach is that it moves SWOT analysis beyond the traditional emphasis on creating "laundry lists" of factors, and instead provides a means by which HRD professionals can develop defensible, data-based estimations of the assets and liabilities impacting their organization internally and externally.

Figure 3 shows a CUDA grid that HRD practitioners can use in focus groups, interviews, and surveys to collect independently verifiable data regarding the influence of SWOTs on an organization. In traditional SWOT analysis,

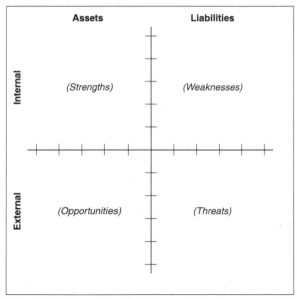

Figure 3. The CUDA Grid

stakeholders are asked to generate lists of strengths, weaknesses, opportunities, and threats, then simply match each SWOT to the relevant quadrant (see Figure 2). Causal-utility decision analysis asks stakeholders to graphically plot SWOTs according to estimates of the relative costs and benefits of all factors, and to approximate the degree to which each factor is or is not within the control of the organization.

Based on data collected through CUDA, informed decisions can be made regarding actions an organization should take regarding various strengths (internal assets), weaknesses (internal liabilities), opportunities (external assets), and threats (external liabilities). Factors close to the horizontal center of the grid are least costly (or least beneficial) and most neutral with regard to control. These factors, therefore, probably should be monitored in order to determine their stability over time. More valuable assets that are also under greater control should be sustained or amplified to ensure their perpetuation. Conversely, more costly liabilities should be either improved or fixed immediately. Figure 4 displays the most basic decision thresholds that differentiate decisions and guide plans for action.

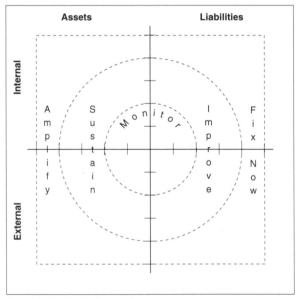

Figure 4. Basic CUDA Decision Thresholds

The diameter of these thresholds can be adjusted according to organizational priorities and requirements. Figure 5 demonstrates one such adaptation in a hypothetical organization that has decided that minimal costs and benefits should be monitored, regardless of the source of control. It chooses to take more aggressive action on factors over which it has greater control and which are more costly or beneficial. On the other hand, it opts to handle factors under substantial external control more conservatively.

Techniques such as CUDA have the potential drawback of allowing stakeholders to look for fits between strengths and current opportunities, rather than to stretch to identify potential opportunities for endorsement (Balamuralikrishna & Dugger, 1995). Consequently, it is often useful to establish decision rules (for example, the diameter of decision thresholds) prior to identifying and ranking factors so that decision makers can be held accountable for the actions they recommend. A second, related threat involves what Jones and Nisbett term "actor-observer bias"—attributing success internally and failure externally (Weiner, 1992). This tendency manifests in CUDA when strengths and threats are over-represented, and weaknesses and

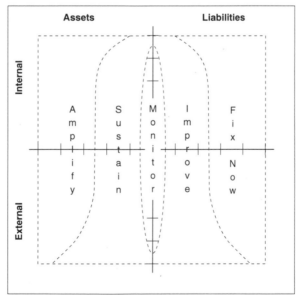

Figure 5. Conservative CUDA Decision Thresholds

opportunities are overlooked. As a facilitator of CUDA focus groups, it is the HRD professional's responsibility to ensure that all four quadrants of a CUDA grid are sufficiently represented.

To facilitate CUDA data collection, Figure 6 may be used in a focus group setting to generate factors related to any organization's internal and external influences in terms of cost and control. Participants first offer internal and external issues affecting their own organization or department that are currently or potentially functioning as assets or liabilities. Next, participants specify which quadrant they believe each factor belongs in. To best rep-

		Assets			Liabilities	
Internal	Issue	Estimated Cost/Value	Control	Issue	Estimated Cost/Value	Control
External	Issue	Estimated Cost/Value	Control	Issue	Estimated Cost/Value	Control

Figure 6. CUDA Factor Chart

resent an organization's strengths, weaknesses, opportunities, and threats, this process should be continued until at least five to ten issues appear in each quadrant. After writing the factor in the appropriate quadrant, the facilitator asks the participants to estimate the cost or value of each factor in monetary terms. On a scale of 0 (neutral) to 5 (complete), the participants then rate the degree to which the issue is within (strengths and weaknesses) or outside (opportunities and threats) the control of the organization or department. The facilitator then plots these factors on the grid presented in Figure 3 to determine the relative influence of each factor on the organization. Decision thresholds are then superimposed over the grid and negotiated if necessary, so that policy makers can take appropriate and responsible action.

ELEMENTS OF COST

A simple way to conceptualize most costs is in terms of the extent to which the factor acts as either an asset or a liability to the organization. Cost analysis is a commonly employed process of calculating the cost of something. Scriven (1991) discusses costs in terms of "what it takes to acquire (or make) and keep" something of value. Differentiating "cost" from "price" (the dollar cost paid for a product or service), Scriven proposes that the full range of costs can be determined by defining three elements: the payer, the type of cost, and the duration over which a cost is incurred.

Although CUDA is best conducted at the organizational level most impacted by the consequences of identified factors (Kaufman & Grise, 1995), this is not to say that the costs and benefits of SWOTs do not impact multiple stakeholders. Both fiscal payers and consumers should be considered when determining cost. Some typical stakeholders are staff members, supervisors, managers, executives, volunteers, contractors, taxpayers, students, and community representatives (Balamuralikrishna & Dugger, 1995; McKenna & Whiteside, 1998; Scriven, 1991). Such stakeholders are excellent sources of data regarding the costs and causality of SWOTs and should be included in the CUDA data collection. Research indicates that collecting CUDA data in a group setting with these and other stakeholders is especially effective in "providing structure, objectivity, clarity and focus to discussions about strategy, which might otherwise tend to wander or else be strongly influenced by politics and personalities" (Glass, 1991).

Regarding "types of cost" Scriven (1991) suggests that cost analysis include such outlays as fees, time, materials and equipment, space, energy, environmental impact, labor, transportation, quality of life, and societal and opportunity costs, including the costs of intended and unintended side effects. Using money as a proxy, cost-benefit analysis can be used as a means to estimate the overall costs and benefits of alternate SWOTs (Kaufman & Carron, 1980; Sobel & Kaufman, 1989). The advantage to using this measure of cost and benefit is that various SWOT factors can be compared against a common yardstick to determine the extent to which each is an asset or liability to the organization. For SWOTs that are less amenable to this process, such as aesthetic or ethical costs, the stakeholders should reach consensus on the relative costs and benefits of each factor. Even more than for factors with fiscal impacts, these types of costs require objectivity on the part of stakeholders (Kaufman, 1992).

Scriven's third element of cost, "duration over which a cost is incurred," can be considered in terms of preparation, installation, operation, and termination. In general, these time phases can be thought of in terms of planning, setup, implementation, and maintenance/cessation.

Cost-consequences analysis (CCA) is a relatively new form of cost analysis that defines the return on investment of any intervention on the basis of "what an organization gives and what it gets" for the results it achieves (Kaufman & Watkins, 1996; Muir, Watkins, Kaufman, & Leigh, 1998). Cost-consequence analysis is useful during the conduct of needs assessments and strategic planning in that it helps quantify the various costs to ignore gaps in results (needs). Causal-utility decision analysis acts as a counterpart to this process by better defining the costs and benefits of closing such gaps according to the resources the organization is currently implementing and the results the organization's processes are accomplishing.

LOCUS OF CAUSILITY

Since Rotter's introduction of the concept in 1966, locus of control has become one of the most popular indicators of causal attribution. Belief that one's behaviors will or will not influence the attainment of a goal is one determinant of expectancies for success or failure (Weiner, 1992). Internal control denotes a self-perception that an individual has control over influential experiential factors, while external control represents a perception that such factors are controlled by fate, chance, or "powerful others" (Levenson, 1972). Arnold, Porterfield, & Smith (1996) maintain that the consideration of strengths, weaknesses, opportunities, and threats can also be thought of in terms of organizational control.

As Scriven (1991) points out, taking steps toward the internalization of locus of control for any given factor might not necessarily be advantageous or necessary; indeed, it may be an indication of unrealistic or unfounded aspirations. Similarly, just because a factor is under external control, it is not necessarily "uncontrollable" or "out of control." Attribution theory (Weiner, 1992) indicates that consequences are accounted for according to three interrelated variables: locus of causality, stability, and controllability. Understanding the interaction among these three variables is particularly important to policy makers and market analysts; they must consider the potential interactive effects on all factors of action taken on one or more factors. It is critical that the interactions among the three variables be studied on a regular basis in order to track stability and controllability. Techniques such as CUDA provide "snapshots" of past and current factors that influence an organization.

Conclusion

In addition to designing and presenting training, HRD professionals today must be able to conduct needs assessments and performance systems analyses in order to contribute to organizational strategic planning, evaluation, and continuous improvement. Human resource development professionals have found that organizational success is at least as dependent on what occurs outside an organization as it is on what goes on within the organization. As Gardner points out, "Leaders unwilling to seek mutually workable arrangements with systems external to their own are not serving the long-term interest of their constituents" (1990).

While the CUDA framework presented here provides useful, measurable data regarding SWOTs, an organization is best served by transforming weaknesses to strengths and threats to opportunities. Anecdotes such as Henry Kaiser's maxim that "problems are only opportunities in work clothes" may be inspirational, but most HRD practitioners require more formalized methods to move their organizations to the desired states. Used in conjunction, needs assessment, CUDA, and CCA provide a rational basis by which HRD professionals can plan for the success of their departments, organizations, external clients, and surrounding communities.

References

Arnold, D.R., Porterfield, R.I., & Smith, C.D. (1996). *E-SWOT analysis: An extension of a practical tool for small businesses.* Online: http://www.lowe.org/data/2/2758.txt [1999, January 1].

Balamuralikrishna, R., & Dugger, J.C. (1995, fall). SWOT analysis: A management tool for initiating new programs in vocational schools. *Journal of Vocational and Technical Education, 12*(1).

Capon, C., & Disbury, A. (1999). *Understanding organisational context.* London, England, United Kingdom: Financial Times Management.

Crosbie, L., & Knight, K. (1995). *Strategy for sustainable business: Environmental opportunity and strategic choice.* London, England, United Kingdom: McGraw-Hill.

Dean, P.J., Dean, M.R., & Rebalsky, R.M. (1996). Employee perceptions of workplace factors that will most improve their performance. *Performance Improvement Quarterly, 9*(2), 75–89.

Gardner, J.W. (1990). *On leadership.* New York: The Free Press.

Glass, N.M. (1991). *Pro-active management: How to improve your management performance.* East Brunswick, NJ: Nichols.

Kaufman, R. (1992). *Strategic planning plus: An organizational guide* (rev. ed.). Thousand Oaks, CA: Sage.

Kaufman, R. (1998). *Strategic thinking: A guide to identifying and solving problems* (rev. ed.). Arlington, VA & Washington, DC: Jointly published by the American Society for Training & Development and the International Society for Performance Improvement.

Kaufman, R., & Carron, A.S. (1980). Utility and self-sufficiency in the selection of educational alternatives. *Journal of Instructional Development, 4*(1), 14–18, 23–26.

Kaufman, R., & Grise, P. (1995). *Auditing your educational strategic plan.* Thousand Oaks, CA: Corwin Press.

Kaufman, R., & Watkins, R. (1996, Spring). Cost-consequences analysis. *Human Resource Development Quarterly, 7*(1).

Leigh, D. (1998). *A brief history of instructional design.* ISPI Global Network Chapter. Online: http://www.pigncispi.com/articles/education/brief/20history.htm [1998, January 1].

Leigh, D., Watkins, R., Platt, W., & Kaufman, R. (1999). Several models of needs assessment . . . which one is right for your organization? *Human Resource Development Quarterly, 10*(2).

Levenson, H. (1972). Distinctions within the concept of internal-external control: Development of a new scale. *Proceedings of the 80th Annual Convention, American Psychological Association.*

Marshall, S. (1997). *Strategy formulation: SWOT analysis—An indictment.* Online: http://www.mindspring.com/~stevenmarshall/Strategy.htm [1999, January 1].

McKenna, M.M., & Whiteside, K.S. (1998, March). *Building organizational scanning tools.* Session presented at the annual conference of the International Society for Performance Improvement. Chicago, IL.

Muir, M., Watkins, R., Kaufman, R., and Leigh, D. (1998). Costs-consequences analysis: A primer. *Performance Improvement, 37*(4), 8–17.

Rotter, J.B. (1966). Generalized expectancies for internal versus external control of reinforcement. *Psychological Monograph,* 80 (1, Whole No. 609).

Scriven, M. (1991). *Evaluation thesaurus* (4th ed). Thousand Oaks, CA: Sage.

Sovel, I., & Kaufman, R. (1989). Toward a "hard" metric for educational utility. *Performance Improvement Quarterly, 2*(1).

Stevens, S.S. (1951). Mathematics, measurement, and psychophysics. *Handbook of experimental psychology.* (pp. 1–149). New York: John Wiley.

Triner, D., Greenberry, A., & Watkins, R. (1996). Training needs assessment: A contradiction in terms. *Educational Technology, 36*(6), 51–55.

Weihrich, H. (1982). The TOWS matrix: A tool for situational analysis. *Long Range Planning, 15*(2).

Weiner, B. (1992). *Human motivation: Metaphors, theories, and research.* Thousand Oaks, CA: Sage.

Doug Leigh *holds a master's degree in instructional systems design from Florida State University and is completing his doctoral work in the same program. Mr. Leigh is the associate director of Roger Kaufman and Associates and a faculty member at the Office for Needs Assessment and Planning in Tallahassee, Florida, where he currently resides. He consults in the areas of needs assessment, evaluation, and strategic planning and is a frequent author and lecturer regarding these and related topics.*

KEY STAKEHOLDER ANALYSIS: PREPARING TO INTRODUCE A NEW ORGANIZATIONAL IDEA

Neil J. Simon

Abstract: Improving or changing an organization often requires integrating new or different tools, technology, and/or work processes into the work environment. If you are the person attempting to bring in something new, you need to gain a thorough understanding of the key organizational stakeholders; their views; and how your proposed tool, technology, or work process will fit into the existing organization. If what you propose is congruent with the needs of the key stakeholders as well as the needs of the existing system, your proposal is likely to meet with success.

This article focuses on the information you need about key stakeholder perceptions and needs in order to determine how successful your proposal will be. A tool used to conduct the key stakeholder analysis is described and presented.

What You Face in Introducing an Idea

Assume that you have a great idea about something that you would like an organization to adopt—something that you genuinely believe will benefit the organization. Success in gaining acceptance of your idea depends on how you introduce it to the organization and how it meshes with the organization's structure. People's natural resistance to anything new will be a significant factor. Acceptance is often determined by just a few people: the key stakeholders. These are the individuals who have a vested interest in the organization's processes and practices and are accountable for the results produced; they may include any other employees who have joined you in sponsoring or championing your idea, the managers of relevant units, key nonmanagerial employees (technical experts in relevant fields, for example), and those who will be responsible for implementing your idea.

Integration theory (Simon, 1998) tells us a great deal about incorporating new ideas into organizations. It suggests the following principles, which have been derived from repeated observations in organizational settings:

- If those at the top of the organizational hierarchy impose a change on those at lower levels, that change may be implemented, but only under duress or in ways that are less than optimal. What generally happens is that employees are asked to adopt tasks and ways of doing business that do not make sense to them or that do not have relevance from their perspective.

- If employees from the lower levels of the hierarchy try to impose their wants on the organization, the change attempt also goes awry. What generally happens is that those who design and propose the change do not take into account the needs and perspectives of those at the top. In addition, those at lower levels do not command the resources, power, or authority to implement changes that run counter to executives' needs.

Increasing the Odds for Success

Monitoring for and Creating the Right Conditions

The most successful implementation of a new idea is one in which the organization acts as a magnet for the idea and actually *pulls* that idea into its processes and practices, meeting the needs of key stakeholders, including end users. In other words, you should be on the lookout for (and help to create, if possible) a situation in which your idea is so right for the organization that existing conditions, both internal and external, will actually facilitate the implementation of your idea. Other circumstances that facilitate implementation include the following:

- The organization has a recognized need for your idea (product or process). (In other words, employees at all relevant levels have been experiencing "pain" as a result of a condition or set of conditions that your idea will fix.)

- Those responsible for implementation understand the organization's need for your idea in terms of meeting both short-term and long-term objectives.

- Those responsible for implementing your idea have a say in which processes, tools, and technology they will use to accomplish implementation.

Ameliorating Stakeholder Fears

Key stakeholders often find a new idea threatening for any or all of the following reasons:

- Fear of something new, which often involves not understanding the change and its impact on organizational effectiveness;

- Fear of being seen as incompetent or as adopting an idea that turns out to be obsolete; or

- Fear of losing control or ownership (the "not-invented-here" syndrome).

To ameliorate these fears, interview the key stakeholders, obtain information about their needs and concerns, and use that information in preparing a presentation for them that will emphasize how they may benefit from your idea. The interviews will not only further your understanding of the inner workings of the organization, but also enable you to identify those who are likely to be *supporters* of your idea as well as those who are likely to be *detractors* or *fence sitters*.

STAKEHOLDER INTERVIEWS: FOUR AREAS OF EMPHASIS

During the interviews you need to gain insight into the stakeholders' perceptions of four specific areas:

- The organization's direction as well as the direction of each stakeholder's unit;
- The functional structure and political structure of the organization;
- The organization's norms; and
- The stakeholders' individual needs.

These four areas and the interview questions that pertain to them are discussed in the following paragraphs.

1. Organizational and Unit Direction

Each stakeholder will have a unique perception of the organization's direction as well as the direction of his or her unit within the organization. To identify those perceptions, you need to ask specific questions such as the following:

- "What is your vision of the organization?"
- "What is your mission within the organization?"
- "What is your vision for your unit? What does your unit contribute to the organization in terms of services or products?"
- "What is your unit's mission? How does that mission align with the organization's vision and mission?"

2. Functional Structure and Political Structure

There are two kinds of organizational structure, functional and political. In order to introduce your idea successfully, you will need to develop an understanding of both. Often the functional structure is formally recorded in an organizational chart denoting who does what, who is accountable for what, and who is responsible to whom. If the organization has such a chart, you can easily obtain a copy.

However, no organizational chart reveals the organization's political structure—how the organization actually works. If you want to know that (and you will), during your interviews you will have to ask questions designed to identify the stakeholders' perceptions of the informal structures and processes that people have developed to get things done. You will also want to elicit information about the stakeholders' perceptions of their own roles in the political structure. Samples of appropriate questions are as follows:

- "What is the purpose of the organization?"
- "What service or product does it provide?"
- "What do you personally do to contribute to the work that the organization does?"
- "Who are the key organizational leaders, and what do they do to contribute to the work of the organization?"
- "Who are the supporters and detractors of these key leaders?"
- "What do the supporters as a group and the detractors as a group do in terms of furthering the organization's goals?"
- "In your opinion, do these different groups value what you provide?"

3. Organizational Norms

An organization consists of people who work together and follow set ways of working and behaving (called "conventions"). As an organization evolves, it creates rules and regulations that establish boundaries (things people are not allowed to do) as well as preferred behaviors (things people not only are allowed to do, but are encouraged to do). These rules and regulations are called "norms"; they can be either formal (written or orally expressed) or informal (unwritten and transmitted orally or demonstrated nonverbally). People who want to start or continue working for an organization—in other words, those who want to belong—adhere to its norms. Also, every organization expects its employees to work with concepts and processes that are consistent with its norms.

Following are examples of interview questions that are appropriate for eliciting information about norms:

- "What does this organization value?"
- "What are the organization's rules concerning its work?"
- "How does work get done in this organization?"

- "What are the organization's rules concerning tools and processes that can be used to get work done?"

- "What are the formal and informal rewards of this organization?"

- "What part or role do you play in how the organization functions and what happens to new ideas that are introduced?"

- "How are people's contributions to the organization recognized and rewarded?"

4. Stakeholder Needs

Each stakeholder needs something from the organization in return for his or her contributions. Everyone you interview will be able to help you in identifying not only his or her own needs, but also those of other key stakeholders.

Developing an understanding of the key stakeholders' needs is critical. Once you have such an understanding, you can determine whether and in what way your proposed idea will meet those needs; then you will be able to appeal to stakeholders on that basis. Those whose needs are congruent with your idea may be inclined to become your allies—or perhaps even sponsors. Even if you discover no way in which your idea can meet a particular person's needs, at least you will know not to expend too much time and effort in converting that person into a supporter. (If your idea does not meet a stakeholder's needs but does not necessarily impede him or her in meeting those needs, that person may be a fence sitter; you may eventually want to appeal to him or her on the basis of the overall benefits of your idea to others or to the organization as a whole.)

Questions such as the following are useful in eliciting needs:

- "Who leads the organization?"

- "What are those leaders' needs?"

- "Which organizational issues or problems especially concern or interest the leaders?"

- "Which organizational members are capable of influencing the leaders?"

- "Which leaders support the services or products that you offer?"

- "Which leaders oppose your services or products?"

- "Who could informally assist you in establishing a connection with the leaders and those who influence them?"

Summary: Optimizing the Introduction of a New Idea

When you want to introduce a new idea to an organization, you need to obtain specific information to be used in determining the likelihood of success in gaining approval, developing a presentation strategy, and implementing the idea. The following process is useful (also see Exhibit 1 for a sample matrix that can be used in collecting and analyzing data):

1. Identify key stakeholders.

2. Create a format and specific questions to use in interviewing the key stakeholders.

3. Set up the interviews.

4. Determine how you will record responses during the interviews. *Note:* If you paraphrase responses, be careful not to indicate any biases.

5. During the interviews record responses as accurately as possible, using the interviewee's own words. (The exact words will help you to gain an appreciation of how the person thinks and processes ideas.)

6. After all interviews have been conducted, compile the data in a way that facilitates review and analysis.

7. Review the data in different ways. For example, you will want to review all of each interviewee's data to obtain a profile of that person; you will also want to consider the questions one by one, reviewing all responses to each question so that you can see the spectrum of viewpoints.

8. On the basis of the data, determine the likelihood of success in presenting your idea and gaining approval. Remember to consider conditions in both the organization's internal and external environments in order to determine the best time for your presentation.

Area	Question	Respondent 1	Respondent 2	Respondent 3	Horizontal Analysis
Organizational and Unit Direction	What is your vision of the organization?				
	What is your mission within the organization?				
	What is your vision for your unit? What services or products does your unit contribute?				
	What is your unit's mission? How does that mission align with the organization's vision and mission?				
Functional and Political Structure	What is the organization's purpose?				
	What service or product does the organization provide?				
	What do you contribute to the organization's work?				
	Who are the key leaders, and what do they do to contribute to the organization's work?				
	Who are the key leaders' supporters and detractors?				
	What do the supporters as a group and the detractors as a group do to further the organization's goals?				
	Do the supporters and detractors value your contributions?				
Organizational Norms	What does your organization value?				
	What are the organization's rules concerning its work?				

Exhibit 1. Sample Matrix for Introducing a New Idea

(continued on next page)

Area	Question	Respon-dent 1	Respon-dent 2	Respon-dent 3	Horizontal Analysis
	How does work get done? How does the work get done in the organization?				
	What are the organization's rules about tools and pro-cesses that can be used to get work done?				
	What formal and informal things are used as organiza-tional currency?				
	What role do you play in the organization's functioning and what happens to new ideas that are introduced?				
Stakeholder Needs	How are people's contribu-tions to the organization recognized and rewarded?				
	Who leads the organization?				
	What are the leaders' needs?				
	Which organizational issues or problems concern the leaders?				
	Which organizational mem-bers are capable of influen-cing the leaders?				
	Which members are opposed to what you offer?				
	Who could informally assist in establishing a connection with the leaders and those who influence them?				

This matrix was created for use in the A²D⁴ Self-Designing Organization Approach © 1996 by Business Development Group, Inc.

Exhibit 1. Sample Matrix for Introducing a New Idea *(continued)*

Reference

Simon, N.J. The A²D⁴ process for designing and improving organizational processes. (1998). *The 1998 annual: Volume 2, consulting.* San Francisco, CA: Jossey-Bass/Pfeiffer.

Neil J. Simon *is the president of Business Development Group, Inc., based in Ann Arbor, Michigan. Mr. Simon has more than twenty years of experience in improving organizational and individual performance. He works with organizational clients to innovate, design, or redesign departments, divisions, or entire organizations. He guides clients in designing their own processes for sustainable change. In addition to consulting, he lectures and presents interactive workshops nationally and internationally in areas relating to organizational culture, organizational change, and organizational and individual performance. He has published numerous articles in business, clinical, and health care journals. Mr. Simon holds an M.S. degree in educational psychology from Eastern Michigan University and conducted his post-graduate studies at the Fielding Institute in Santa Barbara, California. He holds staff appointments at several colleges and universities.*

THE RELATIONSHIP BETWEEN LEADER BEHAVIOR AND TEAM PERFORMANCE AND SATISFACTION

Mary Ann Burress

Abstract: The relationship between team leader behavior and team performance and satisfaction was investigated by field research that tested dimensions of leader behavior based on two theoretical models of team effectiveness: Hackman's (1992) "expert available coaching" and Cohen's (1994) "encouraging supervisory behaviors." The results indicated that leader behavior is a less important component of team effectiveness than expected.

The research determined some essential skills for managing high-performance teams, improving employee satisfaction, and creating an empowered environment. Managers in a team environment may need to develop new skills, such as building and developing the organization's business, creating in-depth relationships with customers, and establishing alliances and partnerships with other organizations. These new roles may lead to high performance, employee and manager job satisfaction, and increased managerial value to the organization.

$\mathbf{A}$n enormous body of literature suggests that leader behavior impacts the effectiveness of self-managing teams. Theoretical models of team leadership indicate leaders should be coaches and mentors, not supervisors or directive managers (Cohen, 1994; Hackman, 1992; Manz & Sims, 1987). Few empirical studies have tested these theories. Thus, there is a lack of knowledge about the appropriate managerial behaviors for leading self-managing individuals and teams.

A study was conducted to increase knowledge about the impact of managerial behavior on the performance of self-managing teams and the effect of encouraging supervisory behavior on employee satisfaction with the supervisor. The leader behavior measures used in the study were developed from the Manz and Sims theory of team leadership. The following were key focal areas:

- Specific leader skills that are critical for managing high-performance teams;

- The relationship between leader behaviors and employee satisfaction with supervision; and

- Leader behaviors that are most strongly associated with customer satisfaction.

METHODOLOGY

Forty-three first-level customer service field managers and one hundred seventy-five work group members participated in the study. Managers were primarily white males between the ages of forty and forty-nine with sixteen to thirty years' tenure. Work group members were primarily white males thirty to forty-nine years old with six to twenty-five years' tenure.

The study was conducted in Xerox's U.S. Customer Services Organization (USCO). The USCO Division maintains and repairs office equipment. At the time of the study, USCO employed approximately sixteen thousand people in sixty-eight districts across the United States. Each district is divided geographically and/or by the type of machine serviced. Field managers are responsible for the approximately twenty to thirty customer service technicians who report to them. The service technicians are organized into work groups and repair office equipment in customer locations. Xerox's field employees have worked in empowered work groups since 1988.

MEASURES

The Team Leader Survey

Leading self-directed teams requires different skills from leading traditional teams or individuals. The Team Leader Survey collects behavioral data that leaders and teams can use to improve the way they work together. The survey allows leaders to receive behavioral feedback from their managers, their peers, and their teams. This 360-degree feedback provides information about the managers' unique strengths and developmental needs. The purpose of the survey is to promote the development of effective leadership skills. Its emphasis on strengths helps leaders build on their successes.

The Team Leader Survey has six scales; the scales and reliability coefficients are: Influence (.85), Interpersonal Skills (.87), Administration (.83), Communication (.81), Thinking (.81), and Flexibility (.89).

- Influence is defined as influencing, encouraging, and developing people.

- Interpersonal skills include valuing diversity and input from everyone on the team, and addressing the group rather than the individual.

- Administration includes coordination, process improvement, juggling priorities, scheduling, and resource acquisition.

- Communication comprises listening, sharing information, presenting ideas, and giving feedback.

- Thinking skills include analytical and anticipatory problem solving, attending to nonverbal cues, and exploring multiple sides of an issue.

- Flexibility is defined as responding to unanticipated change, coping with uncertainty, and deviating from an initial strategy when new contradictory information is available.

The survey focuses on abilities found most important for effective team leadership. It is a research-based tool suitable for team leader training and development programs (Burress, 1992, 1993, 1995).

Employee Satisfaction

Every year, USCO monitors its employees' satisfaction with the company and their immediate managers. The Immediate Manager Index (IMI), a twelve-item subscale from the employee satisfaction survey, indicates the satisfaction level of employees on topics that are within a local manager's control. Employee responses on the IMI are part of a manager's performance evaluation process.

The IMI asks employees about their work, company expectations regarding performance, and how well managers communicate and share information. Employees are asked whether cooperation exists in their department, whether opportunities exist for their professional growth and development, and whether they receive recognition for their performance. These data were obtained from company archival records.

Customer Satisfaction

Archival records provided performance data for the six months prior to and six months after data collection. Performance criteria included parts expense, response time, repair time, machine reliability, and customer satisfaction, the performance measure most relevant to this study. Customer satisfaction data were obtained from periodic customer surveys. These indicate the customers' satisfaction with their machines and service. Based on the survey responses, customers are coded as either satisfied or as dissatisfied with Xerox's performance. Group performance is measured by the percent of the group's customers who describe themselves as "satisfied" or "very satisfied."

FINDINGS

This section is composed of three primary topics: major findings, the implications of these findings for leadership development, and implications for organizational design.

Major Findings

The study investigated the overall contribution of leader behavior to team effectiveness and satisfaction.

- Not surprisingly, high-performing teams are more likely to satisfy customers and are more satisfied with their managers than low-performing teams.

- Surprisingly, in light of the team-performance literature, flexibility on the part of the manager had a negative correlation to high team performance and employee satisfaction. The flexibility scale differentiated managers of high and low performing teams more than any other.

- Managerial interpersonal skills were associated with high team performance, while leadership was associated with high team performance and employee satisfaction.

- The relationship between leader behaviors and customer satisfaction was not linear; the sample size was a likely limitation.

Wageman (1997) tested Hackman's theoretical model for leading self-managing teams. Wageman found that coaching influenced team member satisfaction and group process and that performance was more strongly influenced by organizational design conditions and self-management. The most important organizational design conditions were (1) a clear direction and (2) tasks and rewards designed for teams and not individuals. Wageman determined that leader behavior accounted for approximately 20 percent of the variance between high-performing and low-performing teams.

Wageman's findings are consistent with the current study. Both studies concluded that leader behavior is a less important component of team effectiveness than initially expected, accounting for only 10 percent of the variance between high-performing and low-performing teams.

Leader Behaviors That Help

The findings indicate that interpersonal skills and leadership are associated with high-performing teams and that administration and coordination activities by the manager nurture employee satisfaction.

Interpersonal Skills. High levels of interpersonal skills by managers predicted high team performance. Interpersonal skills include how well the manager encourages collaboration, fosters smooth team interaction, and works through conflicts. Capitalizing on diversity and valuing input from everyone on the team are also important leader skills. Encouraging the team to address interpersonal problems as a group is another key manager skill. Establishing personal growth opportunities for team members also was found to be important.

These positive managerial behaviors are consistent with the team effectiveness literature and the research of Manz and Sims (1987). The conclusions also support Bass's (1981) recommendation that today's managers must balance technical, conceptual, and interpersonal skills.

Influence. High-performing team leaders encourage responsibility, accountability, and the team's monitoring of their own performance goals. These leader skills encourage teamwork and foster an environment in which the team coordinates its own work. The leader who exhibits these skills places decision-making authority with the team, based on team member knowledge and skills. Such leadership fosters team member learning and provides opportunities for teams to acquire and apply new skills. The leader also challenges the status quo and demonstrates willingness to change.

Coaching leaders who encourage, influence, and provide developmental opportunities are more likely to have high-performing teams and satisfied employees. Treating job openings in their departments as developmental opportunities for employees also helps to increase employee satisfaction. The findings also suggest that high-performing employees receive a sense of personal accomplishment at work and are satisfied with their workload and how they are recognized for their performance.

The positive relationship between employee satisfaction and managers' providing developmental opportunities also supports Miles and Snow's (1994) managerial philosophy of human investment, which assumes that employees are trustworthy and have the potential to develop new skills and increase their business understanding. Providing development opportunities is the manager's basic task. Employee acquisition of new skills builds the organization's adaptive capacity and ensures its future.

Administration. Leaders who coordinate activities between teams, implement process improvements, and handle scheduling requirements create environments that support their teams. Other important leader skills include the ability to acquire resources and attention to detail. The positive relationship between manager administrative activities and employee satisfaction was expected. These findings suggest employees welcome inter-team coordination and assistance with process improvements. They also imply that designing organizational processes is an important managerial role.

Another important managerial role is establishing and coordinating relationships within and between other organizations. The work of Miles and Snow (1994) on new organizational forms supports this, which is especially important because many companies are creating inter-organizational alliances and new network structures and are using contract employees and other outsourcing arrangements.

Leader Behaviors That Hinder

Several findings of the study are inconsistent with the team leadership and team effectiveness literature. A negative relationship was found between leader skill flexibility and high team performance and satisfaction. Communication skills and thinking skills both had marginally negative relationships with high team performance.

Flexibility. Flexibility refers to the leader's ability to respond to unanticipated changes and cope with uncertainty. Although flexibility was the skill that most differentiated managers of high-performing and low-performing teams, the relationship between leader behavior and team performance and customer satisfaction was negative. This means that managers of low-performing teams demonstrated more flexible behavior than managers of high-performing teams.

Taking advantage of opportunities and deviating from an initial strategy in the face of new information have been considered important leader skills. Generating options and presenting alternative ideas for team consideration and handling multiple assignments are also regarded as important for team leadership. All these skills seem critical for organizations adapting to changing environments and increasing competition. So, why were these skills negatively related to team performance and customer satisfaction? A discussion with employees and internal organization development experts offered some explanations for this apparent inconsistency.

The team members in the study were technicians who repair office equipment and copy machines. The work is procedurally oriented, held to rigid codes with low tolerance for error and precise measurements on machines. Machines are taken apart and put back together systematically and are then expected to run. The technical part of the work is highly structured, and it is performed by individuals who value sameness and consistency.

There is much potential variety in the human element of the work, as each customer call is different. The technician initiates customer interactions in a negative environment, that is, the customer's equipment is not working properly. Repairing the machine usually satisfies the customer and changes this environment. Each customer call is different because of the problem, the human element, and the service issue.

It is likely that managers give high-performing teams more autonomy in their work. It is also likely that high-performing teams have better problem-solving and technical skills, so do not need their managers' intervention or input as much.

Task intervention by managers of low-performing teams is mentioned by other researchers as a negative leader behavior (Wageman, 1997). Managers of low-performing teams may focus on how the work gets done, become more involved in day-to-day operations, and monitor the team members' problem solving and customer interactions more closely. The coaching behavior "present alternative ideas to team members" may be an attempt to stimulate team member thinking and resolution of customer issues. Their higher flexibility scores could reflect managers' frustration with low performance and their attempts to increase performance by using many different coaching skills, rather than directive behavior, because that is what the literature recommends.

The organizational design context also is an important predictor of high performance (Wageman, 1997). Wageman found that clear direction and tasks and rewards designed for teams, rather than individuals, contributed most to high team performance. Managers may need organizational design skills as well as coaching skills.

It also is possible that the managers of low-performing work groups did not anticipate environmental and organizational changes. These findings suggest questions for further study.

Communication. Contrary to what the literature indicates, the relationship between managerial communication skills and team performance was negative. Communication skills are defined as how clearly the manager presents ideas and how proficient the leader is in giving constructive feedback, which allows team members to build on their successes and correct any deficits. By definition, a leader with good communication skills shares customer and company information, fosters an atmosphere in which team members express ideas and opinions freely, and is adept at listening and reflecting back what people say to ensure understanding and the feeling of being heard. Sharing company and customer information has long been considered an important managerial role. In fact, managers are the information conduits in most organizations. So why was the relationship between communication and performance negative?

One possible explanation is that self-directed teams at USCO receive performance data and management information directly from headquarters and not from their managers. High-performing teams were more autonomous and did not interact so much with their managers. Perhaps it does not matter where or in what form company and customer information originates. Maybe teams do not need communication and information to come from a manager. Integrated databases with all customer information and virtual office environments worked just as well in this company. This indicates that integrated data-bases that permit a free flow of customer information throughout an organization should become essential supportive mechanisms for high-performance teams. A more effective role for managers in organizations with virtual offices is interpreting reports and other organizational information.

However, the communication skills defined above were positively associated with customer satisfaction. Managers of high-performing teams were more likely to express ideas, share information, and give feedback about customers.

These findings suggest that managers and high-performing teams should communicate about the results that need to be produced, rather than about how the work gets done.

Thinking. Anticipating, identifying, and solving team problems are leader behaviors that reduce employee satisfaction and have no effect on team performance. These finding are consistent with the literature, which states that effective teams are responsible for solving their own problems. Wageman (1997) and Manz and Sims (1987) also found that manager intervention undermines work satisfaction.

CUSTOMER SATISFACTION

Customer satisfaction is a measure of team performance used by many organizations. Organization development experts at USCO think that customer satisfaction is the most important predictor of corporate profitability. Managers are indirectly responsible for customer satisfaction and spend approximately 25 percent of their time addressing customer issues. Solving customer problems was the focus for the work groups.

There were two important findings in the study regarding customer satisfaction and leader behavior. First, there was a significant difference between high-performing and low-performing teams on customer satisfaction. Second, the overall relationship between leader behavior and customer satisfaction was positive. The number of participants in the study limited further conclusions about customer satisfaction.

IMPLICATIONS FOR LEADERSHIP DEVELOPMENT

The findings in this study resolved some issues about the leader behaviors appropriate for self-directed teams and raised additional questions for leadership development.

Manager-Subordinate Interaction

That managers intervene more with low-performing teams than with high-performing teams is not surprising. Perhaps accountability for performance outcomes increases managerial intervention. The questions raised by the results of this study are whether knowledge of organizational design concepts would help managers to identify the causes of low performance and whether managerial intervention or the lack of team-member skills, experience, or motivation cause low performance. The leadership literature offers some potential answers.

Graen et al. (1975) found that managers give better assignments and more influence and autonomy to "in-group" members. Subordinate performance and positive personal interaction were significant predictors of this leader-employee interaction. Green and Mitchell (1979) suggest that leaders interpret employee performance information and respond with interactions based on attributions, the thought processes we use to determine the cause of our own or others' behavior. A manager will try to change a situation when it is attributed to an external or environmental cause. However, if the cause is attributed to an internal trait in the employee, the manager will provide detailed instruction, coach and monitor the subordinate more closely, or set easier goals and deadlines.

Educating managers about their attributions and the potential effects on their employees would be invaluable for a couple of reasons. It is possible that internal attributions would set in place a negative downward spiral, that is, closely monitoring subordinates, giving more detailed instruction for how to do the work, and setting easier goals and deadlines.

Wageman (1997) found the organizational design context the most significant predictor of performance. This indicates that managers should evaluate the environments and create appropriate contexts rather than provide close supervision.

These findings also reflect Wolford's (1982) emphasis on the macro level influences of the situation. The leader increases performance and motivation with incentives, participation, job redesign, and high expectations. The leader uses diagnostic behavior to assess deficiencies and take corrective action by changing the context, modifying the technology, removing physical constraints and providing resources. Hackman (1992) also indicates that manager actions should include diagnosing the organizational context and taking action where necessary. In this way managers can ensure that problems are solved without undermining the team.

There are fundamental differences between traditionally structured organizations and team-based systems. In a team-based design, employees are not as dependent on the leader. Years of nontheoretical leadership research found that the more subordinates are dependent on the leader for things they need, the higher will be the relationship between leader consideration and structure and subordinate satisfaction and performance. This relationship is based on subordinate dependence on the leader and the amount the leader can deliver. Team-based organizations reduce subordinate dependence on the leader, and systems thinking indicates that changing this dependence relationship will require other changes. This is obviously a question for further research.

Organizational Design

The fact that leader behavior accounts for a small percentage of the difference between high and low performance indicates that other factors matter more. Wageman (1997) determined that a clear, engaging direction was the most important organizational predictor of high performance. A clear direction reflects corporate strategy and directs employee activities. Clear objectives imply knowledge of the organization's key markets, the application of products and services to each market, and customer requirements.

Consistent goals and objectives are only possible with cross-functional collaboration (Mohrman, Mohrman, & Cohen, 1994). Understanding the customers' business means that managers should have broad industry knowledge, understand the opportunities and challenges within each sector, and have knowledge about the productivity drivers for each industry. Thus, scanning the environment and knowing what is going on in the marketplace are increasingly important responsibilities for managers. Getting managers in the marketplace, making external alliances, and building the company's business are expanding roles. Creating inter-organizational alliances, joint ventures, and other network arrangements are key future management activities. Entrepreneurial skills that include business development, revenue generation, and investment management will be required. Learning how to negotiate and create "win-win" situations will be critical in ensuring trust and long-term alliances and relationships.

For example, at USCO, in-depth customer relationships are a prerequisite to offering document solutions. Resolutions of customer problems are necessary to maintain good customer relationships. Managers must work in collaborative, cross-functional ways with customers. This means that developing general managers with cross-functional perspectives will be useful in the future. Managers also will need the ability to establish inter-organizational trust and set a clear, engaging direction for the work.

Mohrman, Mohrman, & Cohen (1994) suggest that changes in corporate systems (that is, rewards, performance evaluation, information, and communication) are necessary for a successful and sustained implementation of teamwork. Wageman (1997) determined that tasks and rewards designed for teams are key enabling conditions and predictors of high performance. Designing corporate systems suitable for high-performance teams should be a primary obligation of managers. Managers need to have diagnostic and design capabilities in order to determine the systems that are appropriate for their organizational situations. Managers should ensure that teams are necessary to accomplish the work, and that the work is designed for interdependence if teams are necessary. Ensuring that other corporate support systems are designed to support the team is another component of this organizational design role. In addition, teaching managers the diagnostic skills necessary to evaluate the impact of their designs on the team is critical. Diagnosing and taking action regarding the organizational context for each team will likely enhance high performance (Hackman, 1992). Organizational design skills should become a significant component of leader development programs.

Assessment of Leader Behavior

Although leader behavior accounts for a small percentage of the difference between high and low team performance, knowledge of what that behavior is and its impact on the team is important. Behavioral assessment and feedback can establish strengths and developmental opportunities while opening communication between the manager and team.

All managers need to understand the effects of various aspects of their behavior on team performance, employee satisfaction, and customer satisfaction. Managers need to move away from managing individuals and concentrate on leading and interacting with the team.

To improve performance, leaders should have high interpersonal skills, which means that they encourage collaboration, help to smooth team interchanges and resolve conflict, appreciate diversity, and value input from everyone. This also means that growth opportunities are made available to everyone in the organization.

Holding teams responsible and accountable for work outcomes changes who has the authority and responsibility for results. If high employee satisfaction is a desired outcome, the manager's role is keeping the organization and teams focused on the results that need to be produced. Managers should set strategic direction, create a vision for the organization, and let the team determine how the work is done. This framework gives the team room to operate within a defined structure and with definite expectations. Appropriate leadership skills include influencing and encouraging responsibility, accountability, and self-management by team members. Such leadership fosters team learning, provides developmental opportunities, teaches appropriate decision making, and encourages teamwork. The leader gives people the information, knowledge, and skills to make intelligent decisions and then steps aside. The team members solve their own problems and determine how they do their work. Team members should generate options for solving customer problems and identify different ways to accomplish goals. The team should shift priorities to juggle assignments, obligations, and change with the circumstances. This is only possible if the team has the knowledge, skills, and authority to make effective decisions. The manager should provide a consistent message about direction and expectations and ensure that the team has the requisite knowledge, skills, abilities, and resources to perform. In today's competitive, global environment, leaders need high-performance teams that are partners in building the business.

Leaders who coordinate between teams and establish processes that support their teams' work are likely to achieve high performance. Establishing inter-organizational alliances that encourage collaboration is a key leader role. Letting teams interact directly with external customers and suppliers encourages high performance and resolution of problems.

Managers also must anticipate environmental and organizational changes. Appropriate customer and market research can help managers to determine a consistent strategic direction for the organization's products and services which, in turn, can be used to present employees with guidelines for decisions and actions. Such a focus would result in higher performance and customer satisfaction.

Limitations of the Study

The small sample was the most pronounced limitation of the study. Work groups in the study were nominated based on either high or low performance, which caused statistical problems. Differences between high-performing and low-performing groups were easily identified, however, which created a trade-off.

Because a single firm was used in the study, generalizing the findings to other organizations requires caution.

The findings of this study regarding communication and customer satisfaction are inconsistent with literature on team effectiveness, thus raising questions for further research. The results imply that high-performance teams communicate less with their managers and that the nature of the communication is different than with low-performing teams. The type of communication appropriate for high performance or where the information originates (that is, manager or database), however, is not clear. An important question for future research is determining whether the flexibility scale really measures what it is intended to measure. Determining the construct validity of the instrument, and in particular the flexibility scale, would help answer some the psychometric questions.

Future answers to questions about communication, flexibility, and customer satisfaction can broaden our understanding of the requirements for high-performance work systems.

References

Bass, B.M. (1981). *Handbook of leadership: Revised and expanded edition.* New York: New York Press.

Burress, M.A. (1992). *Development of a model of leadership for self-managed teams in a greenfield environment.* (MicS 160 no. 6788).

Burress, M.A. (1993). *Leader behaviors for self-managing teams.* Unpublished manuscript.

Burress, M.A. (1995). *A reliability study and factor analysis of the team leader survey.* Unpublished manuscript.

Cohen, S. (1994). Designing effective self-managing work teams. In M. Beyerlein and D. Johnson (Eds.), *Advances in interdisciplinary studies of work teams.* (pp. 67–102). Greenwich, CT: JAI Press.

Graen, D.F., Graen, G.B., et al. (1975, February). A vertical dyad linage approach to leadership within formal organizations. *Organizational Behavior and Human Performance, 31*(1), 46–78.

Graen, G.B., Scandura, T.A., & Graen, M.R. (1986). A field experimental test of the moderating effects of growth need strength on productivity. *Journal of Applied Psychology, 71*(3), 484–491.

Green, S.G., & Mitchell, T.R. (1979). Attributional processes of leaders in leader-member interactions. *Organizational Behavior and Human Performance, 23,* 429–458.

Hackman, J.R. (1987). The design of work teams. In J.W. Lorsch (Ed.), *Handbook of organizational behavior* (pp. 315–342). Englewood Cliffs, NJ: Prentice Hall.

Hackman, J.R. (1992). The psychology of self-management in organizations. In R. Glaser (Ed.), *Classic readings in self-managing teamwork* (pp. 143–193). King of Prussia, PA: Organization Design and Development.

Manz, C.C., & Sims, H.P., Jr. (1987). Leading workers to lead themselves. *Administrative Science Quarterly, 32*(1), 106–128.

Miles, R.E., & Snow, C.C. (1994). *Fit, failure, & the hall of fame.* New York: The Free Press.

Mohrman, S.A., Mohrman, A.M., Jr. & Cohen, S.G. (1995). *Designing team-based organizations.* San Francisco, CA: Jossey-Bass.

Wageman, R. (1993). *Fostering productive interdependence at work: The interactive effects of task design, reward strategy, and individual preference for autonomy.* Unpublished doctoral dissertation, Harvard University, Boston, MA.

Wageman, R. (1997, Summer) Critical success factors for creating superb self-managing teams. *Organizational Dynamics, 25*(1), 49 (13).

Wolford, J.C. (1982). An integrative theory of leadership. *Journal of Management, 8,* 27–47.

Mary Ann Burress, Ph.D., has twenty years of business experience, including over twelve years of organizational development consulting with Fortune 500 corporations on various transformation processes. Her work embodies change by conducting organizational assessments, helping organizations implement high-performing work systems, serving on the steering committees responsible for designing and implementing change, evaluating managerial competencies, assessing leadership development requirements, and developing new businesses emphasizing marketing and profitability. Primary corporate clients are Shell Exploration and Production Company, Xerox Corporation, NCH, Interdisciplinary Center for Study of Work Teams, Russian-American Business Development Center, GTE Directories, Texas Instruments, Boeing, International Marble, and Wang Information Services Corporation.

VIEWS OF THE 21ST CENTURY ORGANIZATION

Elizabeth A. Smith

Abstract: The shape, structure, and functions of organizations that survive in the 21st Century will be very different from today's traditional organizations. This article predicts some ways that those differences will be manifest and the ways in which work will be done. Among the predictions are that employees will be considered a very valuable resource, recognized and rewarded for their unique contributions, and that intrinsic motivation and self-motivated creativity will be key variables in attracting and retaining a capable, dedicated, loyal workforce. The author also describes ways in which communication will be enhanced in the future and how learners will have control over the educational environment. It is predicted that personal and organizational change will be accepted as an inevitable way of life—an opportunity to stimulate innovation and develop new perspectives for maximizing contact with people within and outside the organization.

$\mathbf{H}$ow will the function, shape, strategy, and structure of organizations differ in the 21st Century? Will peoples' unique skills, abilities, and knowledge be recognized and used effectively? What role will information, knowledge, and intellectual capital play in the organizations of the future? Will creating and brokering knowledge replace or exceed the standard financial exchanges currently in use?

The author interviewed twenty-five leaders from academia, banking, communications, computer hardware, construction, energy, management consulting, manufacturing, and nonprofit service organizations. These business leaders provided a wide range of answers to these questions and also expressed their beliefs, concerns, and expectations about the future.

Major content areas covered were: people as a valuable resource; leadership; motivation; information, knowledge, intellectual capital, and human intellect; communication; training and learning; customers; the organization; systems; and change. Steps that these leaders felt would lead to a more secure future are presented below in their consolidated form.

PEOPLE AS A VALUABLE RESOURCE

People are the most valuable, powerful, and dynamic resource in any organization. Their abilities to think and create are the greatest underused, untapped resources of all. Currently, management is just starting to recognize the value of developing human capital, or the knowledge, professional skills, experiences, and creativity of their employees. Difficult, but necessary, first steps are to build a firm foundation based on trust, loyalty, and shared values. Everyone in the organization, including the chief financial officer and the chief knowledge officer, must support these efforts in the future.

Recruiting, hiring, and retaining qualified people will be even more essential to the stability and to the ultimate success of any organization. A comprehensive orientation for these new, select groups of people will set guidelines and expectations for performance. This initial clarification process will help employees align their actions with the organization's vision, goals, core competencies, and strategies. A good orientation program can also help new employees understand and assimilate the culture of the organization as quickly as possible. Employees who know how their unique talents are to be used and actually are able to use these talents on the job are generally satisfied with their jobs. Job satisfaction may also result in increased motivation and productivity.

When people throughout the organization have a passion for business, they understand not only what they do, but also how their jobs fit into the overall scheme of things. If workers are to perform their jobs well, they need to know how to begin the demanding, time-consuming process of selecting and transforming important data and information into useful knowledge. People use their expertise and experience to add their unique brand of value or worth to complex knowledge creating and distribution processes. In the future, it's important that meaningful, readily understood terms or a common vocabulary be used to communicate this knowledge to others within and beyond the organization.

LEADERSHIP

Command and control management methods are not being replaced rapidly enough by informed, inspired, consistent, proactive leaders who "walk the talk." Managers must be gradually transformed into leaders who develop, nurture, and support their employees—who share their knowledge and power. To be successful, leaders must have a clear vision of the future and work toward this vision by openly supporting continuous change and lifelong learning.

Unless leaders understand the basics of business and possess both business sense and technical skills, they will not totally understand what is going on around them in the future. Being an empathetic, reflective listener will be even more important, as will excellent verbal and written communication skills to use in workplaces in which the use of networking and group-centered activities is increasing.

Leaders need to be able to gather, sort, select, store, send, retrieve, and share useful data and information and transform these valuable resources into useful units of knowledge. This process will enable leaders to improve the way information and knowledge are used. Increased understanding will lead to better application of advanced technologies.

The creation of environments in which good leadership "happens" is crucial to organizational success in the future. Because leadership is really about relationships with people, social intelligence will continue to be a highly prized human relations skill. Leaders are also expected to have intuitive interpersonal skills and humility. They should be able to foster collaboration and sharing for the common good, be good role models, and live balanced lives. Leaders who have outstanding personal and professional values can build these into their organization's culture.

MOTIVATION

Rewarding performance based on compliance should be replaced with developing and reinforcing performance based on trust. Good performance must be recognized and rewarded, not critiqued annually at performance appraisal time. For example, what is heard and verified through 360-degree feedback may eventually become a constructive basis for making positive changes throughout the organization.

Appropriately reinforcing and recognizing people on an individual basis is a key factor in motivation. People thrive on peer recognition, increased personal and professional visibility, and the opportunity to participate in open communication throughout and beyond the organization. Many individuals want personalized nonmonetary motivators, such as interesting, challenging work and involvement and ownership in decisions. They also want independence, autonomy, and flexibility in the way they view and perform their jobs (Smith, 1998).

A work environment must be developed that openly encourages and rewards creativity and innovation—greatly enhancing levels of motivation. Redefining and rewriting the social employment contract between management and employees can also increase motivation. Factors often written into contracts, and that will become more popular, relate to equitable pay and appropriate ways to identify, recognize, and reward individual and group efforts adequately (Strebel, 1996).

INFORMATION, KNOWLEDGE, INTELLECTUAL CAPITAL, AND HUMAN INTELLECT

Data, information, and knowledge are the raw materials used to create and deliver innovative, competitively priced, value-added services and products. Knowledge management is the strategic application of collective company knowledge and know-how to build profits and expand market share. It is imperative that clear distinctions be made among data, information, and knowledge.

Many cross-disciplinary efforts share information and have common or generic processes, for example, to gather, store, and retrieve data and information. When diverse work forces share information, people who transform this information into knowledge often enhance its worth by adding their unique perspectives. Companies that build knowledge-sharing relationships with their customers and suppliers may find that additional value can be created and then sold (Tobin, 1998). Possessing and applying "expert" knowledge and adding value to services and products are major factors in any form of competition. Reportedly, the new source of wealth is in creating and marketing information that has been transformed into knowledge. Value is created when this knowledge is applied in the workplace.

The number of knowledge-based and knowledge-enabled organizations that consider intellectual capital a prime resource continues to grow (Edvinsson & Malone, 1997; Stewart, 1997; Tobin, 1998). Knowledge is an invisible corporate asset, as are patents, management systems, brand identity, customer relations, and corporate reputation. Knowledge represents much of the gap between a company's book value and the market value of its stock (Pascarella, 1997). Institutionalized knowledge that is used to build and maintain a strong culture should be shared with everyone in the organization. Better ways to turn the unique resources, experience, and learning power of the individual into corporate knowledge need to be devised for the future.

It is important to reduce or handle the information overload more efficiently to direct vital information to those who need it. Retrieving and using small bits of information on an as-needed basis is beginning to be accepted as a way of life in many organizations. Creating a just-in-time, just-enough-knowledge base is not a trivial exercise. The key is to get enough of the "right" information in the "right" format to people when they need it.

Intellectual capital includes human brainpower, leadership, ongoing employee training, technology, and other tangible and intangible assets, such as brand names, customer goodwill, and speed of response to client service calls.

Human or professional intellect is a body of knowledge in a discipline, such as software engineering. This body of knowledge needs to be updated continually. Professional intellect creates most of the value in the economy. Professional people have all four levels: cognitive knowledge; advanced skills; systems understanding; and self-motivated creativity (Quinn, Anderson, & Finkelstein, 1996). The first three levels also exist in the organization's systems, databases, or operating technologies. The fourth level is found in the organization's culture.

Cognitive knowledge, or "know-what," involves the basic mastery of a discipline that is achieved through extensive training, certification, or licensing. This level of knowledge is essential, but does not guarantee success.

Advanced skills, or know-how, transforms "book learning" into effective action. Rules of a discipline are used to solve complex real-world problems in specific areas. This level creates most of the value in organizations.

Systems understanding, or "know-why," is deep knowledge of the web of cause-and-effect relationships underlying a specific discipline. Professionals who have systems understanding use their intuition to create extraordinary value by solving large, complex problems.

Self-motivated creativity, or "care-why," includes will, motivation, and adaptability for success. People with self-motivated creativity select the problems they want to work on and use their own unique methods to solve these problems. Self-motivated creativity plays a major role in intrinsic motivation.

Most organizations spend time and money developing basic, first-level skills. Advanced or second-level skills are usually ignored. Few current managers believe systems understanding and self-motivated creativity are important. A major focus in most organizations of the future must be to create realistic, cost-effective ways to acquire, analyze, store, disseminate, and share knowledge in the most expedient way possible. A small number of organizations already have employees who possess the necessary knowledge-management skills and methods to change data into information, strategies, ideas, and appropriate actions effectively. According to Drucker (1992), the major output of organizations is knowledge that must be managed, measured, and understood.

COMMUNICATION

Corporate leaders should keep everyone informed of the company's plans, goals, and current status. Senior managers must get facts into the hands of the supervisors and managers who lead and coach the front-line workers. Talk, or the simple process of communicating eye-to-eye with people at work, provides first-hand feedback. Everyone needs regular dialogue and feedback. Feedback from various levels of employees plays a major role in bringing about positive change.

Cross-disciplinary communication should be encouraged and supported within and beyond the organization of the future. Information obtained from an array of sources can be relayed through knowledge workers from various disciplines. Linking databases and forming various types and levels of communication networks will be the great equalizer that enables companies throughout the world to access vital information and communicate with anyone, regardless of location.

"Organizational listening," or knowing what is going on in the heart and mind of an organization, is of growing importance. Organizations are dynamic, living entities. The culture of the organization is conveyed through all forms of verbal, nonverbal, print, and electronic communication. Knowledge sharing is really about the entire communication process.

TRAINING AND LEARNING

Major concerns presently relate to the fact that much in-house training is being outsourced and that training is often directed at the wrong level. Only a select few are being trained well. For example, top managers who lead an array of major change and improvement efforts often receive little or no training, and when training is started at the lower levels in the organization, those at the top seldom understand, support, or reinforce change that has occurred.

The financial return on training efforts is about 1 percent at present. Most training is evaluated at only the reaction level—the lowest level. Surveys and questionnaires are used to determine trainees' reactions, thoughts, and feelings about the training. Higher levels of evaluation, such as determining behavioral change, the amount of training that is actually used on the job, and return on investment, are seldom used (Phillips, 1997). In the future, more effort must be directed at evaluating the behavioral outcomes and overall effectiveness of training.

Successful training efforts will enable people to master and apply cutting-edge tools to leverage their overall talents. Tobin (1998) emphasizes the value of moving from "training" to "learning" to meet business goals. Mentoring and training through action learning, or learning by doing, is crucial. Mentoring and coaching work best when combined with continuous learning processes. Cross-cultural apprenticeships abroad can serve as key factors in employees' success. When educational institutions become closely aligned with the business world, it will be possible to provide specialized job training so desperately needed in the workplace. The academic and business worlds are beginning to work together to achieve a common understanding of what each needs and can provide.

Learners who use the language of their own thought processes discover the real meaning of concepts and relationships, while activating their capacity to learn. Learning styles that are closely matched with training styles and media format, such as seeing versus hearing, expedite learning. Few people learn exactly the same way. Feedback is often used to enable people to monitor their progress, but because there is minimal follow-up on training effectiveness and retention of new information, very little newly acquired knowledge is applied on the job at present.

Nearly all phases of training, ranging from traditional classroom training to virtual classrooms, must be viewed in new ways. Multi-disciplinary, multi-media training will move people out of the standard classroom, perhaps on to intranets and Internets (Smith, 1997). The number of "wired" universities that offer the full spectrum of college degrees and continuing education courses is growing rapidly. Networking with knowledge experts from around the world is commonplace and takes a variety of forms.

Individualized training and independent study use a wide range of media. These popular forms of training are designed to strengthen areas of weakness and provide the necessary information when it is needed. However, people must be encouraged to identify their needs and develop their unique skills, abilities, and knowledge so they can become architects of their own careers. A crucial first step is to create and maintain a lifetime career passport of one's spectrum of talents, knowledge, experience, goals, vision, and mission (Smith, in press). Only then will people begin to accept responsibility for their own training, learning, and careers.

CUSTOMERS

A prime purpose of the organization is to create and satisfy customers. And those customers have begun to expect more from the people serving them. If asked, customers can provide valuable information on what exemplary service is and how it can be achieved. Humility and good interpersonal skills are high on customers' lists of wants. However, what customers say they want and what they need are often quite different.

External and internal customers dictate functions to be performed and the form and shape of the organizational structure required to provide services and products. Ongoing customer feedback on the usefulness and quality of products and services is an important ingredient in creating new added value. Some customers form partnerships with suppliers in order to help design and pay for new products and services they need. In general, customers will play steadily growing roles in the development, design, and implementation of services and products in the future, so it is extremely important to tie customers into the company's external and internal knowledge networks (Tobin, 1998).

In the computer industry, for instance, staying ahead of the competition means working on products and services that are two or three levels ahead of what is currently being marketed. In highly competitive markets, it is imperative to develop solutions customers will need in the future.

THE ORGANIZATION

The future physical shape and structure of organizations is believed to range from free-form to a very tangible structure that can be described in specific terms. The organization of the future will not have any specific shape, but may be virtual—anywhere and everywhere—and exist only in people's heads. Each person will have a slightly different image of the organization.

Wheatley (1993) believes that organizations do not have specific boundaries. The future organization will be fluid in terms of what people can do and what customers actually need. Work may be done "any time, any place," and may involve scheduling an office or work station only when needed. The current job that requires sitting at a desk, going to meetings in a nearby conference room, and meeting with customers on a regular, face-to-face basis is disappearing slowly.

Organizations are becoming increasingly flat, decentralized, and empowered. Flattening effects are caused partly by reengineering, downsizing, and the need to restructure in order to operate closer to the customer. As the number of management layers continues to decrease, communication will be decentralized and made accessible to everyone through computer and human networks and readily accessible databases.

Organizational shape will evolve, depending on the nature of the business, the type of customer, the products and services provided, and on technology. Handy (1994) suggests that organizations may be shaped like a doughnut in the future. The hole in the doughnut represents the core of the organization that contains all central operations and services necessary to transact business. An individual's core contains things that must be done in a job if that person is to succeed.

Vision (what) and mission (how) statements are being enacted on the shop floor, but talk currently outweighs action. Core ideology, or the organization's soul, guides, inspires, and embodies the organization's reason for being and also the idealistic motives people have for doing the company's work. Some core ideologies that incorporate enduring personality characteristics, such as integrity, honesty and loyalty, values, and purpose, are being (re)discovered. There will be more realization that an organization is a living entity focused on the essential factors of shared values and trust.

The culture of the organization, as represented by stories, lore, and history, defines what is happening in the present. The Hewlett-Packard way, for example, is founded on solid core values—deep respect for people, trust, dedication to affordable quality and reliability, continuous innovation, and commitment to community responsibility. There is no universally "right" set of core values. Few companies have the same core values, due to differences in culture, customer base, processes, and products produced. Ideology must be meaningful and inspirational only to the people inside the organization, not necessarily exciting or inspiring to others. Core ideology transcends management fads, changes of leadership, market life cycles, and technological breakthroughs.

The decentralization of many organizations puts people closer to the action. In the future, people will be more empowered and customer-focused. Individual prosperity and organizational prosperity must be aligned as closely as possible. Employees, shareholders, partners, and other stakeholders should share in this overall feeling of satisfaction and well-being. Decentralization will foster an environment enabling people to perform to their potential.

The organization's environment now mirrors marketplace stability—turbulence. A noncritical, supportive, nurturing atmosphere, in which creativity, innovation, and risk taking are encouraged and appropriately rewarded, is essential for the future. Worker-friendly organizations that are customer-oriented, participative, and progressive will enable people to mobilize their strengths, take risks, and develop realistic, cost-effective solutions to numerous problems.

Reality is a moving target for people and the organization, for example, lifetime employability versus lifetime employment. Organizations want well-trained, self-reliant, loyal, dedicated, cooperative, productive employees. Employees want stable, strong-culture organizations that provide meaningful work, appropriately encourage, reward, and reinforce risk taking, have adequate training, and ensure a secure future. Both organizations and employees must move toward a middle ground in the future.

Systems

Everyone is part of a system, whether a family, work team, or social group. A system consists of separate parts that are arranged in a particular order or design to make a whole. Changing one part of a system often produces unexpected changes in other parts. Systems must be open—or dynamic. A closed, static system or person cannot know itself or assimilate or adjust to changing environments. Organizations of the future, as parts of larger, global systems, must be able to process and use information or feedback from their external environments and subsystems to adjust to new realities, demands, and expectations.

Humans are vital gears and stabilizers in group processes. Employees in the future must be encouraged to be the best they can be, not become replaceable parts in static systems. Evolutionary and natural systems approaches, as holistic ways to view and assess people, organizations, and change, are gaining favor. Natural systems theory proposes that people and organizations have active emotional components. The development of the whole person requires an emotional base. The emotional components related to motivation, surprise, fear, anger, and inability to concentrate, among others, play alternately helpful and harmful roles in people's work and personal worlds.

Change

Change is an inevitable, nagging constant and also an opportunity. Many people dread the unknown, uncontrollable, unpredictable consequences of change. Some people fear taking risks. "Bad" change that disrupts personal values, beliefs, and expectations is usually resisted or ignored. "Good" change, viewed in terms of self-interest or personal advantage, is more readily accepted. Many barriers to change are emotional, not intellectual. Perceptions and longstanding beliefs may cloud, even obscure, reality.

Organizations that change continually, yet retain their underlying structure and culture, operate at the edge of flexibility, or dynamic equilibrium. Expertise in analyzing and changing strategy, management techniques, and business processes will become ever more essential in all change efforts.

People with the courage and ability to confront their "inner selves" can reframe or refocus change and view it in a different light. By personally envisioning their responses to change and putting themselves in the picture, people can gradually become active participants in change and growth processes. Currently, few change efforts, like downsizing, reengineering, and restructuring, reward people for growing, developing, and learning. The long run consists of a series of short runs. All change is gradual, or evolutionary. Most minor change is invisible until something major happens.

Steps Leading to a More Secure Future

The following statements summarize major concerns and statements made by the various leaders who were interviewed for this article.

Measure Against Yourself. Use self-reference to see where your strengths and unique abilities fit into the organization's overall vision, mission, strategies, and goals. Plan for and manage your career by establishing criteria for learning and accomplishment. Set milestones to achieve certain goals. Monitor and document progress toward these goals regularly.

Become More Trusting. Expand your radius of trust. Widespread distrust levies burdens on humans and on economic activity. Distrust also increases the need for more hierarchy and vertical integration or control—the exact opposite of empowerment. Eliminate fear from working and learning.

Learn in Multiple Ways. Employ many user-friendly, individually tailored, multi-level learning materials and delivery methods. There is no one "best" way to learn. Reframe what you learn in terms of the organization's strategic business needs, goals, and core competencies. "Unlearn" irrelevant material that blocks or hinders new learning.

Reward New Behaviors. Be creative and fair when you reward behaviors, belief systems, and overall outcomes to be achieved in the workplace. Foster cooperation, facilitate communication, and tolerate risk.

Share What You Know. Share expertise and knowledge across functions, disciplines, generations, organizations, cultures—nations. The synergy of working together in cross-functional teams fuels the fire for innovative breakthroughs.

Collect Information. Document and assess people's core competencies in logical, cost-effective ways. Create and maintain databases that include information on a wide range of job-related training activities that can be used to provide information on capabilities of an organization's entire workforce. Individuals may develop a portfolio of work activities, or create a career passport. In some instances, jobs can be brokered or negotiated.

Think Win/Win. Use consensus or synergistic methods to break down either/or and win/lose dichotomies. Everyone benefits under win/win situations when processes and actions flow together to create a seamless, unified result.

Intervene Across the Organization. Use information on personal and organizational alignment to make major, constructive, powerful, multi-level interventions to initiate change. Use the core competencies of individuals and the organization to develop realistic solutions to the major business problems. Avoid easy, tempting "quick fixes."

State Your Vision. Start building a visionary organization that has a strong corporate culture. Be patient. Accept small, positive, steady gains. It takes ten to thirty years to progress toward an envisioned future. Visionary companies are built with 1 percent vision and 99 percent alignment. Visionary companies, such as Johnson & Johnson, IBM, and Intel, have survived many tidal waves of change.

Use Talented Experts. Develop multi-talented, human relations experts who can plan for and anticipate the future. They must be able to listen to, inspire, and encourage others.

SUMMARY

Common concerns for the future include the steadily growing challenges, counterforces, and undercurrents in the global marketplace. Using technology as a panacea or "cure-all" was seriously questioned. Keeping up with one's job on a daily basis, given shrinking resources, less than adequate support staff, and insufficient training budgets, was almost a preoccupation.

Key success factors most often mentioned were shared values, trust, and loyalty to an ideal, not to an entity. Regular tracking and aligning of business strategy with the interests of employees, customers, suppliers, partners, shareholders, and the community help organizations achieve and maintain balance. Internships, mentoring programs, co-ops, and industry-based liaisons with schools and universities are starting to reduce the size of the gap between what students learn in school and what they need to know to perform successfully on the job.

Evolutionary change that keeps organizations in constant transition, even turmoil, fosters creativity and innovation. Insightful, proactive leaders must create and maintain a stimulating, supportive organizational culture that individually recognizes, rewards, and maximizes people's talents. Organizations and employees may need to create a new business contract jointly based on a liberating rather than on a constraining philosophy. Long-term success requires self-reliance, self-knowledge, lifelong learning, and—most of all—flexibility.

The new organizational structure will likely be flat and be connected through overlapping (electronic) networks, similar to spider webs (Quinn, Anderson, & Finkelstein, 1996). The new organizational structure will include a knowledge-based environment that enables knowledge experts to transform information into useful, cost-effective, just-in-time knowledge. The environment must support a myriad of activities and provide a culture that rewards knowledge experts.

The next paradigm shift is predicted to be based on values and beliefs, or on an organizational culture that grows gradually and becomes stronger. It is imperative to invest in the quality of the social fabric of a company and create a sense of values and purpose. This will be a tough task in our rapidly changing global marketplace, but it can be done!

References

Drucker, P. (1992, September/October). The new society for organizations. *Harvard Business Review*, pp. 95–104.

Edvinsson, L., & Malone, M.S. (1997). *Intellectual capital.* New York: HarperCollins.

Handy, (1994). *Age of paradox.* Boston, MA: Harvard Business School Press.

Pascarella, P. (1997, October). Harnessing knowledge. *Management Review*, pp. 37–40.

Phillips, J.J. (1997). *Handbook of training evaluation and measurement methods* (3rd ed.). Houston, TX: Gulf.

Quinn, J.M., Anderson, P., & Finkelstein, S. (1996, March/April). Managing professional intellect: Making the most of the best. *Harvard Business Review*, pp. 71–80.

Smith, B. (1997, October). Career development: Compliments of your employer? *Management Review*, pp. 25–27.

Smith, E.A. (1998). The role of creativity and motivation in productivity. In D.J. Sumanth, W.B. Werther, & J.A. Edosomwan (Eds.), *Proceedings of the Seventh International Conference on Productivity and Quality Research* (pp. 11–23). Norcross, GA: Engineering & Management Press.

Smith, E.A. (in press). The core-unique-expanding model: The career passport for performance. *International Journal of Business Performance Management*.

Strebel, P. (1996, May/June). Why do employees resist change? *Harvard Business Review*, pp. 86–92.

Stewart, T.A. (1997). *Intellectual capital*. New York: Currency/Doubleday.

Tobin, D.R. (1998). *The knowledge-enabled organization*. New York: AMACOM.

Wheatley, M.J. (1993). *Leadership and the new science*. San Francisco, CA: Berrett-Koehler.

Elizabeth A. Smith, Ph.D., is currently visiting assistant professor in industrial/ organizational psychology at the University of Houston, Clear Lake, Texas, and vice president of Summit Resources, Inc. She teaches graduate courses in organizational development, training and development, and industrial/organizational psychology. She has published numerous books and articles on productivity, creativity, motivation, and evaluation and published tests to assess managerial behavior. Dr. Smith has a bachelor's degree in psychology from the University of Alberta, Canada, and a master's and Ph.D. in psychology from the University of Wyoming.

CONTRIBUTORS

Kristin J. Arnold, MBA, CPCM
Quality Process Consultants, Inc.
48 West Queens Way
Hampton, VA 23669
  (757) 728-0191
  fax: (757) 728-0192
  e-mail: karnold@qpcteam.com

Ron Ashkenas
Robert H. Schaffer & Associates
Four High Ridge Park
Stamford, CT 06905-1325
  (203) 322-1604
  fax: (203) 322-3599
  e-mail: Info@rhsa.com

Andy Beaulieu
10713 Lady Slipper Terrace
North Bethesda, MD 20852
  (301) 231-0077
  e-mail: andy-beaulieu@erols.com

Mary Ann Burress, Ph.D.
9550 Ella Lee Lane #1403
Houston, TX 77063
  (713) 784-3085
  e-mail: maburress@sellus.com

Marilee Crosby
1650 Mohr Road
Portage, WI 53901
  (608) 742-1966
  e-mail: mcrosby@cardinalcorp.com

Daniel Dana, Ph.D.
Mediator-Consultant-Speaker
10210 Robinson
Overland Park, KS 66212-2512
  (913) 341-2888
  e-mail: dmi@mediationworks.com
  URL: www.mediationworks.com

John D. Delcarmen, M.S.
Department of Psychology
VCU Box 842018
Richmond, VA 23284
  (804) 828-1193
  e-mail: s0jddelc@titan.vcu.edu

Melissa I. Figueiredo, M.S.
Department of Psychology
VCU Box 842018
Richmond, VA 23284
  (804) 225-3866
  e-mail: psy5mif@titan.vcu.edu

Gary Gemmill, Ph.D.
School of Management
Syracuse University
Syracuse, NY 13244-2130
  (315) 437-1727
  fax: (315) 443-5457
  e-mail: ggemmill@waldenu.edu

Barbara Pate Glacel, Ph.D.
VIMA International
5390 Lygate Court
Burke, VA 22015
  (703) 764-0780
  fax: (703) 764-0789

David R. Glaser
Vogel/Glaser & Associates, Inc.
5188 Even Star Place
Columbia, MD 21044
(301) 596-0170
fax: (410) 730-9590
e-mail: DRGlaser@aol.com

Edward Earl Hampton, Jr.
Performance Perspectives
2578 Danielle Drive
Oviedo, FL 32765
(407) 823-3940
fax: (407) 977-9194
e-mail: champton@mail.ucf.edu

Barbara Hanson, M.S.
107 Burlington Drive
Manlius, NY 13104
(315) 682-2486

Terry L. Hight, M.S., M.A.
Department of Psychology
VCU Box 842018
Richmond, VA 23284
(804) 225-3866
e-mail: psy5tlh@titan.vcu.edu

M.K. Key, Ph.D.
Key Associates, LLC
144 Second Avenue, North
Suite 150
Nashville, TN 37201
(615) 255-0011
fax: (615) 665-1622
e-mail: keyassocs@mindspring.com

Krista Kurth, Ph.D.
Renewal Resources
9428 Garden Court
Potomac, MD 20854-3964
(301) 765-9551
fax: (301) 765-9099
e-mail: RenewalKK@aol.com

Doug Leigh
LSI/ONAP
3500 University Center, Building C
Tallahassee, FL 32306
(850) 644-0232
e-mail: dleigh@email.com

James L. Moseley, Ed.D., L.P.C.
University Health Center
4201 St. Antoine Boulevard, Suite 9D
Detroit, MI 48201
(313) 577-7948
e-mail: jmosele@med.wayne.edu

Terry Murray
Creative Solutions
8 Ferguson Road
Cornwall, NY 12518
(914) 534-4713
fax: (914) 534-4609
e-mail: tmurray@cresol.net
URL: www.cresol.net

Julie O'Mara
O'Mara and Associates
5979 Greenridge Road
Castro Valley, CA 94552
(510) 582-7744
fax: (510) 582-4826
e-mail: OMaraAssoc@aol.com

Aja Oakman
20111 Westridge Court #26
Castro Valley, CA 94546
  (510) 582-7744
  fax: (510) 582-4826
  e-mail: ajao@aol.com

Scott B. Parry
Training House, Inc.
P.O. Box 3090
Princeton, NJ 08543
(100 Bear Brook Road
Princeton, NJ 08540)
  (609) 452-1505
  fax: (609) 243-9668

Richard G. Peters
53 Sheldrake Avenue
Larchmont, NY 10538
  (914) 833-7750
  fax: (914) 833-7750
  e-mail: rpeters714@aol.com

Richard Phillips
Technologies Division
Mountain Empire Community College
Drawer 700
Big Stone Gap, VA 24219
  (540) 523-2400
  fax: (540) 523-4130
  e-mail: Rphillips@me.cc.va.us

Steven L. Phillips, Ph.D.
CEO/President
Phillips Associates
23440 Civic Center Way, Suite 100
Malibu, CA 90265
  (310) 456-3532
  fax: (310) 456-8744
  e-mail: sphillips@phillipsassociates.
    net
URL: www.phillipsassociates.net

Frank A. Prince
Involvement Systems, Inc.
10635 Buccaneer Point
Frisco, TX 75034
  (972) 625-1099
  fax: (972) 625-6330
  e-mail: unleashyourmind@
    mindspring.com

Robert C. Preziosi
School of Business &
  Entrepreneurship
Nova Southeastern University
3100 SW 9th Avenue
Ft. Lauderdale, FL 33315
  (954) 262-5111
  fax: (954) 262-3965
  e-mail: preziosi@sbe.nova.edu

Emile A. Robert, Jr., Ph.D.
VIMA International
5390 Lygate Court
Burke, VA 22015
  (703) 764-0780
  fax: (703) 764-0789
  e-mail: chumrob@vima.com

Suzanne Adele Schmidt, Ph.D.
Renewal Resources
19046 Partridge Wood Drive
Germantown, MD 20874-5354
  (301) 601-1990
  fax: (301) 540-1990
  e-mail: RenewalSAS@aol.com

Neil Simon
220 East Huron, Suite 250
Ann Arbor, MI, 48104
  (734) 741-4150
  fax: (248) 552-1924
  e-mail: njsimon@aol.com

Elizabeth A. Smith, Ph.D.
Summit Resources, Inc.
2825 Wilcrest, Suite 259
Houston, TX 77042
(713) 785-4818
e-mail: smithce@flash.net

Michael Stanleigh
Business Improvement Architects
85 Scarsdale Road, Suite 302
Toronto, Ontario M3B 2R2
Canada
(416) 444-8225
fax: (416) 444-6743
e-mail: mstanleigh@bia.ca
ULR: www.bia.ca

Steve Sugar
The Game Group
10320 Kettledrum Court
Ellicott City, MD 21042
(410) 418-4930
fax: (410) 418-4162

Douglas J. Swiatkowski, M.Ed.
Fairlane Training and
   Development Center
P.O. Box 6055
1900 Hubbard Drive
Dearborn, MI 48121
(313) 322-5065
e-mail: dswiatko@ford.com

Lee Towe
Innovators International, Inc.
9700 Valdez Drive
Des Moines, IA 50322-1325
(800) 829-5550
URL: www.innovatorsinc.com

Karon West
258 Glengrove Avenue West
Toronto, Ontario M5N 1W1
Canada
(416) 484-4549
fax: (416) 482-1790
e-mail: wcg@total.net

Susan B. Wilkes, Ph.D.
Department of Psychology
VCU Box 842018
Richmond, VA 23284
(804) 828-1191
e-mail: swilkes@vcu.edu

Joseph G. Wojtecki, Jr.
P.O. Box 291
Stevensville, MD 21666
(412 Blenni Lane
Chester, MD 21619)
(410) 643-9061
fax: (410) 643-8524
e-mail: wojtecki@crosslink.net

Michele Matt Yanna
The TRAINERS Group, Inc.
2008 Fuller Road, Suite B
West Des Moines, IA 50265-5528
(515) 225-1249
fax: (515) 225-9396

Sherene Zolno, M.S.
Executive Director
The Leading Clinic
25900 Pillsbury Road SW
Vashon, WA 98070
(206) 463-6374
fax: (206) 463-6328
e-mail: COACHPB@worldnet.att.net

CONTENTS OF THE COMPANION VOLUME, THE 2000 ANNUAL: VOLUME 1, TRAINING

---

*See Experiential Learning Activities Categories, p. 6, for an explanation of the numbering system.

**Topic is "cutting edge."

5736

NOTES